Doing Right
by
Our Kids

Protecting Child Safety at All Levels

Doing Right
by
Our Kids

Protecting Child Safety at All Levels

Amy Tiemann, PhD

and Irene van der Zande,
Founder of Kidpower®

spark press™

CHAPEL HILL, NC

Published by Spark Press
1289 Fordham Blvd. #333
spark|press·   Chapel Hill, NC 27514

www.DoingRightByOurKids.com

The authors gratefully acknowledge permission to reprint from the following works:
Darkness to Light's *5 Steps to Protecting Our Children*™ and
Darkness to Light's *Stewards of Children*® training.
Information from Positive Coaching Alliance: The ELM Tree of Mastery™,
The Double-Goal Coach®, The ROOTS of Honoring the Game™,
The Second-Goal Parent®, and The Triple-Impact Competitor™.

For information about special discounts available for bulk purchases,
sales promotions, fund-raising and educational needs, contact Spark Press
at 1-919-391-4899 or info@sparkproductions.media

Publisher's Cataloging-In-Publication Data
(Prepared by The Donohue Group, Inc.)

Names: Tiemann, Amy. | Van der Zande, Irene.
Heath, Dan, 1973- writer of supplementary textual content.
Title: Doing right by our kids : protecting child safety at all levels / Amy Tiemann, PhD and
Irene van der Zande, Founder of Kidpower ; [foreword by Dan Heath].
Description: Chapel Hill, NC : Spark Press, [2018]
Includes bibliographical references and index.
Identifiers: ISBN 9780976498049 (paperback) | ISBN 9780976498056 (ebook)
Subjects: LCSH: Child abuse—Prevention. | Children—Violence against—Prevention.
Bullying—Prevention. | Discrimination—Prevention. | Child rearing. | Safety education.
Classification: LCC HQ770.7 .T54 2018 (print) | LCC HQ770.7 (ebook) | DDC 613.6083223

First printing

Cover and book design by Kathi Dunn, Dunn+Associates Design, www.dunn-design.com
Edited by Diane O'Connell, Write to Sell Your Book, LLC

Doing Right by Our Kids and Spark Press are registered trademarks of Spark Productions LLC

"We did then what we knew how to do,
and when we knew better, we did better."

—Maya Angelou

"Believe nothing,
no matter where you read it or
who has said it,
even if I have said it,
unless it agrees with your own reason
and your own common sense."

—Buddha

Contents

Dan Heath

Jerry Sandusky. Bill Cosby. Harvey Weinstein. Larry Nassar. The Catholic Church and its seemingly unending sexual abuse scandals and cover-ups. We live in an era of spiraling outrage.

At first, we were outraged by the anomalies: How could a coach like Sandusky get away with such evil acts in the midst of an athletic program that prided itself on leadership and integrity? Later, with the birth of the #MeToo movement, we were outraged by the *ubiquity* of harassment. How could we have allowed so much abuse to happen for so long?

The book you're reading, *Doing Right by Our Kids,* is a stake in the ground. Its message is: No more. The people who read this book and follow its principles will help build a world in which we don't just expose abuses after they happen, but stamp them out beforehand. Not just from sexual abuse, but from bullying, hazing, and negligent treatment.

"The safety and self-esteem of a child are more important than anyone's embarrassment, inconvenience, or offense." That's the founding principle of Kidpower®, the child-safety organization run by one of this book's co-authors, Irene van der Zande. It's a simple and even inarguable statement, but living up to it requires courage. The courage to speak up. The courage to ask a difficult question. The courage to interrupt a problematic scene. This book is a call to be more courageous.

But courage is a fickle ally, because troubling situations catch us by surprise. We hesitate: Are we perceiving things correctly? We doubt ourselves: What if I'm wrong about this? We delay: What if I'm overreacting? The ambiguity paralyzes us, and later we kick ourselves for letting the moment pass.

The courage we need is not the type that stiffens our backbone for confrontations with predators. We have that courage; there are few parents who would not throw themselves in harm's way to protect their kids. Rather, the courage we need is the willingness to *act in ambiguous circumstances*.

And that's the kind of courage that needs to be *practiced*. That's something my brother Chip and I learned in researching our book *The Power of Moments*—that people we think of as "naturally courageous" are often people who have diligently practiced the courageous acts required of them. During the civil rights movement, for instance, a group of brave students led a lunch counter sit-in in Nashville. They were harassed and assaulted and jailed, but their courage led to one of the first victories of the movement. What many people don't know about the story is that those protesters had *rehearsed* their resistance. They'd sat at a mockup of the actual lunch counter while confederates cursed at them and shoved them and belittled them. The practice toughened their skin for the real thing. Similarly, soldiers are trained to approximate what they will experience on the battlefield. Specialists training to defuse bombs begin by tinkering with unarmed bombs.

In short, courage isn't a natural trait. It's built with practice. And my hope for this book is that it will become a field guide for practicing courage. It will arm you with the knowledge and skills you need to know when, why, and how to act. Often these guidelines are incredibly simple: For example, do you know what questions you should be asking youth service organizations (camps, sports leagues, gyms, etc.) that supervise your children? (See pages 76-78.) Do you know the warning signs for inappropriate relationships? (See pages 87-89.) Does your child know some simple strategies to avoid risky situations? (See pages 59-63.)

But please don't forget the "practice" part. Learning isn't enough. Understanding isn't enough. If we want to change our environment for the better, we must act. Full stop. And the action required of us will often be something small: A quick clarifying call to a principal or parent or coach. Or a conversation with our kids that specifies our expectations. Unlike civil rights protesters or soldiers, those actions won't expose us to physical risk. But they might annoy other people or make us feel like a nuisance. That's why we need to remember that critical principle: "The safety and self-esteem of a child are more important than anyone's embarrassment, inconvenience, or offense."

It is all too clear that the work of creating a safe world for our children will not start with institutional leaders. It will not start with Catholic bishops or congressmen or university trustees. They have proven themselves insular and reactive. The change will start with parents. It will start with you. You—and we—will be the people who influence these institutions to embrace safety at all levels.

Because what we know about courage is that it's contagious. Studies of conformity show that people will do absurd things to fit in with a group—including agreeing with obviously false statements (e.g., participants in studies will agree that red circles are "orange" if everyone else in their group says so first). But if even one person in the group stands up to the mistaken norm, it becomes far easier for others in the group to speak up as well.

That's how change happens. It starts small, and it snowballs outward. Each act of courage inspires another, and with time, a few brave and dissatisfied people find that they've helped to build a movement.

Be one of those people. And start your journey with the next page.

—DAN HEATH, co-author of the *New York Times* bestsellers
The Power of Moments, Switch, Made to Stick, and *Decisive*

PART I

Safety for Kids = Peace of Mind for Parents

CHAPTER 1

The Heart of Child Protection

Imagine a world where all children are valued and treated with respect—where their well-being is truly more important than anything else. Imagine a world in which all kids grow up with the support they need to have a happy childhood and to become successful, thriving adults, and where all kids are safe and free from harm. Imagine what society would be like if future generations were composed of these successful, thriving adults.

In order to do right by our kids, each of us must work together to create this kind of world.

We the authors, Amy and Irene, have dedicated our lives to creating and providing tools to protect and empower young people. Our personal experiences have fueled our passion for keeping kids safe and have compelled us to write this book.

Irene's Story

The incident that inspired my advocacy work for child safety, including my founding the international nonprofit Kidpower®, happened in 1985 when I suddenly found myself protecting a group of young children, including my own two, from a man who was threatening to kidnap them. We were in a public place in the middle of the day, with people standing all around. I had taken my seven-year-old daughter, six of her friends, and my four-year-old son on a field trip to visit a museum in our hometown of Santa Cruz, California.

On our way back to the bus, a man with a lot of problems got triggered by the sight of a mom with eight small children. He started to follow us, muttering that I had all the cute little kids, and he had no one. When we got to the lobby of the bus station, this man suddenly charged toward us, shouting, "I'm going to take one of these girls to be my bride!"

To this day, I still can see the terrified faces of the children, with my son trying to hide behind his big sister because he was so scared. I cannot forget the frozen faces of the bystanders and the contorted face of the man.

Faced with this emergency, I did what I believe anyone reading this book would do. I put myself in between the man and the kids and started to yell at him to leave us alone. He shouted back that he could do what he wanted until I finally ordered another man standing nearby to "Get over here and help us! Can't you see these kids are scared?" When this bystander came over, the man who was threatening us ran away.

After the attack was over, the kids were fine. What they saw was that I yelled and the "bad guy" ran. But, I wasn't fine. I kept worrying and asking myself, "What if he knocked me down? What if he even tried to touch one of those kids?" I knew I'd try to stop him, but I wasn't sure how.

The following year, I went to my first self-defense program and was grief-stricken by the suffering of some of my fellow students, who had been raped, molested, harassed, or lost family members to violence. Returning home after one class, I suddenly burst into tears at the sight of my innocent eight-year-old daughter, Chantal. My child, used to her emotional mother, sat calmly on my lap. As my tears dripped into her hair, Chantal asked innocently, "What's the matter, Mommy?"

"It's just," I sighed, "that I wish that I could give you a better world to live in."

"Don't worry, Mommy," Chantal said practically. "Look at it this way. If we were living in the time of the dinosaurs, we'd all have to worry about being eaten, all the time!"

Comforted, I hugged my daughter and laughed, reflecting that my dream of a safe, perfect world for my kids was just that—a dream. I realized that my children did not need my despair. They needed my determination to give them the best world I could—and to prepare them to navigate our imperfect world with confidence, courage, wisdom, and joy.

In 1989, I joined with people from all walks of life to establish Kidpower as an international nonprofit with the vision of working together to help create cultures of safety, respect, and kindness for everyone, everywhere.

Even after all these years, I am still moved by the impact of Kidpower's effective and empowering child protection, positive communication, and 'People Safety' skills. Through our work with countless parents, teachers, and other caring adults, I have seen first-hand how knowing what to do and being successful in practicing how to do it reduces anxiety, increases confidence, and develops competence. To do right by our kids, we adults need to know how to advocate for our children's emotional and physical safety—and how to empower them with skills so that they can take charge of their own well-being.

Amy's Story

I was raised by an incredibly strong and caring mother who was an active child advocate, transcending her own traumatic childhood experiences. She grew up in the 1940s and '50s, a time of strict childrearing and "perfect" outward appearances, no matter what else was going on behind closed doors, and this affected her deeply.

In 2002, I was already working in the field of child safety and abuse prevention when a family bombshell exploded: I learned that a powerful family patriarch, beloved and respected by many, had abused children decades ago. My worldview shattered in an instant as I asked myself how someone I cared about, someone who presented himself as a paragon of high morals, could have done such a thing. I was the mother of a three-year-old, and there were several other young children in the budding next generation. What should I do? How would we move forward? In the midst of this chaos, two things helped keep me together: first, a bedrock commitment to protect our children. And second, trust and faith in my family that we could take honest action without letting this revelation rip our whole family apart.

As a family, we navigated this minefield by sticking to the principle *Put Safety First,* and we made sure that the parents of young children learned what they needed to know to make informed judgments about what would be safe for their kids. This was an incredibly challenging process, but my family ultimately came through it with a great deal of grace.

People had a wide variety of reactions to this situation, and words cannot describe how difficult it was. Even so, we managed to maintain our relationships with each other and acted to never let children be alone with this unsafe person until he passed away years later. I did not confront him directly, though my internal relationship to him changed completely. In this complicated situation, I kept my focus on a single goal that we were able to accomplish without confronting him: to protect our children!

Through this and other experiences, I have learned the hard way that every family and organization needs to be well-versed in child safety. We must move beyond the harmful illusion that "the best" schools or families do not need to worry about abuse or other maltreatment. The hard truth is that it is never enough to screen people as they enter a community— whether it is a family, school, or other organization—and then give them a permanent pass as being "safe," even for people whom we know well.

Although well intentioned, anyone, no matter how well-screened, can make an in-the-moment thoughtless choice or decision that causes a child to become more vulnerable to a safety problem. We do not need to be paranoid, either, but we do need to keep an eye on behavior to make sure that everybody, adults and children alike, follows the safety rules at all times, and that our communities know what to do in cases where safety is threatened.

In my search for answers for how to address these issues, I found Kidpower and Irene. I realized that Kidpower's values, skills, and knowledge provide valuable answers to many of society's toughest questions. There is still an information vacuum in our society when it comes to child safety, and these tools and strategies need to become far more widely known and applied everywhere: in families, in organizations, and as a catalyst for positive societal change, which is our inspiration for writing this book.

The Lifelong Impact of Childhood Trauma

The Centers for Disease Control and Kaiser Permanente conducted a long-running research survey of 17,000 patients called the Adverse Childhood Experiences (ACEs) study. As part of their exams, health care providers asked participants about their childhood history of traumatic experiences including physical, sexual, or emotional abuse, drug abuse in the household, domestic violence, or separation of children from parents, and then documented health outcomes going forward. The startling findings showed that these upsetting experiences are strongly correlated with major, expensive health problems including depression, substance abuse, STDs, cancer, heart disease, chronic lung disease, and diabetes.[1]

The impact was cumulative and "dose dependent"—more childhood trauma led to more serious problems over the person's lifetime.

ACEs study primary investigator Dr. Vincent Fellitti boldly states that "Adverse childhood experiences are the most *basic* cause of health risk behaviors, morbidity, disability, mortality and health care costs." Dr. Robert Anda, another primary investigator on the ACEs study, says he believes that dealing with the intergenerational transmission of adversity that causes so many problems is "the most important thing you can ever do."[1]

Epidemiologist David F. Williamson, PhD says that abuse is not just a social worker's problem, it's not just a psychologist's problem, it's not just a pediatrician's problem, it's not just a juvenile court judge's problem—it's everybody's.[1]

Stories Behind the Statistics

Child victimization expert David Finkelhor says, "Children experience far more violence, abuse and crime than do adults. If life were this dangerous for ordinary grown-ups, we'd never tolerate it."[2]

The risk of violence and abuse continues into adulthood. One in five women on college campuses will experience attempted or completed sexual assault.[3] The widespread sexual misconduct in the United States military harms thousands of women and men every year.[4]

Our society has made progress in bringing these problems to light— a big step, to be sure, in the case of problems that had thrived in denial and secrecy. The compelling result is that, almost every day, we see another news story underlining the harm done to children and teens—and the huge need for child protection education to become far more widespread. The flood of #MeToo revelations is both heart-rending about the suffering of the past and inspiring by making it clear that that harassment and sexual abuse will no longer be tolerated in our society.

Each of the examples in the following sections represents countless stories of misery, trauma, and tragedy that might have been prevented. Although identifying names and details have been changed to protect privacy, all of the following stories are real. Through professional counseling, Kidpower training, and other support, the families facing these serious safety problems were able to find solutions:

Current trends predict that one in ten children growing up today will be victimized by sexual abuse before age 18. While abuse rates have declined over the last several decades, sexual abuse is still a serious risk for both girls and boys. The vast majority of sexual abuse is perpetrated by someone in the child's family, or by someone the parents know and trust.[5]

For as long as she could remember, Danielle had been molested by her neighbor, who often took care of her and was a long-time friend of her family. She didn't have the words to say to stop him—and she felt ashamed and as if the abuse was her fault. She was afraid of upsetting her parents by saying anything and felt terribly alone.

Danielle learned that when an adult does something to hurt a child, it is not the child's fault and that it is never too late to tell. She was able to report the abuse being committed by her neighbor. The man has been arrested, and she is getting counseling.

Nearly one in three middle- and high-school students have been bullied at school.[6] *After their family moved and changed schools, both Pedro and Selina were shunned and tormented by a group of other kids. They would get shoved, pushed, and called names. When they asked adults at the school for help, they were forced to sit down and talk with the kids who had bullied them, who denied what had happened and accused them of having started it. The school counselor told Pedro and Selina's parents that they needed time to adjust to a new school and that they should try harder to get along with the other kids.*

Pedro and Selina's parents sought support and practiced how to talk with school officials about the bullying that the children were subjected to by their classmates. They eventually decided to change schools. Pedro and Selina learned how to stay aware, leave a threatening situation, protect their feelings, yell for help, and defend themselves physically as a last resort—and that, even if one adult doesn't listen or help, you should keep asking another until you get the help you need.

One in three students have been in at least one physical fight in the preceding year.[7] *Jeremy knew that he would be suspended if he got into another fight at middle school, but it was hard not to. Kids were constantly teasing him with cruel remarks like, "Your mother is a slut!" He felt like he had to defend her honor and that he would be a bad son if he didn't get back at them.*

Jeremy learned that his mother wanted him to make wise choices and be safe rather than defend her honor by getting into dangerous fistfights. He learned how to identify and manage his emotional triggers and how to walk away from trouble.

- Over 60% of children have been exposed to violence in their lives in the past year, either directly or indirectly, such as witnessing domestic violence committed by one family member hurting another. The National Survey of Children's Exposure to Violence also reveals that more than a third of U.S. children and teens up to age 17 have been direct victims of physical assault, primarily at the hands of siblings and peers.[7]

When Becka's father lost his job, he started drinking a lot and was constantly fighting with her mom, who would scream at him to stop wasting money drinking and to go find work to support their family. Becka felt frightened because sometimes her dad would get so upset that he would shove her mom and even hit her. Her mom said not to tell anyone. When Becka's older brother sometimes scared and hurt his girlfriend, Becka didn't say anything because she didn't want to make more trouble for their family and anyway, she understood that this was just the way men act sometimes.

With counseling and participation in an alcohol and drug abuse prevention program, Becka's parents learned that their fighting violated domestic violence laws and endangered the emotional safety of their children. They developed skills and strategies to resolve conflicts peacefully instead of escalating into violence. Becka and her older brother learned that, instead of trying to hide problems in their family, it was important to get help—and that neither men nor women have the right to threaten or hurt someone else.

The Economic Costs of Abuse

In addition to the suffering caused by abuse, this issue also has a serious economic impact borne by victims and their families and society as a whole. Each year in the United States, the effects of child abuse create lifetime costs of $124 billion.[8, 9] This includes legal costs, absence from school and work, emergency room visits, and other medical and psychological care. While we believe that personal safety of each person is priceless, understanding the economic impact of abuse can help to motivate lawmakers to allocate resources and change policies.

Safety issues also disproportionately affect senior citizens; individuals with physical, mental or developmental disabilities[10]; the diverse LGBTQIA+ community[11, 12]; immigrants; and people of cultures and religions whose voices are not equitably represented in social and civic contexts.[13]

Clearly, each of us needs to learn how to protect ourselves and those we care about, now and throughout our lives.

Although we still have a long way to go, the effort to protect children and end abuse, particularly sexual abuse, has been underway for several generations. The United States has experienced encouraging downward trends in crime and child abuse since the early 1990s. Even so, children are still exposed to an unacceptable level of violence in their lives. Beginning with the Columbine school shooting in 1999, more than 135,000 students in the USA attending at least 164 primary or secondary schools have experienced a shooting on campus. That doesn't include the number of suicides, accidents, and after-school assaults that have also exposed children to gunfire.[14] We each have to do what we can to make sure that all kids are safe, valued, and treated with respect.

Protecting Child Safety at All Levels

We have many roles in our lives—at home, at work, at school, as part of different organizations, in our recreational activities, in our places of worship, and everywhere we or our children go, in person or online. Whether we are participating as a leader, parent, or member, each of our roles at all levels is important in ensuring the safety and well-being of young people. **While being well-versed in personal safety as individuals is essential, that alone is not enough.** Children are often cared for by many different individuals or organizations, from babysitters, neighbors and relatives, to child care centers to educational institutions. Many kids are in sports teams, summer camps, and other recreational activities. Many families are part of religious communities. And when young adults leave the nest, they interact with colleges, the workplace, and other institutions such as the military.

Each of these activities can provide safe and important experiences for young people—and each has the potential for safety concerns to be ignored or left behind. In recent years, abuse scandals that have exploded into the public consciousness have illustrated the worst-case scenario: when organizations fail to protect safety, a situation can develop that is full of dysfunction and corruption that can be continually exploited by individuals who misuse their power. Being trapped in this kind of situation is dangerous.

Protecting young people requires vigilance and action from each of us, because kids get hurt when good people turn a blind eye, fail to see trouble, or do nothing to stop it.

Thinking about our roles as individuals within groups and institutions, large and small, led to the 'Protecting Child Safety at All Levels' approach that we are using in *Doing Right by Our Kids*.

Taking Leadership at All Levels

The goal of this book is to prepare responsible adults at all levels to take leadership by advocating and intervening to protect our kids and by equipping young people with skills to take charge of their safety as they gain independence.

Being aware of the risks and addressing the problems does not mean that we should be spending our lives in fear, or locking our children away, or over-sharing our worries with them about the risks they might face. On the contrary, we want to ensure that kids get many wonderful experiences in ways that are safe—and to prepare children and teens to take charge of their own safety and well-being as their independence grows.

Chapter 2 introduces Kidpower's core safety principles for adults and Chapter 3 introduces everyday safety skills that parents and caregivers can teach their children. We will share Kidpower's approach for *what to do and how to do it,* always teaching kids in a fun and upbeat way that is success-based rather than scary.

From this foundation based on Kidpower's skills and principles, we will work our way outward to explore what schools, youth groups, sports teams, camps, faith communities, and other youth-serving organizations need to know about creating safe environments, preventing abuses of power, and dealing effectively with problems when they arise.

Finally, we will look at "safety at the top"—a 10,000-foot view of societal forces that are bigger than any one of us but affect all of us.

Safety Checkup

✓ **Child abuse and maltreatment,** an accumulation of Adverse Childhood Experiences, are the basic underlying causes of many long-term societal and health problems.

✓ **While there are encouraging trends** in reduced rates of crime and child abuse, there is still much work to do: children experience too much violence, abuse, and neglect.

✓ **Child protection requires** a 'Safety at All Levels' approach as we advocate for safety everywhere we go, in-person and online.

Kidpower's Core Safety Principles for Adults

Kidpower's Founding Board President Ellen Bass is the co-author of a ground-breaking book for survivors of childhood sexual abuse, The Courage to Heal. *In 1989, Ellen and Irene were at the bank signing the papers to incorporate Kidpower as a nonprofit. Suddenly, Ellen said, "What we are doing here is revolutionary. We are saying that the safety and well-being of a child are more important than anyone's embarrassment, inconvenience, or offense!"*

Irene asked Ellen, "Can you repeat that please?" She borrowed a pen and wrote what became Kidpower's founding principle on the back of an envelope. Since then, millions of people around the world have used this principle to find the courage to overcome discomfort, so they can advocate effectively both for their kids and themselves.

I n this chapter, we will describe Kidpower's three core safety principles that form the foundation of our approach to child protection:

1. Put Safety First.

2. Use Your Awareness.

3. Take Effective Action.

Principle 1: **Put Safety First**

"Put Safety First" is so simple to say and yet can be so hard to do. As co-authors, we have found that, by taking this principle to heart, it has helped us to see things clearly and make better choices in ways that have changed our lives.

Putting safety first means using Kidpower's founding principle as your guide to assess the choices you make for yourself and your children.

On the surface, this idea seems obvious. *Of course* a child's safety and well-being are more important than *anyone's* embarrassment, inconvenience, or offense!

The problem is that fear of embarrassment, inconvenience, and offense are powerful feelings that often get in the way.

In Kidpower parent workshops, we sometimes ask participants, "How many of you hate to be embarrassed? … dislike embarrassing others? … don't want to be bothered when you are busy? … usually dislike bothering other people? …. don't like to have people be mad at you? … dislike the feeling of being angry yourself?"

And, with each question, most people will raise their hands! Then we ask, "Do you think your kids might feel the same way?" And most adults will nod their heads.

As families, we need to prepare ourselves—and our children—to accept the discomfort of embarrassment, inconvenience, and offense because we have made a commitment to Put Safety First. Although it can be difficult, deciding to Put Safety First can become the rock-solid guiding principle that will lead you through times of confusion, conflict, or uncertainty. When you prioritize safety, the protective effect on your family's choices and behavior can save you time, spare you misery, and also help to prevent problems for others.

Principle 2: **Use Your Awareness**

As parents and other responsible adults, we need to understand what the potential issues are that can harm the safety of our children and pay attention to what is happening with our children everywhere they go. Awareness can help us recognize trouble in advance, which in turn prepares us to avoid a vast number of safety problems by seeing a problem as it develops and taking charge of it by doing something to stop it.

One night, many years ago, Irene was camping with her husband Ed and their two young children at Lassen Volcanic National Park. As they were about to turn in for the night, Ed noticed that many people had gone to sleep without putting out their campfires. The wind had come up, causing the fires to flare up and send out sparks. There was a huge field of dry Manzanita bushes bordering the campground that would have gone up like a torch from even a few sparks.

Ed spent more than two hours going around the campground putting water on people's fires until they were completely out and pointing out the danger so that others would do the same. Thankfully, Ed was successful in putting out all the fires.

If Ed and Irene had thought there were still live embers in this dangerous situation, they would have woken up their two sleeping children, taken down their tent, and left, even though they had just set up camp after a seven-hour drive to get there, calling out warnings to other campers before they went.

Using your awareness also means noticing the messages that come from your intuition. From a scientific perspective, intuition is not supernatural or ESP; it is often perception that lies just beyond your conscious awareness. You need to train yourself to pay attention, listen to these important survival signals, and be willing to change your behavior based on what you sense at the edges of your perception.

Often the "storytelling" part of your brain (the neocortex) will try to "talk you out of" these perceptions that it does not understand. The first step in using your intuition is to be open to these perceptions, even when they seem strange, uncomfortable, or counterintuitive, rather than brushing off or explaining away a real danger.

"I just felt something."

One night on the way home from one of Amy's Kidpower parent education seminars, participant Kimberly Green had a life-altering experience. Acting on her intuition saved her life, the lives of her two children, and the baby she was pregnant with at the time. Here is Kimberly's story:[1]

> It was too late and chilly of a January evening for me to have my kids out, but I really wanted to attend Amy's 'Safe Kids in an Uncertain World' lecture at our school. My husband was working late, so I took them with me to school and put them in the childcare program.
>
> I had a lot on my mind when I gathered my kids a little after 9:00 p.m. and helped them get buckled into my Prius, concentrating on talking with them about the lessons learned in the seminar while it was fresh in my mind. There was a line of cars behind me leaving the school parking lot waiting at the red light to turn on to the main road, but I was first behind the light. The light turned green.
>
> Even though I was distracted trying to have this important discussion with my kids about their safety, I just felt something. I don't know how else to describe it. Although I normally have a bit of a lead foot, I hesitated. I gingerly stepped on the accelerator and then stopped myself and re-applied the brake.
>
> I still have no idea what really made me continue to pause. I remember two flashes of light: 1) the SUV's headlights behind me that was also waiting in line to turn, blinding me in my rearview mirror, and 2) another set of headlights in my left-hand periphery that were accompanied by a ... Zoom! The car flew, and I mean literally FLEW and BLEW through the red light on the main road. It was a sleek-looking sports car and it had those fancy high-intensity xenon headlights. This car was going so fast that it was gone from sight within seconds.
>
> What made me pause for several seconds at a green light? It was two to three seconds and that's a long time when you're first in line and leading the pack to get your pregnant self home—with your overtired toddlers in the back seat. I'm assuming my brain saw those headlights

before they really registered in my conscious mind, and I chose in that moment to heed that impulse. That's intuition. Or it was that night.

My family, including the baby in my belly, wouldn't have stood a chance in our small car had we been broadsided by another car traveling at high speed. If Amy had not spoken about the most important part of parenting being following your instincts, paying attention to that little voice or that gut feeling, would we have all been killed that night? Like Amy says, we all have intuition, but we do not all heed it.

Using Your Awareness is one of the most essential safety skills we have. Awareness is a tool that is always with us, if we can remain present in the moment and pay attention.

Principle 3: **Take Effective Action**

Kimberly's stoplight story and Ed's campfire experience show us that once you perceive a safety problem, your challenge is to do something about it. If a situation or person seems unsafe, change your plans. Be prepared to leave. Know how to be persistent in setting boundaries, advocating for your kids, and getting help.

People often feel helpless when they don't know how to approach a problem or navigate past obstacles that get in the way. Obstacle-busting options for a wide range of problems will be explored throughout this book.

Young people are especially likely to need adult help when adults are the ones causing the problem. When Irene's daughter Chantal was twelve years old, she was one of only four girls in her advanced math class. She complained because her math teacher kept looking at her in a leering way and making suggestive remarks. After talking it over with her parents, Chantal told her math teacher the next time he started this behavior, "I feel uncomfortable when you talk about how I look. Please don't do that."

Instead of respecting her boundary, her math teacher made fun of Chantal. He increased his remarks and started making drawings of women's breasts on the blackboard. Although Chantal didn't like the idea, Irene persuaded her daughter that it was time for an adult to tell this math teacher that what he was doing was not okay, not only for Chantal's sake but also for the three other girls in her class.

Irene made an appointment to meet the math teacher after school and said very respectfully, "I think you're an excellent teacher. You may not be aware of some things you're doing that make Chantal uncomfortable. I feel that your teasing remarks about how she looks are just not appropriate."

The math teacher, who was a large man, seemed to get bigger and bigger and redder and redder in the face as Irene was talking, until he exploded, "In my thirty-two years of teaching, no one has ever spoken to me like this!"

"Well," Irene said cheerfully, feeling thankful for all of her self-defense training, "after thirty-two years, it's probably about time."

"Get real!" he snapped. "Your daughter needs to stop being oversensitive when someone just makes a joke! Anyway, who are you to talk to me like this?"

I'm her mother, Irene thought indignantly, *and the founder of Kidpower!*

Instead of saying this out loud, in a firm quiet voice, Irene explained, "There are probably women right now who are sitting in therapists' offices saying that they stopped studying math or other subjects important to them because of those kind of 'just jokes.' And there are probably boys who are making girls' lives miserable by following your poor example. What you're doing is a form of sexual harassment, and I want you to stop. If need be, we can ask the school counselor to help us understand each other."

In the face of this adult version of "Stop or I'll tell," the math teacher deflated like a pricked balloon. "I'll do whatever you want," he said. He then added plaintively, "But I feel bad because your daughter doesn't like me!"

With a friendly smile, Irene said gently, "She might like you if you'd stop teasing her! However, it's not her job to like you, and it's not your job to like her. It's your job to teach her math, and it's her job to learn it."

After that, the math teacher's behavior changed not only toward Chantal but toward all the girls, and they did well in the class.

There often needs to be one person in a situation who speaks up and won't settle for inaction. Irene feels fortunate that her years of experience made it possible for her to put her own outraged feelings aside and advocate for her daughter's needs powerfully, respectfully, and persistently, even in the face of this teacher becoming very upset.

Another effective way of taking action is to move out of harm's way. In Kidpower we often tell kids, "the best martial arts technique of all time is Target Denial, which means *Don't Be There* when trouble happens." We practice and strongly reinforce that message before we teach the emergency-only physical self-defense skills that can help kids escape from someone who is about to harm them.

Using your awareness and moving out of reach means:

- If you notice someone acting creepy and following you on the street, you change your plan and go into a store.

- If someone knocks on your front door, you notice who is there and think before opening it—and teach your children to check with you instead of opening the door themselves.

- If you realize you have a bad impression of a coach who bullies kids, you decide to choose a different team, even if the location or timing is less convenient.

Put Safety First. Use Your Awareness. Take Effective Action. Are there times in your life when following these guiding principles might have spared you or someone important to you from a harmful experience?

Do you see the ways in which these principles can help you to protect the most precious thing in any of our lives—our children—from someone's thoughtless or destructive behavior?

The Bottom Line: Don't Give Your Power Away!

As parents and other caring adults, we need to be careful not to give our own power away, especially when faced with the opinions of people who have more expertise, authority, or knowledge than we do. When 14-year-old Tom started having a high fever and vomiting, his mother took him to urgent care. After his symptoms got worse, he ended up in the hospital. His mother kept asking the doctors to test him for West Nile virus, but it was very rare in their area and he didn't have the typical symptoms. Finally, when Tom's mother kept pressuring the doctors and they couldn't figure out what else might be wrong with him, they did the test, and it turned out that Tom had the first case of West Nile virus reported in their county that year.

One doctor said ruefully, "We should listen more to mothers!" In this case, Tom's mother listened to her intuition—the feeling of "something is not right"—and didn't let the judgment of the experts stop her from insisting that Tom get tested for West Nile virus.

Most health care professionals are extremely dedicated and competent people. However, they have lots of patients and not enough time. Even the best doctors might overlook something or make a mistake.

Most parents know their own kids better—and care more deeply—than even the most excellent experts can. The heart-wrenching vulnerability we feel when our kids get injured or sick—or need medical care for their special needs—requires a special kind of advocacy. We are often dealing with professionals who have a great deal more knowledge than we do about disease and injury, so we need to learn what we can. However, if the answers don't make sense or don't fit with what we know about our child, keep persisting, and, if need be, get a second or even a third or fourth opinion. Our job is to listen, to learn from the experts, and to keep asking until we get answers that work well for our child.

Working Together to Give Our Kids a Better World to Live In

Changing societal attitudes and behavior can be daunting. Overwhelm and denial often get in the way of what we need to do to address crucial issues that affect the well-being of our kids. Facing the facts and finding that there are other people who care about these issues and are willing to stand up to advocate for child safety can be tremendously empowering. Participating in a positive social process where each of us does what we can in partnership with others will increase our effectiveness by allowing us to find allies, so that we can work together constructively rather than feeling hopeless or struggling in isolation.

As South African bishop and human rights activist Desmond Tutu said, "Do your little bit of good where you are; it's those little bits of good put together that overwhelm the world."

In the following chapters, we will describe best practices, strategies, and skills for noticing problems, overcoming obstacles, and being proactive in keeping kids safe.

Safety Checkup

✓ **Put Safety First.** Don't let uncomfortable feelings get in the way of your speaking up for the well-being of your child or yourself.

✓ **Use your awareness.** Pay attention to potential dangers. Don't let disbelief or distraction stop you from staying aware of what is happening everywhere, with everyone, all the time.

✓ **Take effective action.** If you see a problem, don't just hope it will go away. Instead, make a plan to do something about it. If you aren't sure what to do, get help. If one thing doesn't work, try another action.

CHAPTER 3

Kidpower Tools for Protecting Children and Empowering Families

At age 16, Irene's son Arend left home for his first big trip on his own to go to a summer research program at Columbia University in New York City. Arend knew that for his mother and father, this was a bittersweet moment. As they walked together through the airport, Arend put his arm around Irene's shoulders and asked kindly, "Do you have any advice for me?"

Knowing that having permission to give advice was a rare opportunity, Irene thought for a moment, then sighed and said, "Please … remember to … look both ways before you cross the street!"

Arend stood tall and said, "In other words, Mom, you want me to Walk with Awareness and Confidence!"—a phrase he had heard hundreds of times growing up in a home infused with Kidpower skills. When it was time to separate, he hugged his parents tightly for a moment.

As they watched their son stride away from them on his own, Irene reflected that Walking with Awareness and Confidence is the first skill children practice in Kidpower classes and that Arend was going out into the world far better prepared than his parents had been.

This chapter shows how to apply the knowledge and skills created by Kidpower to protect young people from harm, and to empower them to take charge of their own well-being. Since 1989, Kidpower has worked with educators, mental health professionals, public safety officials, martial artists, health care providers, and parents—and with their children—to develop simple and effective tools and skills practices for keeping kids (and people who used to be kids) safe.

Don't Let Discomfort Get in The Way of Safety

As discussed in Chapter 2, Kidpower's *Put Safety First* principle is easy to say, and it can be hard to follow. Too many children have been harmed because uncomfortable feelings got in the way of their safety or made it hard for their adults to take action.

For example, not wanting to embarrass a friend can stop a parent from asking questions that should be asked before a play date, such as, "Do you have a gun in your home?" or "Who else will be there?"

Often, children are so embarrassed about having been tricked into some kind of sexual activity that they don't say anything to anyone.

Embarrassment makes parents more likely to second-guess their perceptions that something is wrong, such as when they learn about a teacher telling a child to keep a favor a secret. Instead of expressing concerns, too often adults discount their discomfort by telling themselves, "He didn't mean anything by it. I'm overreacting."

Fear of creating an embarrassing scene can stop parents and children alike from yelling for help in public in an emergency.

Fear of offending a popular teacher, parent, or coach can make it difficult to speak up when this person makes disrespectful comments or fails to intervene when children are saying or doing hurtful things.

Children who have urgently needed help with a safety problem, such as having been lost or bothered in a store, will say later, "All the grown-ups were busy. I know it's rude to bother them by interrupting, so I didn't know what to do." Kidpower skills and practices are designed to overcome the barriers of embarrassment, inconvenience, and offense so that safety problems CAN be addressed effectively.

What is 'People Safety'?

Kidpower defines 'People Safety' as how people can be safe with and around people. People Safety knowledge and skills prepare us to prevent and solve problems with people by taking charge of the emotional and physical safety of ourselves and others.

People of all ages have the right to be emotionally and physically safe—and the responsibility to act safely and respectfully toward others. What changes as we get older are some of our abilities and level of independence, some of our responsibilities, some of our legal rights, and some of the situations we face.

Fire Safety does not just mean "burning prevention"—it means learning to use fire for heat, cooking, and pleasure. Water Safety doesn't just mean "drowning prevention"—it means learning to swim and enjoy the water. And, People Safety does not just mean avoiding danger with people—it means learning to have joyful, respectful, and caring relationships and interactions with people, including our own inner relationship with ourselves.

Improving our physical health helps protect people from all kinds of diseases and increases their enjoyment of life. And gaining strong People Safety knowledge and skills can help everyone to have more fun and fewer problems with people—while keeping them safe from most bullying, sexual abuse, kidnapping, assault, harassment, and other emotional and physical violence.

Ten Core Kidpower 'People Safety' Skills

As adults, we must first develop a strong foundation of People Safety knowledge and skills for ourselves before we can teach children how to use these skills. Acting as leaders in creating positive social climates for young people requires being prepared to:

• Advocate and intervene effectively to protect children from harm;

- Set a good example by showing our kids our commitment to our own safety;

- Teach children how to take charge of their own safety and how to act safely and respectfully toward others; and,

- Enjoy life more through increased confidence, better relationships, and fewer problems with people.

The skills for safety with people are also the skills for success at school, at play, at work, and in life. When we believe that we are powerful, competent, and valuable, we are more likely to act in ways that will improve our relationships and increase our ability to be successful at whatever we undertake. These ten People Safety skills can prevent and stop experiences that take away from this belief—and can create experiences that develop this belief—for ourselves and our children. The Bonus Toolkit in the final section of this book features Kidpower Skills and Strategies, with detailed descriptions and how to practice and use them, starting on page 193. Here is an overview:

Kidpower's Ten Core People Safety Skills for Both Adults and Children

These skills are at the heart of what we teach and practice in Kidpower workshops:

- Stay aware and act confident.
- Protect your feelings from hurtful words or behavior.
- Stay in charge of what you say and do by managing your emotional triggers.
- Recognize what is and is not safe.
- Move away from trouble and toward safety.
- Check First and Think First.
- Set powerful and respectful boundaries.
- Follow the safety rules about touch, teasing, and play in healthy relationships.
- Persist until you get the help you need.
- Be prepared to use your voice and body to stop an attack.

Replacing Denial, Fear, and Panic with Preparation, Skills, and Prevention

Many times, parents don't want to discuss potential problems with their children because they are afraid of damaging their children's trust in the world as a safe and happy place. Then, when something frightening happens in the news or in their community, the same parents might try to make themselves feel safer by venting their fears to their children and making changes to family rules that they can't sustain.

For example, after a kidnapping or a sexual abuse case, parents often start driving their kids to school every day and talking in a way that makes the world sound scary. After a few months have gone by and things have calmed down, most parents allow their kids to start walking again. The problem is, unless parents have prepared their children with relevant skills, nothing has changed. This kind of inconsistency can make children feel anxious.

We need to separate our fears from our children's needs. We can discuss our worries with other adults, but our children do not need our anxiety. They need our commitment to protect them as best we can, our faith that they can learn to protect themselves most of the time, and our help in learning how.

When bad things happen, managing our children's information diet is every bit as important as managing their food diet. Hearing vivid details over and over and seeing the adults in their lives upset can be emotionally damaging for children. As parents, our job is to stay aware of what our children are hearing from adults, their friends, and the news—and to be careful about what we are saying when they can overhear us, even if they don't seem to be paying attention. In a calm, reassuring way, we can address any questions they might have about what they've heard, without providing upsetting details. Instead of dwelling on the bad things that have happened, we can give them tools for keeping themselves safe most of the time.

When people are taken by surprise in an emergency like a natural disaster, car accident, or attack, their first feeling is likely to be one of denial.

When faced with any unexpected situation, good or bad, it's normal to think, "I don't believe it! This can't really be happening!"

Disbelief can cause people to try to ignore a problem, making the situation more dangerous. Getting stuck for an instant in denial is normal, but we can train our children, and ourselves, to get unstuck quickly. The sooner we can let go of our denial and pay attention, the sooner we can start taking appropriate action.

When people feel threatened by danger, their fear triggers a flood of adrenaline in their bodies. Often, this rush of adrenaline causes us to go on "automatic pilot." Think of a deer that stands frozen in the middle of the road and then suddenly dashes right into an oncoming car. Standing still and then zigzagging fast can help a deer escape from a mountain lion, but the same response creates a safety problem when the danger is an automobile. Like deer, people commonly panic when they are full of adrenaline. We often do not recognize potential problems nor make our safest choices if we go on automatic pilot and start acting out of habit.

Unless you are going to a safer place, running away from a threat in a panic can make a situation more dangerous. As an upset uncle once told Irene, "My nephew and his friends were waiting for me to pick them up outside a big store in downtown San Francisco. A gang of older teens drove up and threatened them. The boys panicked and ran in all directions. A couple of them were caught and beaten up. A car almost hit one because he ran into the street. If only they had kept their wits about them, they would have realized that the big, self-opening doors of the store were directly behind them. They could have stayed together, backed up, and gotten help inside the store."

Automatic behaviors can lead to many kinds of trouble if kids don't know when they can make a different choice. For example, most adults try to teach children to be kind, friendly, polite, and cooperative. But children need to know when not doing what they're told is a better choice for their safety. A mother told Irene this story about her son Chad:

My six-year-old, Chad, is a pleaser. I've always told him to be a good boy, and his teacher has praised him for being so obedient. Yesterday, Chad suddenly had to go to the toilet urgently, but he listened quietly when his teacher told all the children to sit down and work. He eventually got so desperate that he couldn't talk at all and ended up wetting his pants. I feel awful that Chad was embarrassed, but I'm glad that nothing worse happened. We're going to be changing that "always do what adults tell you" habit to a "notice what you need and speak up to take care of yourself" habit!

We don't have to beat ourselves up every time we learn a life lesson like this one. We don't have to hold ourselves to perfect ideals. We do need to have the courage to learn from our mistakes! To paraphrase poet Maya Angelou, "We did then what we knew how to do, and when we knew better, we did better." This is true for us, and our children.

Life is always throwing out new challenges, especially for growing kids. Rehearsing solutions for different problems prepares children to make conscious decisions instead of getting stuck in denial or reacting in a panic without thinking.

Understanding the Power of Positive Practice

Kidpower's Positive Practice Method™ of teaching gives students the opportunity to be successful in rehearsing the ten People Safety skills through structured problem-solving role-plays, based on situations that are age-appropriate and relevant to their lives.

Adults tend to feel more awkward about these rehearsals than kids! If you're nervous about role-playing, remember to capture the spirit of your children's imaginative play. Remember that *how* someone practices is as important as the practice itself. Instead of letting a child struggle, first teach the skill.

Next, pretend to be the person who is causing a problem. If the child isn't sure what to do or say right away, pause and shift roles to coach the child like the prompter in a play who is telling the child what to say and do. Avoid asking, "What would you do next?" Instead, coach them in the moment so they know what you want them to do next. Then continue the role-play, going step-by-step and back-and-forth between acting like the problem person and being the coach as needed.

Here are some key tips for how to use Kidpower's Positive Practice Method effectively:

- *Stay calm.* You can set up safe positive practices for yourself and your children by remembering that getting anxious will interfere with everyone's learning. No matter how difficult or upsetting the issue is, you and anyone you are trying to help will learn better if you are calm.

- *Know your purpose.* Be clear about what you want the outcome of the practices to be, and what you or others need to be able to do or say to make that happen.

- *Look for progress, not perfection.* People are far more likely to accept practicing if they are being encouraged rather than criticized. Be patient with yourself and with anyone you are trying to teach. If someone feels upset about making a mistake, say something encouraging like, "Mistakes are part of learning. That is why we practice." You can use a very popular Kidpower saying by reminding everyone that, "You do not have to be perfect to be great."

- *Coach to ensure success.* When you or others take on a role, remember you are just pretending for the purpose of practice. This is not a test for you or anyone else. To ensure success, go step-by-step and provide in-the-moment coaching like a prompter in a play. People often need to be walked through a practice several times using different examples before being able to do it effectively. They are more motivated if they can see progress each step of the way.

- *Walk your talk.* If you are teaching respect and responsibility to others, be sure that you are modeling this behavior yourself. For example, if you make put-down jokes, use sarcastic humor, gossip about others when you talk to your friends on the phone, or chronically miss commitments—like being on time—don't be surprised if your students, children, or coworkers do the same.

Studies have shown that just raising awareness about problems, without practicing skills to deal with them, can raise anxiety. Using Positive Practice to rehearse how to handle different situations almost always reduces anxiety by building competence and increasing confidence.

Accepting That There Are No Guarantees

In a Kidpower parent workshop, one mother asked desperately, "How old is my daughter going to be before I get to stop worrying? I'm so tired of being so afraid!"

Her daughter was four years old.

With a great deal of sympathy, Irene had to give this worried mother some bad news: "My children are adults now and do a great job of taking care of themselves. But I never get to stop feeling protective as their mom, and my heart still skips a beat any time I think of a possible threat to them! And do you know what? My parents are over 90, and I'm almost 70—and they *still* worry about me!"

Accepting that there are no guarantees helps us to regain our perspective and sense of calm. Uncertainty is a reality of life. Constant worrying about what might happen will just make everyone miserable without making anyone safer. Instead, we can learn to manage our anxiety by taking effective actions that will keep our children safe most of the time.

As author Elizabeth Stone wrote, "Making the decision to have a child . . . is to decide forever to have your heart go walking outside your body." When we are lucky enough to have children in our lives, we have to surrender our children and ourselves to the occasionally dangerous fates of the world.

That's just the way life is. Letting our fears stop us from enjoying our own lives does not make our children safer. Letting our fears cause us to be constantly anxious and restrictive can make our children's lives more stressful and less enjoyable, but it won't make them safer. Ariel's mother learned this lesson through life experience:

I tried to protect my daughter Ariel from everything. I never let her climb up on a play structure for fear of falling. I didn't let her play in a swimming pool because of germs. And I kept her away from other kids and families who might stress her out too much.

When she was almost eight, Ariel got terribly sick. As I sat in her hospital room, I thought about all the fun my fear had kept my child from having. When she, thankfully, got better, I decided to set my fear aside and take more risks. Ariel has broken her arm, gotten head lice, and coped with being bullied. But her joy in doing new things has been worth it.

The reality is that, statistically, a child's major risk of being killed in the United States is from accidents, most often caused by being a passenger in a vehicle, something that is part of most people's everyday lives. However, by taking reasonable precautions such as using seat belts and car seats, and not texting while behind the wheel or driving under the influence, we can reduce the risks and keep the benefits of using our cars. We can apply the same common-sense approach to other decisions we make for our children.

We need to accept that, no matter how careful we are, bad things might happen that are simply out of our control. Yet we should not let those possibilities rule our lives or unnecessarily restrict our kids' experiences. Instead, we can take reasonable precautions and teach our children the skills they need to safely, confidently enjoy their lives, rather than living in an unnecessarily fearful little bubble. We want our children to see their lives as an adventure, rather than seeing uncertainty as a cause for worry and fear. When problems come up, we want our children to see themselves as explorers of life overcoming challenges, not as victims of the unexpected.

Managing Our Emotional Triggers

Being reminded about past upsetting experiences from our own lives, or thinking about the vulnerability of our children when hearing the stories of others, can trigger a flood of overwhelming feelings that make it difficult to stay calm. When we are overwhelmed with upset or anxious feelings, it is hard to think clearly and hard to make safe and wise choices for our kids.

For example, well-meaning, worried adults have made their children watch a video about an abduction over and over, or taken them to the place where a child has been harmed, or tried to test them by agreeing to have someone trick them into going with a stranger to find a lost puppy. These actions can raise awareness, but they do not make kids safer—they make them anxious.

Instead, we can get support for our feelings by talking about them with adults away from our kids—and, if need be, getting professional help.

Kidpower provides a number of emotional safety tools for managing triggers. In parent or teacher workshops, especially after something upsetting has occurred, we sometimes teach Calm Down Power—squeeze the palms of your hands together, take a breath, straighten your back, squeeze your toes down toward the ground, and let your breath out slowly. When you are connected to your body and breath, you are far better able to stay calm. Sometimes we have whole groups of parents pressing their palms together and breathing deeply and quietly as we discuss how they can protect their kids.

Being Prepared for Change

Although change is a reality at any stage of life, children tend to change more quickly and suddenly than adults. For parents and caregivers of children, this means that we are constantly readjusting the parameters for the supervision and limits we impose on our children to protect their well-being, while keeping up with their development.

At age one, Irene's daughter, Chantal, had just started to pull herself up to a standing position. With Irene and her husband, Ed, sitting right next to her talking, Chantal reached up to a table that had previously been out of her reach and pulled a just-poured cup of hot coffee onto her face. Thanks to good luck and the miracle of ice water, their baby was fine, but they have never forgotten the trauma of this experience.

The problem was that Irene and Ed were simply not yet prepared for the fact that their daughter could reach more from a standing position than she could when she was crawling on the floor. As soon as they understood this change, they moved things out of her way, watched her as best they could, and worked hard at teaching her to understand phrases like *Hot!* and *Don't touch.*

Adults can prevent many upsetting experiences by anticipating what is going to change when a child reaches a new level of development. Whether the issues are about People Safety or anything else, each change in skill, awareness, and situation leads to a need for reassessment. As children get older, we can expect changes in several areas:

- *Their abilities increase.* Being able to do more means that children can move around more easily, which brings more risks, more freedom, and more opportunities to learn.

- *Their understanding and curiosity increases.* Children may worry or wonder about new situations or problems as they become more aware of them. As their understanding and knowledge of the world grows, our ability to discuss their concerns and questions with them also grows.

- *Their boundaries change.* The preschooler who sat for hours on our laps and told us everything, grows into a preteen with a great need for privacy and personal space.

- *They go to more places and meet more people.* Part of what makes life interesting and exciting is being able to have new experiences, but simply assuming we know that each new place and person will be okay, or not okay, is a mistake. Instead, our job is to pay attention to potential problems and give children tools to notice what is and is not safe, tell us their concerns, and find solutions.

- *Their need for independence grows.* We do not want to abandon children before they are ready, and we want to support their development by fostering their independence and ability to care for themselves.

Over time, children will eventually grow from being in our arms, to holding our hands, to being within our reach, to staying where we can see and hear them, to being close enough to get back to us quickly, to being required to tell us what they are doing and where, to going many places without our supervision.

By preparing for the many changes that life brings, we can protect our children from most harm while teaching them how to protect themselves.

Making 'People Safety' a Habit

Teaching safety works best when the topic becomes an ongoing, upbeat conversation focused on what we can do to keep ourselves safe, rather than a one-time talk, or constant anxiety-ridden lectures. We must also set a positive example because what we do—the behavior and attitudes we model—is much more powerful than any words we say.

In order to help children develop strong People Safety habits, parents first need to agree on what the safety rules are for our children and families. We then need to communicate our expectations and boundaries with every individual, school, and organization responsible for the care of our kids. As soon as they are old enough to understand, we also need to teach and practice People Safety skills together with our children, so everyone knows how to follow the safety rules and what to do if something happens that is against these rules.

Finally, parents, teachers, and other caregivers need to coach children to keep following our established safety rules and applying our safety skills in daily life, so that they become established habits. Many of Kidpower's success stories come from children who have practiced these skills in our safety workshops. When they have relied on these skills later on, facing real-world safety challenges, Kidpower-trained kids have reported back, "I didn't have to figure anything out, because my body knew just what to do!"

Raising awareness is important. However, telling children and teens about the dangers of bullying, violence, and abuse—without practicing skills—can increase their anxiety without making them safer. Talking about these dangers and worrying about child safety can feel as if you are taking action, but the reality is that talking and worrying are not enough. Child protection requires recognizing unsafe behavior and intervening to change it; as well as rehearsing safety skills with young people, so that they know how to prevent and solve problems or get help to solve them when we are not with them.

Making these skills and habits part of your life will have a profound impact on your children. As one Kidpower student told us, "One day I was riding my bike in our neighborhood. Suddenly, a man yelled at me to 'get over here.' I didn't have to stop and think because my body remembered what we'd practiced in class. I yelled 'I NEED HELP!' Then I raced on my bike all the way home and told my mom what happened."

Kidpower's Six-Step Process for Preparing Young People for More Independence

1. Make realistic assessments about the situation and the child.
2. Teach about safety in ways that build confidence, not fear.
3. Learn, practice, and coach the use of the People Safety skills.
4. Co-pilot with your child to field-test the use of safety skills in the real world.
5. Conduct trial runs to rehearse independence in controlled doses with adult backup.
6. Keep communications open with listening, ongoing checking in, and review.

This process is described in detail, with examples of how to follow it, in the Bonus Toolkit on page 217.

Making SURE Kids Know You Care!

When teaching Kidpower in a classroom, we often ask the students, "Who would you go to for help if you have a safety problem?"

We encourage them to come up with lots of ideas—and then sometimes we turn to their teacher and ask, "What about YOU? Suppose your kids here have a safety problem, can they come to YOU for help?"

Of course, each teacher will immediately turn to their students and say in a heartfelt way, "YES! You CAN come to me no matter what. And I WILL help you!"

The problem is that far more often kids hear messages that can conflict with the idea of getting help—such as "Don't bother me. I'm too busy." "Don't upset anyone." "Be polite." "That's private."

For this reason, we encourage you to stop for a moment to make sure kids know you care by discussing the following Kidpower Protection Promise™ and asking other adults in your children's lives to do the same:

You are VERY important to me!

If you have a safety problem, I want to know —
  even if I seem too busy,
  even if someone we care about will be upset,
  even if it is embarrassing,
  even if you promised not to tell, and
  even if you made a mistake.

Please tell me, and I will do everything in my power to help you.

At any age, secrecy and shame are likely to accompany sexual assault, bullying, harassment, and other social or physical aggression, leaving people isolated, allowing this destructive behavior to continue, and making it harder to get help. Also, adult depression, domestic violence, and misuse of alcohol or drugs can have a devastating impact on the children in a family. For these reasons, we also recommend that adults make the Kidpower Protection Promise to each other—because we *all* deserve to have help instead of dealing with problems in isolation.

Sometimes a few words said at just the right time can create a bridge to help for someone who is suffering. Reminding kids and adults alike that you care, and that they are worthy of love and support, matters!

To prepare teens and young adults to overcome the difficult feelings that can get in the way of making wise choices, please encourage them to make the Kidpower Put Safety First commitment™ for themselves:

"I WILL put the safety and well-being of myself and others ahead of anyone's embarrassment, inconvenience, or offense, including my own."

Keeping these commitments in mind is useful for everyone in defining values, establishing priorities, communicating under pressure, and setting boundaries when other people act unsafely or disrespectfully—and is important in ensuring the safety and success of our kids!

Safety Checkup

✓ Separate your fears from your children's needs. We can discuss our worries with other adults, but our children do not need our anxiety.

✓ When there is a safety problem, getting stuck for an instant in denial is normal. The sooner we can let go of our denial and pay attention, the sooner we can start taking appropriate action.

✓ When problems come up, help your children to see themselves as explorers of life overcoming challenges, not as victims of the unexpected.

✓ Recognize that over time, children will eventually grow from being in your arms, to holding your hands, to being within your reach, to staying where you can see and hear them, to being close enough to get back to you quickly, to being required to tell you what they are doing and where, to going many places without our supervision.

✓ Protecting young people requires that you recognize unsafe behavior and intervene to change it, as well as rehearsing safety skills, so that young people know how to prevent and solve problems when you are not with them.

✓ Make sure that children and adults in your life truly know that you care and want to know if they are having safety problems.

CHAPTER 4

Creating Safety Within the Inner Circle:

Family, Friends, Neighbors, Babysitters

"Looking back to my childhood," recalls a successful physician, "I remember an elderly woman who lived across the street. Our family was not as wealthy as others, and some people looked down on us, but she always had a kind word for me. She offered opportunities to do chores so I could earn money, and even though I didn't do things perfectly, she expressed gratitude instead of criticism. She helped me feel proud of what I could do instead of feeling bad about my mistakes."

Experiences with kids' families, friends, neighbors, teachers, coaches, babysitters, and other caregivers shape our children's worldview. Although most people have good intentions, children are tremendously vulnerable to those whom they know, love, trust, want to please, or are told to obey. At the same time, at its best, the 'Inner Circle' of people with close personal access to children can have a profoundly positive influence on their lives, as the physician's elderly neighbor did.

As we think back to our own childhoods, we are grateful to the family members, friends, and neighbors who were mentors and who facilitated our joy and interest in life, encouraging us to play, learn, and grow. Irene still thinks of how her grandmother was so excited about every letter she sent and kept saying, "Irene, honey, I think you should *write*!"

We also each remember people who confused us by sometimes being an important source of affection, attention, and fun—and other times being unkind or abusive. According to a father of three, "I adored my older cousins and followed them around at family gatherings. Sometimes we played wonderful games. But a few times, these games became cruel jokes at my expense. I cringe each time one of those memories pops into my mind. Because of this, I watch my kids closely when we have large family gatherings. I step in to redirect hurtful teasing and encourage all the kids to be supportive of one another."

And we each have heard many stories about children who were harmed by an important person in their life who they feared and couldn't avoid. As a famous musician told Irene, "I was so good at playing the flute that my parents arranged for me to have private lessons with a talented teacher. He taught me so much that I became something of a child prodigy, playing at many public performances. But one day, when I was about 12, my flute teacher shocked me by suddenly kissing me on the lips and telling me that he wanted to teach me other things as well. It was hard for me to ever trust a man again."

If we look back to memories of our own experiences, we know how much the actions of adults close to us have harmed or helped us—and we want to make sure that our children's experiences with other people are as positive as possible.

Of course, parents and guardians have the right to choose the people they allow into their children's Inner Circle. However, in real life, the process of deciding who these people are gets complicated. Family members have expectations. Neighbors live close by. Children need and want to participate in various activities led by different adults, and these experiences often enrich their lives. And once parents have hired a babysitter, nanny, or caregiver for their kids, they often grow dependent on that person.

We call these people our Inner Circle and not our Circle of Trust because, no matter what our relationship is with someone, each person needs to earn and maintain trust. This takes time and a history of shared, positive experiences where respect for boundaries and openness are clearly shown.

What Do We Need to Know About Inner Circles?

We need to keep in mind that giving someone close personal access to children also means that we are potentially giving them privacy and control. Privacy means being alone, without another responsible adult there. Control means that someone has more power than the child.

Safety expert Gavin de Becker, best-selling author of *The Gift of Fear* and *Protecting the Gift,* describes how having more privacy and control creates a higher-stakes situation, making children more vulnerable to potential abuse.[1] A neighbor who walks by your yard with his dog, waves, and says hello to your family does not have direct access to your kids. Walking by and waving is a lower-stakes situation, especially if you or another caregiver are present, because the neighbor does not have privacy and control. If, however, your children go into the neighbor's home to play with their dog without you there, that becomes a higher-stakes situation because there is close personal access with privacy and control.

When adults are in charge of children, they have more control over those children. Most of the time, they use this position of power to protect children, to have fun together, and to help them to learn and grow. Adults in leadership positions, such as teachers or religious leaders, have additional levels of power and control because of their special roles.

Young people have similar power differences within peer groups. When kids or teens are in a group on their own, power differences can occur because of age, size, strength, maturity, ability or even force of personality.

Because it is normal for some kids to experiment with negative uses of their power, adult leadership is important to ensure that a potentially higher-stakes situation does not develop between kids, including friends and siblings.

Staying aware of the impact of privacy and control on a child's safety is important because ordinary, everyday relationships and activities often include, or quickly become, high-stakes situations. Following are some examples:

Babysitting. Choosing a babysitter is a high-stakes situation, even if we are "just" hiring the teenager next door whom we've known as a neighbor for years. We can increase our children's safety and reduce the babysitter's privacy and control by:

- Being clear about the rules—discussing them in advance and putting them in writing.

- Returning home unexpectedly from time to time.

- As soon as our children are old enough to understand, teaching them not to keep problems, games, or other activities secret.

- Regularly and consistently conveying the message, "Everybody needs to follow the safety rules" rather than, "Do what the babysitter says."

A teenage babysitter getting a ride home from one of the adults is also in a high-stakes situation. We can increase our teen's safety by making sure that they have the skills to stay aware, speak up, set boundaries, and tell you if anything uncomfortable happens.

In some situations, we might have our teen arrange their own ride home to avoiding being alone in a car with an adult they do not know well. This helps the babysitter avoid having to make judgment calls about drunk driving, as well as eliminating an opportunity for sexual advances to take place.

Playdates. When children graduate from playdates with their parents present to having playdates on their own in other homes, even with other adults present, that becomes a high-stakes situation. The key to safety is communication with the adults in charge. Instead of assuming that other parents will know our standards of supervision, we need to talk it through with them. Will the parent be home, or will a nanny or babysitter be in charge? Who else will be there? Are there older siblings present, perhaps with their friends too? How closely will the children be supervised? Are there guns in the home, and if so, how are they secured?

Are these conversations awkward? Yes, sometimes. But they are important, and other parents' willingness to talk about these issues is a good gauge of how close a relationship we might want to develop with their family. This is a good time to remember Kidpower's Core Principle to *Put Safety First*—ahead of potential embarrassment, inconvenience, or offense.

We all have our life lessons in this area. The first time Amy let her three-year-old go home for a playdate with a four-year-old boy from preschool, it didn't turn out as she had expected. She made the mistake of assuming that since they all chose the same Montessori preschool, their families would share the same kind of parenting approach, so she didn't talk to the other child's parent in detail ahead of time.

When Amy picked up her child at the end of the playdate, she discovered that the nanny had been in charge rather than a parent and that the preschoolers had played unsupervised in a yard with a pond. The two kids had spent a lot of time watching TV together while snuggling. The little boy's nine-year-old brother also had friends over, and none of the kids were closely supervised.

Amy remembers having a sick feeling in the pit of her stomach because things had been so loosely supervised and unpredictable. After that, Amy started her Kidpower training and became much more proactive in her conversations with other parents about what to expect on a playdate. She also decided that a parent's response to her questions would determine how much she would trust them to care for her child. Amy's child remained good friends with this classmate, but they didn't arrange more playdates outside of school.

Sleepovers. All the previous assessment questions apply, and a few other precautions are needed since a sleepover raises the stakes even higher, as kids are together overnight without direct supervision. For most children, it is likely to be harder to call home at 3 a.m. than 3 p.m. if a problem arises. We can't assume that children will automatically know that it is important to call, even in the middle of the night, if they have a safety problem. We can explain what we want our kids to do and then practice how to make the call.

Teen parties. Teenagers holding an unsupervised party are clearly in a high-stakes situation. Safety can be increased by making sure that adults are present and paying attention, rather than leaving teens alone. We can also increase a teen's control by agreeing on clear rules that will be communicated to everyone—and ensuring that they are prepared to take charge and stop unsafe behavior—or leave to get help if they ever find themselves in a situation that is getting out of hand.

Dating. Dates often start out with less privacy and therefore lower stakes, perhaps by meeting someone at a coffee shop or a group activity such as a football game. Over time, dating is likely to progress to situations with greater privacy by driving together or spending time alone together in a room. For both teens and adults, dating safety means avoiding being in high-stakes situations until you know people well enough to trust them.

As adult leaders, we can teach our teens to pay attention, whether or not they are alone with someone, as well as paying attention to changes in behavior that might signal a problem, such as anyone pressuring them to lower their boundaries. Situations can change quickly. Going behind the bleachers at a football game with one person is different than sitting in the stands with that same person or with a group of friends. If one person drives the other home at the end of a coffee shop date, that introduces far greater privacy and control than was possible at the coffee shop. And, at a big party, going into a private room with someone immediately creates a high-stakes situation, especially if alcohol or drugs are being used.

In order to prepare young people to stay safe while increasing their independence, they need to know how to pay attention to changes in context, how to set boundaries, manage their emotional triggers, de-escalate a confrontation, and, if need be, protect themselves from an assault as well as how to persist in getting help, even from a busy, indifferent or grumpy adult.

It is important to remember that if someone is assaulted, it is not the targeted person's fault; the attacker is responsible for their actions. When we talk about reducing the risk of violence, that does not in any way imply that we are blaming victims. Much like car safety or gun safety, it makes sense to know as much as possible to avoid or leave dangerous situations. But if a drunk or reckless driver injures innocent people, the fault ultimately lies with the negligent driver.

Avoiding a bad situation can prevent a lot of misery. As one teen told Irene, "I was at a party that was fun at first but then things started to get kind of intense. People were getting very high and going into back bedrooms and making lots of aggressively sexual comments. I told my friend, 'It's time to go home.' She didn't want to leave but I reminded her that we had agreed to stay together and insisted. Later we heard that the police had been called and found all kinds of drugs. We were totally thankful not to have been there."

Is managing our kids' relationships with other people uncomfortable sometimes? Can it be inconvenient, even embarrassing? Will our kids be annoyed when we remind them of something they think they already know? The answer to each of these questions is, "Of course! And my child's safety is worth it!" Keeping "Put Safety First!" in mind can help us be clear about our priorities and give us the boost of confidence we need to start a potentially difficult conversation.

Situational Awareness Helps to Determine When We Need to Take Action

"Situational awareness" means keeping in mind how the variables around a situation as well the changes in context can affect our perceptions. Lack of situational awareness about the physical and social environment around children risks our making assessment and decision-making mistakes that can lead to devastating consequences. The father in the following story was shocked to realize that he had failed to see a potentially major hazard to his young daughter in what seemed like a very safe place:

> *I was on the outside terrace at a nice restaurant with my three-year-old playing on the lawn—and didn't realize that, instead of being surrounded by a fence, the lawn slopped down to a stream that was out of my line of vision. I could see my toddler's head and thought she was playing in a protected area. I didn't know that at her feet was water, broken glass, and an unconscious man—until, following the Kidpower safety rule of Check First—she came back and told me. Thank goodness for her safety skills. Now we all make sure to practice using them, me included!*

In terms of your own Inner Circle, once you develop a sense of situational awareness, planning for what kind of privacy and control you will allow people to have with your kids can become an automatic habit.

Sometimes people worry, "But this sounds paranoid!" There is a big difference between being anxious all the time and being aware all the time. For a toddler, we do our best to childproof our homes, but we must still stay aware of situational hazards such as a pill dropped on the floor, a hot pan on the stove, or an open window on an upstairs floor.

Whether the issue is traffic, water, animals, people, or other potential hazards, people often fail to see potential problems or notice when a situation changes because familiarity leads to a false sense of security that Kidpower calls the 'Illusion of Safety.'

Staying aware of what is happening anywhere you or your kids might be and what everyone around you is doing is no more paranoid than staying aware of what cars are doing as you cross streets or move through parking lots. And the more capable and mentally present our children are, the more we can trust them to manage these hazards when we are not with them.

Suppose you are at a large, all-ages family gathering, and everyone is together in the backyard. The context makes this a low-stakes situation.

And then, if a group of kids goes to play inside, away from the larger group and adult supervision, the change of context turns this into a higher-stakes situation.

Using situational awareness makes it possible to minimize high-stakes situations most of the time. For example, you might say to the person you are chatting with, "Let's talk in the living room where I can keep an eye on the kids." If you feel your kids are ready to handle a situation on their own, you might say before you let them go to a party, "Let's go over the safety rules so that I have the peace of mind of knowing that you are prepared to handle any problems, that you will leave if someone starts acting unsafely or makes you uncomfortable, and that you will tell me what happens, even if you make a mistake or feel embarrassed, even if someone might get angry or make you promise not to tell, and even if in the end everything turned out fine. You can also call me at any time to come and pick you up without having to explain anything in the moment."

Suppose you are at a pool party and need to leave your children alone just for a few minutes to go to the bathroom. Of course, this is a very high-stakes situation because a child can drown quickly in a crowd without anyone noticing. In addition to being with caring and respectful people, you must make a specific, direct agreement with a responsible adult who understands the risks and agrees to be in charge of watching your child closely until you return.

When you allow someone else to be in charge of a high-stakes situation, here are the steps you can take to prevent and stop problems:

Select a capable and ethical person whom you trust to be in charge of your kids. At the pool party, for example, it is not enough to know that there are a lot of other parents around; make sure that a specific adult agrees to take full responsibility for the safety of your children in your absence.

Communicate your safety rules to the person in charge in a clear, forthright manner.

Make sure that your children know these rules and that everyone needs to follow them, including adults, babysitters, and other people in charge. Make sure to tell your kids you are leaving in someone else's care and who is in charge of their safety during your absence.

Teach your children that they should always tell you if they have a problem or concern—you will take them seriously and help them. As your kids develop, you can teach them age-appropriate skills that will help them become more independent and in charge of their own safety.

Empower your children with knowledge about how to get help if a situation with an adult or other kids becomes unsafe, even with people they know very well.

Ask your kids how things went when you were away.

'The Power of the Situation' Can Make It Harder to Make Wise Choices

In addition to paying attention to privacy and control, understanding how the built-in nature of specific situations is likely to affect decision-making can help us to make realistic assessments. Years of psychological studies have shown that most people tend to believe that our actions are guided by our individual characteristics and judgment.[1] The fact is that we are much more influenced by situations than we typically acknowledge. Not allowing 'The Power of the Situation' to undermine our commitment to safety is challenging for people of any age. This is especially difficult for children and teens who do not have as much life experience as adults.

Despite all of the programs about the dangers of drunken or distracted driving, too many times teens have been killed or injured after getting in a car with a driver who they knew was unsafe because they were caught up in The Power of the Situation of being with their friends or under the influence or power of a positive trigger like excitement or thrill.

Now, suppose you have a 16-year-old daughter who wants to go to a party where you know that the parents might not be supervising closely (or present at all) and that alcohol might be served.

Your teenager may look you in the eye and say honestly, believing it in her heart of hearts, "Dad, I can handle myself at this party. I would never drink alcohol. If someone hands me a beer, I will just carry it around and pour it out into a plant when no one is looking."

If we think back to ourselves and our friends as teenagers, we would be wise as parents to be skeptical about this claim. As sincere as your daughter may be, she can't look into a crystal ball and reliably predict what she would do if another teenager whom she liked approached her and offered her a drink. The Power of the Situation, peer pressure, and the desire to experiment can be hard to resist—and your daughter will be unable to reliably predict her reaction ahead of time. This speaks to basic psychology and inexperience rather than a character flaw.

There is an upside to this fact. For parents and other responsible adults, understanding 'The Power of the Situation' creates a firm and hopefully depersonalized ground to stand on when we draw limits. You might say to a teenager, "I *do* trust you. The problem is that I don't trust that situation, so I can't allow you to go to that party. Let's see what we can set up with another friend instead." Young people need understanding, skills, and life experience in order to be able to resist The Power of the Situation themselves.

The challenge for parents, educators, and other responsible adults is reflected in this saying attributed to Mark Twain:

> *"Good decisions come from experience....*
> *Experience comes from making bad decisions."*

The narrow path that adults must navigate requires giving children and teens enough freedom to explore and make mistakes while avoiding seriously harmful outcomes along the way. This balancing act can be the source of gray hairs and sleepless nights, yet it is the essential challenge we need to take on as guardians of the children in our care and guides in their development into competent adults.

Boundaries and Trust Within Your Inner Circle

Our children's lives will be far richer if they have relationships with a wide variety of people. At the same time, parents can help protect them from harm by setting high, thoughtful thresholds for each level of access they grant to people in their family's Inner Circle along with ongoing evaluations of everyone's safe or respectful behavior. As children become older and more capable, their adults can also increase their safety, physical and emotional, by teaching them the safety rules and the skills they need to follow these rules.

You may not always have complete control over who is in your Inner Circle, but **you do not owe anyone unsupervised access to your kids.** Trust needs to be earned, not granted automatically because of someone's status in the family or in society. How can we know when trust is established? Trust should be based on a history of shared positive experiences that is evaluated by specific, observed behavior and that is continually reassessed.

There are times when even very good people can suddenly stop being trustworthy. When Irene's daughter Chantal was a toddler, she loved staying with a neighbor who was paid for a few hours a week of child care. This woman was respectful and careful and highly recommended by people Irene knew well. One morning when Irene dropped Chantal off, her neighbor mentioned that she was nervous about waiting for some medical test results.

After Irene got to work, she suddenly became worried because it seemed as if the situation might have changed. She called her neighbor, but there was no answer. Even though it was the middle of the morning, she left her job and went back, arriving just as her neighbor was strapping Chantal into a car seat to go with her to the doctor's office to get some more tests involving radiation that they said she needed right away. The Power of the Situation had caused Irene's neighbor to lose her normally good judgment and, instead of asking Irene to come back, she was making choices in the moment that were not safe for Chantal.

Giving people a free pass from scrutiny because they are part of the Inner Circle puts children at risk. Unfortunately, too many times abusive people have worked their way into a family or organization's Inner Circle. Once they were on the inside, other people stopped paying attention to their behavior and either failed to notice problems or didn't take them seriously.

There are too many news stories about well-known people with excellent reputations misusing their access to children. These people used their authority, charm, and fame to work their way into the Inner Circle and then got away with inappropriate behavior including serious abuse because everyone fell under the Illusion of Safety. Once they got into the Inner Circle, too often people stopped asking questions because of their status.

We don't want to let this happen in our own Inner Circles. Until we have seen someone demonstrate trustworthy behavior over time, it is important to be slow and careful to grant unsupervised access to children and to try to minimize high-stakes situations. Examples of red flags to watch out for are:

- Any adult who wants to be your child's friend but not your friend

- Someone who continually asks that you trust them

- Someone who makes unsolicited promises

- A situation that seems too good to be true—because it often is

- Anyone who disregards your safety rules or tries to make you feel wrong for having concerns.

When behavior goes against our safety rules, we need to be prepared to restrict, deny, or revoke access to our kids.

Adults should not single out children with exclusive gifts or favors. For example, an aunt or uncle who gives presents to one child in the family should give equal presents to all the kids in the family. A sports coach might bring a treat for the whole team but should not single out one player for special gifts or privileges.

When an adult does single out a child for exclusive attention, gifts or favors, this is a time to ask questions and set clear boundaries.

Any interaction with our children should be open for discussion. As parents and guardians, we can insist that the people in our Inner Circle don't ask kids to keep secrets even if they are innocent and well-meaning. To help prepare our children in case this happens anyway, when young kids get old enough to understand, we can teach them the difference between secrets that are unsafe because they are just between a few people, and surprises that everyone knows about except the person getting the surprise, who will also know as soon as the party happens, or the gift is given.

There is a big difference between a grandparent pampering the kids by going out for ice cream—even though the parents might not approve—and that grandparent telling the kids to keep the ice cream a secret. This can be an opportunity for dialogue with the grandparents. It's not that Grandma or Grandpa is necessarily doing anything bad or abusive, but that keeping secrets about treats is unsafe. Some rules (dessert before dinner, TV watching) might be a little more relaxed at Grandma's house, but that must be something that everyone knows about.

Another safety rule that often causes concern in families is about not forcing kids to show physical affection through hugging, kissing, rough-housing, lap sitting, or holding hands. Suppose your children don't want to accept or reciprocate a hug or a kiss. You can explain to the family members or friends that you are helping your children understand their personal boundaries and ask that they support that effort by not pressuring your children and not taking their response personally by getting offended or hurt. Most people, including kids, don't enjoy physical affection with everyone they know all the time.

Instead of pressuring kids, we give them other acceptable options to show appreciation, respect, politeness, or kindness. For example, they can wave goodbye or blow kisses rather than give real ones. They can say "thank you" rather than giving a thank you hug. Even young children often enjoy finding alternatives. Kidpower instructor Marylaine tells a story about her son Colin who, as a toddler, disliked being kissed or hugged unless he initiated the affection. Colin made up an alternative where he would pretend to have a spray bottle to squirt air kisses at affectionate relatives.

Setting Boundaries with People Who Have Problems

Suppose you and your kids are going to a gathering of extended family or longtime friends. First, take a few minutes to think about each person who will be there and ask yourself these questions:

- Is there anyone who you know might act unsafely or unkindly, such as a child who often leaves one of your children out?

- Will there be people you don't know well, such as someone's new romantic partner?

- Will there be anyone there who has a drinking problem, gets easily triggered, or has trouble accepting boundaries?

- Is there any adult there who has difficulty supervising kids in ways that are effective and respectful?

- Will anyone be bringing a pet whose behavior might cause a concern?

If the answer is "yes" to any of these questions, you can make a plan about how you are going to keep your kids safe in this specific situation with these specific people and pets —and prepare them to take charge of their own safety as much as they are able. For example, you might take preemptive action about a child who leaves other kids out—depending on how the exclusion happens—by encouraging all the children ahead of time to make a plan so that everyone can feel welcome or to set the rules of a game before they start it to avoid conflicts.

If we cast a wide enough net, all of us know people who have problems, from alcohol misuse and drug addiction to other mental health issues. Some families have a member who has caused domestic violence or other physical harm.

Most people with problems do not do harm to others intentionally and have many good qualities. But if you know people whose problems makes them a potential risk to children, you must make sure that your children are not left alone with them.

Once in a Kidpower parents' workshop, a mother told Irene, "My family is very close to our neighbors, and our kids go back and forth all the time. However, their uncle just got out of jail for child sexual abuse and will be staying with them for a while. I have been wondering whether or not I should let my kids go there anymore. They love playing together, and it is so convenient. And after all, their uncle has served his time. He seems so nice and says it was all a misunderstanding. I don't want to be prejudiced against him—or to stop the friendships between the kids."

Irene made a reassuring gesture to calm the other parents, who were about to burst into outraged comments. She took a big breath and said gently, "I really appreciate that you are thinking about this concern even though changing how you do things would be very inconvenient and might offend your neighbors. I understand that you don't want to be prejudiced or to disrupt your children's friendships."

As the mother nodded, Irene continued, "Unfortunately, people who have molested children are at great risk of doing this again, no matter how much time they have served, how nice they seem, or how good their intentions might be. I recommend that you only have your neighbor's kids come to your house while this man is living with them. And, since they live so close by, tell your kids to Move Away and Check First before going anywhere near this man because he might not know how to follow your safety rules. Have them practice walking away from someone who seems friendly and has hurt feelings while saying, 'I need to Check First.'"

Even people very close to you, such as your own parent, aunt, neighbor, or best friend's husband might be harmful to kids. You may be at family, neighborhood, or school events with someone like this. This is when putting safety first—no matter who is offended or embarrassed and no matter how inconvenient—helps with setting boundaries and making difficult decisions.

The bottom line is that parents or guardians are responsible for setting the ground rules and requiring that people abide by them in order to have access to their kids. As we move outside the Inner Circle, into organizations and schools, we often don't get to choose who will be supervising our kids. Even so, we are responsible for thoughtfully managing and monitoring all relationships involving our kids, both through our own awareness and action and by paying attention to the policies and practices of organizations, schools, and other important institutions in our children's lives.

Safety Checkup

✓ Be aware that children are tremendously vulnerable to those in their Inner Circle whom they know, love, trust, want to please, or are told to obey.

✓ Keep in mind that giving someone close personal access to children also means that we are giving them privacy and control, creating a "high-stakes" situation.

✓ In addition to paying attention to privacy and control, help your child understand how the Power of the Situation can affect decision-making.

✓ Don't allow the Illusion of Safety to give you a false sense of security —whether the issue is traffic, water, animals, people, or other potential hazards.

✓ Trust should be based on a history of shared positive experiences that is evaluated by specific, observed behavior and that is continually reassessed.

✓ Be slow and careful to grant access to your children, and try to minimize high-stakes situations until you have seen a person demonstrate trustworthy behavior over time.

✓ Insist that the people in your Inner Circle don't ask kids to keep secrets even if they are innocent and well-meaning.

✓ Don't let others force kids to show physical affection through hugging, kissing, roughhousing, lap sitting, or holding hands.

✓ If you know people whose problems makes them a potential risk to children, you must make sure that your children are not left alone with them and know how to leave if they are mistakenly alone with them.

✓ The bottom line: you are responsible for setting the ground rules and requiring that people abide by them in order to have access to your kids.

PART II

How Organizations
Can Earn Our Trust

CHAPTER 5

Worthy of Trust
What Youth-Serving Organizations MUST Do to Protect Kids from Harm

When 15-year-old Tyler Madoff's parents sent him on a teen kayaking adventure trip in Hawaii, they trusted the Bold Earth Adventure Company to keep their son safe. Tragically, Tyler's exciting trip ended in his death through the negligence of the guides who failed to follow safety procedures. The company eventually made a settlement after a wrongful death lawsuit because Tyler's guides had violated their park permit by staying later and taking the group into an illegal and unauthorized area, and had ignored a high surf advisory.

According to the Madoff family's lawyers, "A series of large waves came over the lava flats, throwing the teenagers against the walls of the tide pools. The guides assured them that this was the 'fun zone,' and encouraged them to stay. A third large wave hit and an inescapable channel of water, head[ed] directly to the edge of a cliff …. Tyler's body was swept along, and he went over the cliff."[1]

The marketing of the company that Tyler's parents had trusted was not reflected in the safety practices of the people who were actually going to be in charge of their son.

A youth-serving organization (YSO) is any group that is organized for the benefit of young people. Although they may not have seen themselves that way, Bold Earth Adventures is a YSO that must take greater responsibility in the future for the actions of the people or subcontractors they employ in the activities that they provide.

The Many Youth-Serving Organizations in our Kids' Lives

The size of a youth-serving organization can range from a group of two people—such as one adult mentor with one child or teen like a "Little-Big" pair in the Big Brothers Big Sisters program—to a highly institutionalized group of millions, such as the Scouts or 4-H.

Whether led by one person or many, YSOs of any kind can have a tremendous impact for good or for ill on the lives of our children and teens. YSOs are woven into many aspects of our society, including child care, education, recreation, health, spiritual growth, social opportunities, or employment. Our kids could interact with several of them in one day. An elementary school, an arts program, a kids' sports league, a summer camp, or a local YMCA or JCC (Jewish Community Center) are clear examples of YSOs that leap to mind.

Religious communities are definitely youth-serving organizations, under what might feel like a larger umbrella mission of religious worship, education, and fellowship. Health care professionals provide treatments for children, sometimes without other adults present. And any number of businesses or professionals—a driving school, an ice skating rink, a martial arts dojo, a music school, a therapist, a dance instructor, or a drawing teacher—have youth in their care in the course of their work, and must provide for their safety.

Take a moment to think about the YSOs that involve you or your family, personally or professionally. You may find yourself adding to the list over time. Which organizations popped into your mind first? Which had less obvious connections to youth?

Recognizing the Responsibilities of a YSO

Sometimes businesses expand, or a nonprofit's mission evolves, without their realizing that they have now become directly responsible for providing a safe environment for young people as well as a service for adults. Examples might include a gym or resort that starts offering drop-in child care; a business that starts an internship program with a local high school or a health-care provider that lets children stay in the waiting room while parents get treatment.

Many parents mistakenly assume that organizations their family interacts with automatically know what to do to keep kids safe, especially if they are well-established. After the Jerry Sandusky abuse scandal, in which Sandusky used his role as a football coach and Second Mile nonprofit director to serially abuse kids on the Penn State campus and beyond, universities across the country started asking themselves anew, "Do we even have any minors on campus, and if so, what policies are in place to protect them?"

In some cases, the answers were, "Yes, the university has *hundreds* of programs serving *thousands* of minors, and no, there are few to no policies in place to guide these programs." Some programs were led on campus by groups that did recognize their roles as a youth-serving organization—for example, a university planetarium that hosts field trips and after-school programs year-round. But other programs didn't really think of themselves in the framework of serving minors, such as science programs that invited high-school research interns to work in labs, all the way up to week-long residential programs that were operating under little to no guidance about how to run a program for young people.[2]

Parents need to be aware that even when people have the best of intentions and have an impressive reputation for what they do, organizations that are not used to being in charge of kids sometimes make risky mistakes. One well-known university summer sports camp offered programs for elementary, middle, and high-school-aged kids, and then assigned dorm roommates alphabetically, regardless of age. Having a 14-year-old automatically assigned to share a room with an eight-year-old is inappropriate and shows a lack of understanding about camp management on the part of the leaders. Sharing a dorm room provides a great deal of privacy and control, which increases greatly the risk of abuse if a teen is put with a much younger child.

The good news is that more and more organizations are treating the prevention of abuse as a high priority, especially after news stories about decades of abuse that have emerged over the last few years and are still being made public. The result is that many YSOs now provide child protection training and resources for their staff, volunteers, parents, and children.

What Do Parents and Guardians Need to Do?

As a parent or guardian of children and teens, your job is to insist that any individual or institution responsible for your kids for even a short time makes sure that they not only know how to keep kids emotionally and physically safe, but actually are acting on this knowledge in an ongoing way.

You need to check out a program for yourself. Talk to the people who are actually running the program you want your child to participate in, and find out who specifically will be in charge of your kids. If you aren't satisfied that a safe environment is being created, don't be afraid to "vote with your feet" and take your business elsewhere. When you encounter organizations that are doing right by our kids with safe policies and actions, you can let them know you appreciate the job they are doing.

Basic questions to ask program leaders before enrolling your kids in a program:
- Who will be with my child?
- What happens if a staff member leaves? Do you hire each person directly, or work with another provider through a subcontract?
- What do you consider to be best safety practices for the kinds of activities my child will be doing? How are these practices implemented in your program?
- Do you have a statement of values that includes respect for differences?

- How do you train your staff to:
  - Do the activity safely? Parents often ask, "How good are you at teaching [art, canoeing, basketball]?" but don't always ask "How do you do it safely?" Both are important.
  - Prevent bullying and abuse?
  - Understand and demonstrate appropriate, safe standards of behavior of adult staff and volunteers toward kids?
- Do you do criminal background checks on all of your staff and volunteers who work with children?
- What kind of training do your staff and volunteers receive to prevent child sexual abuse and bullying?
- Do you have a code of conduct that all your staff need to sign and comply with? And if so, may I see it?

An adequate code of conduct includes:
- Rules that prohibit staff in group activities from leaving children unsupervised or from being alone with a child except for specific purposes and then only with parental consent. (One-on-one relationships such as for counseling or private lessons require a higher level of screening and are addressed below.)
- Guidelines for appropriate touch, language, and games
- Guidelines for handling and talking about situations, if any, when touch of private areas is mandatory for the child's health and safety (e.g., bathroom cleanliness support for preschool-aged children; removing thorns if a child falls into a sticker bush; and close physical contact, potentially including touch for safety, in certain sports like acrobatic cheerleading, etc.)
- Prohibitions on any kind of sexual activity with a child and requirements for agency and parental approval of any kind of sexual education

- Restrictions on online contact or private relationships outside of the organization

- A transportation policy that bars staff from transporting children except on official trips

- A bullying and harassment prevention policy that requires leaders to intervene early any time they see unsafe or disrespectful behavior toward anyone for any reason and that provides training in how to do this effectively

- Supervision policies to ensure that adult leaders are aware of what children are doing all the time that they are in their care—and that children know how to get help if they need it or anytime someone or something makes them uncomfortable

- Staff requirements to follow safety practices and legal restrictions even if they do something different on their own time

- Rules against giving gifts to children, and a policy about outside relationships, including babysitting.

Kidpower provides model policies and codes of conduct that can be downloaded for free from the *Kidpower.org* website and adapted for each organization's needs.

When choosing a camp program, another option is to look for programs that are accredited by the American Camp Association (ACA). As always, no accreditation should substitute for your own judgment, but an accredited program will have signed on to adopting industry-accepted, government-recognized standards.

Remember that a policy and code of conduct is only as good as its implementation. To be effective, a policy must serve as *rules to live by* in daily use, not just existing on paper in a binder on a shelf, or buried deep on a web page that few people visit. Group leaders should convey and reinforce expectations and policies on a regular basis as part of the organization's culture, and have clear policies for reporting concerns to leadership *and* following up on them.

'Two-Deep Leadership' and Special Relationships

Many youth-serving organizations require 'Two-Deep Leadership' as a best practice, which means having at least two unrelated adult leaders at all times with kids. This practice provides greater safety for the child and avoids having even the potential appearance of impropriety. These kinds of policies are necessary to safeguard children when parents or guardians are trusting an organization to ensure that the people caring for their kids are not going to harm them, as well as to make sure that there is enough adult leadership and back-up to respond to an accident or physical emergency.

Even when private conversations are necessary with a child, making sure that the conversation takes place in an observable location helps ensure safety for everyone. As a high school teacher, Amy would sometimes need to meet with a student in one-on-one meetings for tutoring or discussion. Instead of sitting in her office, which was more isolated, she would have the meeting in a room that had a big window adjacent to the hallway, or at a table in the library. This became standard practice that was easy to follow.

Policies should consider how to handle emergency situations rather than just specify absolutes such as "no adult should ever be alone with a child." For example, if a kid is alone at the end of sports practice and no one comes to pick them up, it would not be safe to leave the child there. A reasonable policy in this situation would be to have the coach call the supervisor and the child's parent, and let them know that the coach will drive the child home if no one else arrives by a stated time, or make sure the YSO has an emergency contact, outside the immediate family, that can be called on to pick the child up in these instances.

Organizations may want to discourage or prohibit outside relationships or have another sort of boundary regarding these rules, while leaving room for real life. For example, even though most Kidpower workshops are one- or two-time lessons, the policy is that there will be no private relationships between instructors and students (or parents of students), unless a relationship already existed, for at least six months after a workshop—and that any contacts with children online or in-person will never be a secret to parents or to the instructor's supervisor in Kidpower.

What About Important One-on-One Relationships?

Most children benefit from time spent with trustworthy adults, and private lessons or counseling sessions can be a huge benefit to young people. If you choose to have a child develop a one-on-one relationship with someone, remember that you are giving this individual a higher level of privacy and control with your child, and use an 'Inner Circle' level of evaluation as discussed in Chapter 3. Even if you are familiar with someone through a sport or other recreational activity, recognize that the situation has changed when you meet outside the bounds of a supervised, readily observable group program. Be sure that:

- Parents or guardians are welcome to drop in anytime—and do so unexpectedly.

- Kids are prepared with knowledge and skills so that they do not keep secrets about anything that happens or anything that bothers them, understand what the safety rules are about touch and about private areas, and are ready to get help if someone breaks these rules.

- The organization provides clear rules and guidance about relationships outside the YSO's official activities. For instance, a summer camp might have a rule that their counselors may not be allowed to be hired to babysit their campers outside the camp program. This type of rule might seem inconvenient, but it serves an important purpose and is not meant to offend anyone or "make them wrong"; the rule just needs to be followed.

Social media interactions can count as one-on-one private conversations. Camp Daggett in Northern Michigan has served many generations of summer campers since 1925, and their leadership has continually adapted to changing times. Even though camp itself remains a rustic, lakeside experience, the leaders have developed a very thoughtful social networking policy that explains the reasons why the camp discourages social media contact between campers and counselors after camp is over. Camp Daggett's policy reads in part:

"Our pledge is to put your children in the company of the most trust-worthy and capable young adults we can hire—counselors who are well suited to the task of caring for campers. The effort we put into screening and selecting our staff is part of that pledge. Our staff members work with your children in the context of a visible, well scrutinized environment that has many built-in checks and balances. Counselors are supervised by senior staff guided by clear, firm policies regarding behavior. Their actions are also visible to co-workers and campers. In general, *we discourage our staff from having contact with your children after camp and from sharing information through social networking sites, blogs, or personal Web sites, since we cannot supervise it.* We hire our staff for the camp season and train them extensively in such policies, but we cannot take responsibility for their behavior off-season. We also respect their desire for continued privacy during the off-season."[3]

The Pitfall of The Illusion of Safety Within Organizations

Good intentions are important but not enough. Kids having fun is great but not enough. Even having an excellent organizational reputation is not enough, because many child predators have not been convicted and will pass a background check.

Even very caring, responsible adults can be lulled into complacency by the Illusion of Safety. The Illusion of Safety happens when people feel so trusting, relaxed, sheltered, or distracted that they fail to ensure that their children and teens have adequate protection, knowledge, and skills to avoid potential dangers. Sadly, the Illusion of Safety can lead to young people experiencing trauma, injury, or even loss of life from problems that could have been prevented.

Two unhelpful habits that contribute to the Illusion of Safety are the 'Wishing Technique' or 'Worrywart Technique.' The Wishing Technique involves hoping that our wishes will make things happen or not happen the way we want without actually doing anything. These are rationalizations that don't actually help! Don't give in to thoughts and statements like, "I'll just be gone for a minute." Or, "This is a safe place. Of course, things like that don't happen here." Remember that children can come to harm within a few seconds and that "here" might mean many square miles filled with thousands of people, if it happens to be a place or a community that the adult feels attached to, such as a special annual festival. A place is only as safe as the people in that space are acting at any given time—and only as safe as the children are either protected from or prepared to avoid hazards like cars, running water, animals, or cliffs.

The Worrywart Technique involves investing time, thought, and energy worrying about all the bad things that might happen without taking any action to build skills to address our worries. The Worrywart Technique can make everyone miserable and does not make children safer.

When you notice yourself or others wishing or worrying, stop and think. What is most likely to cause danger here? What kind of supervision and/or skills does my child need to be safe here?

Intellectually, we know that parents and other adult leaders need to stay aware of potential problems and *take action sooner rather than later* to address them. We know that proper supervision, staying in charge of what is happening with our kids, and speaking up about any concerns can prevent a great deal of suffering.

And yet, all too often, **after** harm has come to a child that could have been prevented, everyone says sadly, "NOW, we realize we should have done things differently." In order to understand how to prevent this from happening, we need to understand what gets in the way of our dealing with problems proactively instead of after something awful has happened.

Why Do We Wait Until It is Too Late to Act on a Potential Problem?

Without adequate safeguards and an ongoing commitment to honoring these safeguards, even very ethical and caring individuals and organizations often have trouble dealing with problems. Understanding these pitfalls helps us overcome obstacles, to make sure that problems are addressed fully. Here is what gets in the way.

As individuals, the drive to preserve our self-image of being a good person is normal. When faced with behavior that might be harmful to a child, taking responsibility requires:

- Strong awareness

- An understanding of the impact of this unsafe behavior

- Healthy boundaries

- Excellent communication skills

- A high level of personal integrity

- Acting respectfully while accepting that others may say you are "being too nice"

- Preparation to stay calm and confident in the face of others' disapproval, anger, bad mouthing, or other strong feelings.

Without all of these qualities and skills, most of us are likely to try to protect our self-image rather than acknowledge and solve the problem.

When confronted with a difficult situation, we might:

- Ignore the concern, hoping it will go away

- Make excuses by saying, "This happened because of things outside my control."

- Deny responsibility, by saying, "But it's not my job to do this." Or "I'm sure someone else is taking care of it."

- Deny that there is a problem by saying, "That didn't really happen."

- Minimize the concern by saying, "It wasn't that bad."

- Counter-attack by saying, "This problem is actually the fault of the other person."

The more prominent or well-known a group is in its community, the more this need to preserve reputation gets magnified. Most people who have a deep need to believe in the integrity of their family or organization will try to avoid information that conflicts with this image. This is why people tend to look the other way, use the Wishing Technique, make excuses, minimize, or blame the victim rather than do something to fix the problem.

The result is that institutions often try to protect their reputations rather than address issues proactively—unless and until their members at all levels decide to do differently.

Speaking Up with Patience and Persistence

Amy found out that her child's school was planning to rent a 12-passenger van to drive the sixth-grade class for their big trip to Washington, DC, almost 300 miles away.

Through discussions with insurance experts, Amy knew that despite being commonly used to transport people, 12-passenger vans are actually inherently unsafe and prone to serious accidents and roll-overs, especially when fully loaded with people and gear.

When Amy told the Assistant Head of School about the risks of using these vans to transport the students, at first the assistant head resisted. She expressed a list of objections including "we already have this planned," "it would be inconvenient to change," "it would cost too much to fly" and "we all want to travel together in one group."

Amy was patient, laying out her case that the 12-passenger van was an unacceptable option, providing facts and research to back up her assertion. Amy acknowledged the Assistant Head's feelings and kept the conversation going by saying things like, "I can understand that this feels like a big change right now. I know you have used these vans in the past and all went well— and this new knowledge about the dangers changes things. I am very concerned about the use of these vans for our kids."

A couple of days later, the Assistant Head responded that the school had decided that they would change the plan. The two teachers on the trip would each drive one car load of kids in their own cars, staying together in a caravan. The one downside was that they would not travel as one big group in the same vehicle, but that was an acceptable trade-off for every-body, and this solution even cost less than renting the van would have.

Anticipating safety concerns when possible makes this process go more smoothly. Having time to spread out the decision-making process over multiple conversations allowed the Assistant Head a chance to think over and agree with Amy's request, rather than just give in grudgingly. And, there are times that in order to Put Safety First, parents will have to put their foot down in the moment and insist on a safer plan, even if people get upset with them.

Making Safety an Ongoing Habit

What we have said about helping kids to develop strong safety habits is also true of organizations: safety needs to be an ongoing conversation, not a one-time event. Written polices and stated practices can become mean-ingless unless the people at all levels constantly uphold their commitment to child protection.

Instead of waiting for others to do something, each person involved in an organization or group must take responsibility for making statements and taking actions that reflect their organization's policies and practices on a daily basis in every situation or problem. People at all levels in an organi-zation—leaders, staff, volunteers, parents, and kids—must work together to create a culture of safety and respect for all their members.

Reporting Potential Child Abuse

Laws about who is required to report child abuse or maltreatment vary from state to state and country to country. Morally, we think all responsible adults should realize that we each have a responsibility to do something to stop someone who is harming kids. If you have a concern about how a child is being treated, in the USA you can reach out to the Childhelp National Child Abuse Hotline, 1-800-4AChild (1-800-422-4453). This hotline is staffed by trained counselors who will help you sort out the situation and decide if a problem is reportable, and they can connect you with resources in your area. Globally, many countries have such hotlines.

Lessons from Safety Leaders: The Redwoods Group—Learning to Look Under the Surface

We can learn from leading innovators in the field of child protection, such The Redwoods Group, based in Morrisville, North Carolina. This innovative insurance company has gained deep knowledge and insight on child safety issues as the insurer of over 500 YMCAs, JCCs, Boys and Girls Clubs, and summer camps across the country.

Co-Founder and CEO Kevin Trapani sums up his guiding philosophy that safety is always his primary concern. If inconvenience or cost come up as obstacles, he states that, "We make it very clear to the groups we insure that if they can't afford to offer a program safely, then they can't afford to offer it at all."

As curators of the awesome responsibility of providing programs for so many children, Redwoods Group trains its member organizations and their staff how to *look below the surface* in ensuring safety for the young people in their care. As part of their work with recreational programs, Redwoods has had to provide crisis response to families and organizations after a drowning has occurred. At the same time, they also analyzed what happened in order to develop best practices for preventing future drownings. They work with so many organizations that they can accumulate more information on these tragic occurrences than any individual organization's executive director could ever accumulate in a lifetime. Redwoods Group President and lawyer Gareth Hedges shared the following organizational wisdom, to add to Kevin Trapani's insights.[4]

Through their research, Redwoods experts realized that some lifeguards were positioned in a low-level chair on the pool deck, providing them poor visibility, so the first step was moving lifeguards up into the position where they could see the whole pool more clearly. Next, lifeguards had to be trained properly *how* to observe and carefully scan the pool. Redwoods staff spent a lot of time training aquatics directors and lifeguards to look below the surface of the water, to scan the pool from the bottom up. They taught them that a drowning victim doesn't look like the person who is splashing and yelling for help that you might see in a movie, but is a fast, silent process. Once drowning victims are under the water, they are extremely difficult to see, so lifeguards must know where to look, what to look for, and how to look actively.[5]

The willingness to "look below the surface" demonstrated in Redwoods' approach also applies to stopping child sexual abuse. Most people will stop abuse if they understand that this is what is happening. However, abusive behavior itself rarely happens out in the open. Instead, community members are more likely to see the warning signs of grooming behavior, and an abuser's attempt to create a close connection with a specific child and their family, in order to eventually gain access to and power over the child.

As part of the Redwoods training, staff, and often parents, are educated about the warning signs of abuse and about the safety rules that are in place to prevent the kind of grooming behavior that increases the risks of abuse, such as singling out some children for special attention, giving gifts or doing favors privately, trying to get time alone with kids, and asking children to keep problems a secret. In addition to making abuse against the rules, Redwood recommends that its members also *make grooming behavior itself against the rules and reportable to the leadership.*

Unfortunately, many abusive relationships happen after a relationship that started at camp or a recreational facility leads to grooming behavior and molestation away from the camp. This is why Redwood recommends that organizations' policies specify strict boundaries about outside relationships between staff and children.

Redwoods recommends that reporting problems should start with making clear rules and asking parents to report when those rules are broken. Unless there is very clear evidence of wrong-doing, it is a very big leap for a parent to say, "I believe that my daughter's soccer coach is a sexual predator." Instead, parents can call the Parks & Recreation director and say, "My daughter's soccer coach gave her a gift. You told me that was against the rules so I'm reporting that it happened." Or, "We have practices twice a week, but the coach has suggested that my son come have private instruction on Saturday morning, and I understand that's not appropriate in this setting unless we check first and get your approval." Identifying observable behaviors that parents can respond to, and bring to the attention of program leaders, is one way that organizations can identify and disrupt the grooming process that can progress to abuse.

The Redwoods Group's mission to use their knowledge and experience to actively create a safer society shines through in their purpose statement, which says in part, "We hold ourselves and our stakeholders to a high moral standard. We courageously share data-driven truth, even when it's inconvenient. Our work—delivered directly, through our customers and through other key partners—catalyzes behavior changes that make our communities safer. Our actions save lives and reduce injuries."[6] One of those key national partners is Darkness to Light.

Darkness to Light: Protecting Children in Community

Darkness to Light is a national advocacy organization that raises awareness about childhood sexual abuse, in order to educate adults and get them to take protective actions. Darkness to Light works with youth-serving organizations and by extension, communities. Inspired by Malcolm Gladwell's work in *The Tipping Point,* Darkness to Light has partnered with groups, including the Y and Redwoods Group Foundation, to train over a million people across the USA. Darkness to Light has a "first milestone" goal of training 5% of the adults in a community, in an effort create a critical mass of trained adults in each community who know how to prevent and detect child sexual abuse to stop it in its tracks.[7]

Darkness to Light *Stewards of Children*© training provides important education for anyone with responsibility for children—from camp counselors who are teenagers themselves, to all staff members up to CEOs. The training can be taught by an in-person facilitator or presented as online education. It is the kind of training that parents could ask their YSO leadership to require for all staff, from camp counselors on up. The training emphasizes "5 Steps to Protecting our Children."

Darkness to Light's 5 Steps to Protecting Our Children™

These steps are a guide to help adults protect children using simple and practical actions to prevent abuse or intervene if abuse is suspected.

Step 1: Learn the Facts

Over 90% of sexually abused children are abused by someone known by the child or family and 1 in 10 children will be sexually abused before their 18th birthday.

Step 2: Minimize Opportunity

More than 80% of child sexual abuse incidents occur when children are in isolated, one-on-one situations with adults or other youth.

Step 3: Talk About It

Open conversations with children about body safety, sex, and boundaries is one of the best defenses against child sexual abuse.

Step 4: Recognize the Signs

The most common symptoms of child sexual abuse are emotional or behavioral changes.

Step 5: React Responsibly

Intervening when boundaries are crossed or reporting suspected abuse is critical to protecting all children from sexual abuse.

An Organizational Point of View: Four Key Decisions to Turn Principles into Action

Each individual and group that cares for children—be this family, religious, educational, social, health, or recreational—can learn how to be open to negative information and address problems in a constructive, balanced fashion. Hiding from potential issues doesn't work, and neither does over-reacting. We encourage parents to study these principles and use them as a standard to hold up for the organizations who care for your kids.

Here are four decisions that organization leaders need to put into action to protect the safety of the children in their organization's care:

1. Protecting child safety is our highest priority—far above protecting our image or reputation. Saving face in the short run can cause terrible harm and can also lead to severe damage to reputations in the long run. To *Put Safety First* means making all forms of emotional and physical violence and abuse explicitly and publicly against the rules.

2. We will make it safe for everyone to speak up. One of Kidpower's fundamental boundary rules is that "Problems should not be secrets." However, people are too often stopped from speaking up about safety concerns because of fear of loss—of credibility, jobs, money, and/or relationships.

Addressing safety concerns sooner rather than later can prevent problems from escalating and can help to build a reputation for integrity and commitment to upholding values.

Making it safe for people to speak up means having everyone in positions of power commit to putting their egos and fear aside and *listening* to someone's story. Often, stories have more than one side, so be prepared to listen without judgment and to look for solutions rather than blame.

3. No one is above the law, and the safety rules apply to everyone. No one's power, charisma, status, job title, financial contributions, or popularity should make any individual exempt from the rules.

However, the rules should be fair, equitable and allow for appropriate consequences depending on the specifics of what happened and who is involved. Applying rules automatically without thought can lead to overreactions that reduce safety. A kindergartner trying to peek under a little girl's skirt should simply be stopped in the moment—and this behavior is not the same as a group of kids pulling off another kid's pants, which requires a higher level of management, in the moment and after the fact. The two situations, even in the same group of children, call for different responses.

Be prepared to take action to stop unsafe behavior without overreacting. If you see a problem, stay calm, interrupt the behavior, make sure you understand the whole story, listen to different perspectives, and think about the purpose of the safety rules.

4. A position of power with children is a privilege, not a right. Within an organization or institution, the privilege of staff or volunteers being in contact with children should depend on their responsible actions in upholding the safety rules.

An adult's failure to manage any privilege safely should logically result in a loss of that privilege. If a person drives or is responsible for children when they are incapacitated by being under the influence of alcohol or other drugs, the logical consequence could be to lose the privilege to drive or to be the person in charge of kids unless there is enough assurance that this will not happen again.

People of any age or position who fail to see or deliberately cross someone's boundaries need to learn how to respect the boundaries of others. If this behavior is hurtful, they need to make amends and show commitment to behaving differently. Depending on the behavior and the role of the person who caused the problem, job termination may be an appropriate response.

Although some causes might be out of our control, we must look carefully anytime a child is harmed to understand what happened and figure out how to prevent future problems.

Safety Checkup

✓ Don't let any group or person's prestige, position, kindness, or authority blind you to potential abuses of power or risks of neglect.

✓ Even if a person, place, or group seems great at first, keep checking in. Drop by unexpectedly. Pay attention to potential safety problems. Be prepared to advocate for solutions rather than just hoping that problems will fix themselves.

✓ Even if other people notice a problem and seem concerned, be persistent in speaking up until your concern is addressed. Even though you may be the only one who does, many people might benefit in the end.

✓ Trust your own intuition and judgment and take action if anything seems wrong to you.

✓ Most of all, stay in good communication with your kids so that you really know what's happening in their lives.

✓ As adults, we are responsible for making safety for children a priority at home, at school, and in our communities. Make sure your words are backed by actions to *put safety first*—ahead of *embarrassment, inconvenience, or offense*—every day, everywhere, with everyone.

CHAPTER 6

Kids Learn Best When They Feel Safe:
Tools for Schools

Twelve-year-old Lloyd enjoyed having long hair but was being constantly ridiculed by a group of his classmates, who called him a girl, a sissy, and gay. When his mother approached the teacher, he said that the problem was Lloyd's long hair and recommended that, instead of trying to be different, her son should just cut it off. When the bullying escalated to a couple of kids pulling Lloyd's hair and knocking him down, the school principal stepped in and gave three-day suspensions to these children, according to the "zero tolerance" policies of the school. The parents of the suspended children then threatened the school with a lawsuit for unfair treatment, since they claimed that students were insulting and pushing each other around all the time.

This story of Lloyd's bullying includes teachers initially minimizing the problem and then administrators over-reacting with three-day suspensions when the problem escalated. Planning and implementing a consistent approach to solving problems can help schools avoid swinging back and forth between the extremes of under-reaction and over-reaction.

Most children ages 5 to 18 spend the majority of their waking hours at school. At their best, schools create safe and joyful learning environments that prepare their students to survive and thrive in today's challenging world. Schools also create caring communities where families and educators work as a team to support children and adults alike. It is crucial that schools invest the time, attention and resources needed to create a safe social climate for all students.

Unfortunately, too many schools are struggling to meet overwhelming and conflicting priorities that often get in the way of achieving their potential. Instead of working together as a team to address challenges to the well-being of the children and teens in their care, parents, teachers, and school administrators are often torn in different directions.

The good news is that almost everyone involved in a school community has the same goals. We want kids to:

- Enjoy school most of the time.

- Be and feel safe and respected all of the time.

- Act safely and respectfully toward others all of the time.

- Develop confidence and competence.

- Learn what they need to know in order to have a happy and successful life.

Achieving these goals takes a commitment to communication, team-work, and problem-solving involving all members of a school community. In this chapter, we will build on the last chapter's foundation of best practices for youth-serving organizations, which apply to schools as well. We will examine with compassion the different perspectives of parents, teachers, and school administrators. Then we will take a look at the specific challenges and mandates that schools are faced with, obstacles that can get in the way of change, and strategies to get unstuck. Finally, we will look at two sets of Kidpower strategies, one for school leaders about creating a culture of safety and respect, and one for parents about what to do if your child is being bullied at school.

The Family's Perspective

Almost every day, upset mothers, fathers, and other family members contact Kidpower and tell us stories about the problems their kids are having at school.

"My seven-year-old son says he doesn't want to go to school anymore because other kids push him and make fun of him at recess, and the teachers don't do anything to stop it."

"My ten-year-old little sister says she feels desperate because her best friend at school suddenly joined a group of other girls who refuse to talk with her at lunchtime."

"My five-year-old had always behaved perfectly at preschool and is now being reprimanded for hitting other kids. He says they hit him first, and the grown-ups don't seem to notice."

"My fourteen-year-old grandson says that he keeps getting an upset stomach after lunch because his history teacher yells at the kids, tells horror stories about war and torture, and can't seem to control the class."

"My twelve-year-old daughter got a sprained back in physical education class because the teacher told the girls to stand in two lines and run into each other. She is small and just got mowed down by a larger girl."

"My noise-sensitive eight-year-old son came home with a headache because his class was at a very loud assembly, and the teacher had told the children not to leave their seats."

"I was horrified when my fifteen-year-old daughter said that a speaker in her health class gave information that I knew was inaccurate and potentially dangerous."

"My thirteen-year-old nephew had his shirt ripped off and was tossed into the trash can at gym. His teacher said it was just a joke."

"When I tried to talk to my child's teacher about what was going on, he said he understood but didn't do anything to solve the problem. When I spoke to the principal, she made a lot of promises but didn't follow up on any of them."

"My granddaughter's teacher is bullying her in class. How can we expect kids not to bully when they have such poor role models?"

The Teacher's Perspective

We also hear from teachers who often feel alone, unappreciated, and unsupported. Here are some of their stories.

From a third-grade teacher: "I work so hard and care so much about my students. But two of them have severe mental health issues that require more help than I can provide and cause them to disrupt the rest of the class. I know I am doing a good job, but I feel like a failure a lot of the time."

From a first-grade teacher: "One mother was so worried that she stood in the hall outside the door of my classroom for hours every day. She obsessed about every little moment where her child didn't like something. No wonder her kid is so anxious!"

From a fifth-grade teacher: "I see another teacher who is bullying her students and wish I could do something to stop it. But she is buddies with the principal, and I don't think he would believe me. In fact, making a report might cause retaliations that would make my job unbearable."

From a yard duty supervisor: "We are so often reacting to emergencies instead of being provided with effective resources to act in a pro-active fashion. An eight-year-old girl was abducted from the playground while waiting for her parents after school. Thankfully, she escaped, but our whole community was traumatized by what happened. We were sent a flyer by the school district office and told to teach the kids about 'Stranger Danger' which I know is against many school parents' wishes and just makes kids more scared."

From a middle school physical education teacher: "One day, I was shocked to be told, without explanation, to leave the school immediately and to not come back or contact anyone at the school until I had an administrative hearing. I was locked out of my email account at the school and was told not to answer questions or take phone calls from my colleagues or students' parents. I had no idea why until the hearing. It turned out that an unknown person had made an anonymous report accusing me of being inappropriate with one of my students. Eventually, my name was cleared, but I am still not supposed to talk about it. My trust, that the school that I have been so loyal to for so many years would respond with loyalty toward me, is broken."

From a high school teacher: "I wish people would just leave me alone so I can do the best job possible teaching my students. I feel squeezed between new rules and requirements from administrators and the powers that be, pressure from parents each lobbying for their own child and not understanding what it takes to make a class work well, and the needs of the kids themselves. It seems like people want us to do more and MORE and MORE!"

The Administration's Perspective

Principals and other school administrators have their own stories of frustration, isolation, and worry as well.

From a high school principal: "When we tried to address a bullying problem, we were threatened with lawsuits by the parents of the kids who were reported for bullying. We didn't have enough proof to take the kind of action I wish we could have, and we certainly did not want to spend our very limited resources on defending a lawsuit. Now the parents of the child who says he was bullied are threatening to sue."

From a middle school vice principal: "We just don't have enough money or time to do everything that needs to get done. We have so much maintenance that is long overdue and so many services that would truly benefit our students. I wish things were different."

From a head of a charter school: "I wish people would just TELL me as soon as things start to go wrong instead of waiting until things blow up into big issues that cause a lot of bad feelings and waste a lot of time. If I don't hear them the first time, I wish they would tell me again!"

From a preschool administrator: "I feel badly when I see how a couple of teachers sometimes bully others and are certainly rude and disrespectful to me. Their behavior is subtle enough that it is hard to confront. What kind of an example are we setting for our students when we model this kind of behavior?"

From a school board member: "I was horrified to find out that a mother was accusing the father of another child of abusing her child. I reported this to Child Protective Services, but no action seems to have been taken. The mother who made the accusation is no longer at the school, and the father says that his name is cleared and wants to keep volunteering in the classroom. I have no idea what to do."

From a school security officer: "Two of our students got into a fight after school. One is in the hospital, and the other is in jail. I wish the outpouring of sorrow and energy from our school community would translate into lasting change."

From an elementary school principal: "Even though we check references carefully and do background checks and have a dedicated and wonderful staff, my nightmare is that one of our teachers will cause harm to our students."

No Wonder We Feel Overwhelmed About Our Schools!

Let's be realistic. Schools face hard problems. And, in the midst of these difficulties, we can still put our talents together to make our schools into places of respect and safety for all their members. Let's take a look at common obstacles that prevent people from taking action under these kinds of pressures.

Denial—"We are all nice people here and that kind of thing doesn't happen in our nice school." Or, "It's really not THAT bad."

Resignation—"I tried and tried to make things better but it didn't work so I'm giving up." Or, "We already tried that, and it didn't make any difference."

Bystander Effect—"Everybody saw what was going on, but no one did anything about it."

Emotional Triggers—"I'm afraid that I'll make things worse. Sometimes I get so upset that I blow up. People think less of me, and I feel embarrassed for overreacting."

Isolation—"I feel as if I am the only person who is bothered by this or who cares."

Perceived Helplessness—"I have no power to do anything about it."

Passing the Buck—"It's not MY responsibility. The people who should be taking care of this are not doing their jobs."

Distractions—"People seem to get so caught up gossiping about someone's private business that they walk right past kids who are acting unsafely."

False Reassurance—"Everybody thanked me for speaking up and said they'd take care of it right away. I waited and waited, but nothing happened!"

Meaningless Apologies—"They kept saying they were really sorry, but they didn't provide any solutions."

Failure to PERCEIVE a safety problem and to BELIEVE that we each have the responsibility and the power to do something about it makes ACTION impossible.

Too often, we end up being like this classic story about the four people named Everybody, Somebody, Anybody, and Nobody.

There was an important job to be done and Everybody was sure that Somebody would do it. Anybody could have done it, but Nobody did. Somebody got angry about this, because it was Everybody's job. Everybody thought Anybody could do it, but Nobody realized that Everybody wouldn't do it. It ended up that Everybody blamed Somebody when Nobody did what Anybody could have done!

Persistence in the Face of Resistance

Too often, people become discouraged and frustrated when they try to address a concern about school safety and, instead of getting an apology or any kind of appreciation, they run into one or more of the above obstacles.

Resistance is normal. Most of us don't like being told that we made a mistake or that we should do something differently. The systems in schools and other institutions also usually have a great deal of inertia that can make getting going or changing directions extra hard.

Instead of giving up or deciding that no one cares, we can decide not to allow overwhelm or resistance to get in the way of our advocating for child safety.

We can use the Kidpower strategy of relentless, cheerful persistence in the face of resistance to overcome these obstacles. Remember that people will listen to you better and bother you less if you seem aware, calm, respectful, and confident when talking with them. Sounding uncertain or whiny is likely to result in your being ignored. If you sound angry, many people are likely to react defensively to your anger rather than being able to listen to your message.

So, take a breath and do your best to focus on finding positive, realistic solutions rather than on assigning blame. Instead of seeing action as a one-time conversation, see advocating for child safety as climbing up a steep trail, requiring a great deal of effort to reach your destination and a great deal of appreciation for each step taken that gets you closer to what you want to accomplish. Be pleasantly surprised if the trail is shorter or easier than expected, but plan to keep on going, step by step, forging through brush and rivers, before getting to the top.

Safety at All Levels for Children with Disabilities

Children with disabilities are at far greater risk of "maltreatment" including bullying, abuse, violence, and neglect, than children who are typically developing. However, objectives for protecting these vulnerable children from these risks have not usually been a part of their educational plans.

In the United States, children with disabilities and their parents are required by law to have fair and equitable treatment. Individual Family Service Plans (IFSP) and Individual Education Plans (IEP) are developed for children and teens identified as having special needs—and become the basis for services that are provided to these young people and their families.

For many years, Dr. Harold Johnson, Emeritus Professor of Education at Kent State University, has been a passionate advocate for protecting children with disabilities by making personal safety knowledge and skills a much higher priority in the special education field. Harold is leading a coalition of organizations including Kidpower in working together to enhance the field of special education by having personal safety objectives included in all the students' educational plans, which will lead to their families and schools having better access to child protection training and resources.

Abuse Prevention in Schools

Although bullying is the most common problem in schools, children have also been sexually abused while in the care of well-known, often beloved, and trusted teachers or other staff, causing a great deal of trauma for everyone involved. In addition, in many states and countries, schools are required to provide sexual abuse prevention education, often inspired by the dedicated work of mother and activist Erin Merryn, who suffered abuse as a child and wants to protect all other children.[1]

Too often, well-intended abuse prevention programs increase awareness in a way that leads to anxiety rather than preparing young people with effective and emotionally safe knowledge and skills. Make sure that any abuse prevention program used upholds these prevention training best practices:

- Being positive and fun rather than on dwelling on the bad things that might happen

- Being age-appropriate rather than putting upsetting images into children's minds unnecessarily

- Being trauma-informed and emotionally safe, especially for children or staff who might already be survivors of abuse or have experienced Adverse Childhood Experiences (ACEs)

- Providing positive and successful practices on boundary-setting and help-seeking skills

- Providing clear, age-appropriate and accurate safety rules about touch, private areas, and other behavior

- Being adapted for different abilities

- Being relevant for different cultures and life situations

[For more information about abuse prevention, please review Chapter 5's basic safety principles for Youth-Serving Organizations.]

Avoiding Automatic Steamroller Systems

When systems get into motion, sometimes they roll over innocent people without making anyone safer—and end up doing more harm than good. According to the Merriam-Webster Online Dictionary, "A juggernaut is a massive inexorable force, campaign, movement, or object that crushes whatever is in its path." Fear of the juggernaut of policies mindlessly applied steamrolling everyone in its path can cause students, parents, teachers, and school officials to avoid reporting or addressing safety concerns.

The solution is for everyone involved to be pro-active in addressing potential problems while they are small, to be accurate and specific in describing any concerns, and to find solutions that are based on common sense and help reach a policy's intended spirit rather than thoughtless application of policies.

Safety rules and consequences for breaking them are essential in schools and other institutions. Unfortunately, when schools automatically follow "zero tolerance" policies without the benefit of good judgment, these policies can become like a juggernaut steamrolling over people's lives.

Heavy-handed and unreasonable reactions are harmful and cost schools time and money without making kids safer. Kids of all ages who have suffered months or years of bullying have been suspended for getting caught fighting back even once. Following are three news stories about examples of policies being misapplied:

- According to the *Austin Daily Herald* in 2014, model student seventeen-year-old Alyssa Drescher was expelled for up to twelve months for accidentally bringing a pocketknife to school that she had used the day before for cutting hay bales and left in her purse.[2]

- In a story reported on CNN in 2013, six-year-old Hunter Yelton was suspended and accused of sexual harassment after he kissed a girl in his reading group on the hand.[3]

- According to the *New York Post* in 2016, hundreds of teachers in district schools waiting to be investigated for possible disciplinary action are paid to sit in a room—called the "Rubber Room"—where they just sit and wait for days, weeks, months, and even years. Even if their names are cleared, many end up feeling so stigmatized that they change careers.[4]

These are not stories from 20 years ago or more; they happened in the last five years.

Even when anti-bullying policies are required by law, schools can have a great deal of control over *how* they are implemented. Before taking action, ask questions like:

- How will this policy help?

- Does everyone understand what needs to be done?

- Do all of these actions make sense?

- What are possible unintended negative consequences we need to keep in mind?

As the saying goes, "To a hammer, everything is a nail." But school officials are not hammers and children and teachers are not nails. When we try to apply rules without thought, we create injustice, not safety.

What Stops Schools from Protecting Kids from Bullying?

Unless an abuse case, attempted abduction, assault, or injury accident has recently happened in or near a school community, the most common school safety concerns are about bullying. The principles, strategies, and skills described in the previous chapters are all relevant in preventing the suffering caused by this complex issue.

The documentary film "Bully" provided an intimate and moving look into the lives of families devastated by the loss of kids who have taken their lives after being bullied, the struggles of kids dealing with bullying, and the frustration of parents trying to find solutions. Most of this bullying happened at school or at school-related activities such as riding on the bus or at a school dance.[5]

This film and many other bullying-awareness books, speakers, and programs do an excellent job of showing the impact of this issue and of motivating people to feel that bullying is unacceptable.

The problem is that just increasing awareness is not enough. Thinking about bullying, wanting a change, worrying about kids, and talking about bullying can become all-consuming activities that take time and energy. Thinking, wanting, worrying, and talking can even *feel* like action, but effective action requires that people find and use solutions that lead to positive change.

Taking action to intervene to stop bullying in the moment, when unkind or unsafe behavior is happening between kids or adults, can be uncomfortable for most people. This discomfort can bring positive change to a grinding halt if people are not willing or able to push through it and advocate for the person being bullied or to get help from someone who can.

Unfortunately, the intensity of feelings many kids face every day brought on by disrespectful and unkind behavior is exponentially worse than discomfort. If we, as adults, do not push through our own discomfort and make significant changes, the price will continue to be paid by our children. They will not "figure it out themselves," and they will not "get tough enough to deal with it." Thousands are paying the price today in physical and emotional injury, anxiety, depression, dysfunctional relationships, self-mutilation, and/or suicide. Just as we now know that certain kinds of germs are dangerous to our health and that washing hands is important, studies documenting the long-term damage from bullying show that we should not be accepting this harmful behavior as a normal part of growing up.

That being said, lots of adults who care about kids don't know how to handle conflict, how to speak up in the face of authority, how to set boundaries, or how to talk to upset children and parents. They find themselves either frozen in inaction or repeatedly trying the same solution over and over, even though it's making things worse. And these are adults. Kids are usually less competent than adults. So, we can imagine what kids who are faced with bullying behavior can feel like if they do not have effective People Safety skills to counter this problem!

Have you ever shaken a soda bottle and then opened it? It makes a big mess. Kidpower calls this reaction the 'Soda Bottle Effect.' Too often, adults use the Wishing Technique and hope that the bullying will stop by itself. When it doesn't, tension slowly builds up inside until adults explode in ways that set a terrible example for how to handle problems when you are upset.

Activities like putting "NO BULLYING" and "Respect Everyone" signs up all over a school are not going to work as well as figuring out why people are stuck and providing tools and support for them to supervise the young people in their care and take charge proactively, respectfully, and effectively to stop unsafe or disrespectful behavior.

Even One Adult Leader Can Truly Make a Difference

Even one adult leader can change the "steamroller" effect of a system acting automatically and unfairly into one of compassion and effective action.

When 10-year-old Chloé was in the fifth grade, her school principal used his judgment about how to apply the 'no hitting' school policy. For many years, an older girl, Joséphine, had been bullying Chloé through severe verbal attacks and shunning. Suddenly, Joséphine started to strangle Chloé from behind, and Chloé protected herself by elbowing Joséphine in the face. A teacher saw the fight and stepped in and punished both girls by sending them to the principal's office.

The principal stopped Joséphine's accusations firmly after hearing her version of what had happened. He took the time to hear Chloé's side of the story, took into account that she usually didn't create trouble or get into fights. He simply responded by saying to Chloé in a matter-of-fact tone: "I don't want you to hit her again and my response to you will be very different if you are back in my office for this reason."

Then the principal added, "*That said…* Congratulations for protecting yourself. I am proud of you. Now you can go back to recess and play. I will deal with Joséphine now. Please make sure to tell me if she tries to hurt you again. I will make sure to let the other teachers know about our talk."

With that response and the effect of the principal's support toward Chloé on the school community, he stopped years of bullying directed at Chloé from this specific girl as well as the huge amounts of hurtful behavior of many other students who had been following Joséphine's leadership in targeting her.

Creating a Culture of Safety and Respect in Schools: Six Actions for School Leaders

Parents and other caring adults must be prepared to take leadership themselves to prevent and solve many problems at school—and must be clear about their expectations of safety leadership from their principals, heads of school, and other administrators.

Just like a stool needs at least three legs to be stable, so does change in human behavior. Best-selling authors Chip and Dan Heath describe these three strategies in their exceptional book, *Switch: How to Change Things When Change is Hard:* "Direct the Rider, Motivate the Elephant, and Shape the Path." The Rider is our intellectual mind. The Elephant is our emotional being. And the Path is what defines how we can get where we need to go.

In order to create school cultures of respect and safety, the "Rider" requires awareness so that people understand how big the problem is and what it looks like, the "Elephant" requires motivation so most people will feel strongly that what happens in schools is important for everyone, and the "Path" requires skills so that people will know what to do to intervene in the moment, persist in the face of resistance, make valid assessments, and provide support to others speaking up, even when all of these actions are uncomfortable. Awareness, motivation, *and* skills are all necessary for concerns in schools to be addressed consistently, effectively, and practically.

Whether you are a school administrator, teacher, counselor, yard duty supervisor, or parent volunteer, here are six actions recommended by Kidpower that *you*, as a leader, can take to *Make SURE* that your school becomes an environment where bullying, violence, and abuse will have trouble taking root and growing while leaving room for respect, kindness, and safety for all to become the main crop.

1. Make SURE everyone sees your personal commitment to safety, dignity, kindness, and respect.
2. Make SURE you know what is going on.
3. Make SURE safety is truly your priority in how you use time and resources.
4. Make SURE people who report safety problems are understood and appreciated.
5. Make SURE you support your staff through the process of working out problems.
6. Make SURE that you and others take meaningful action.

Descriptions about HOW to take these "Make SURE" steps are on page 225 in the *Kidpower Skills and Action Plans* section of the book.

"What If My Child Is Being Bullied at School?" Solutions for Parents and Guardians

Kidpower hears countless stories from parents, grandparents, aunts, and uncles who are upset because a child or teen in their life is being bullied, teased, or harassed at school—and because the school seems unable to take action.

School is a big part of kids' lives, and it is usually parents who make the decisions about how and where their children get an education. This means that most young people have no choice about where they go to school.

As a parent, you have the right to expect schools to provide an environment that is emotionally and physically safe for your children. It's normal to feel terrified and enraged about any kind of threat to your kid's well-being, especially in a place where they have to be.

We need to remember that most schools are working valiantly to meet an overwhelming array of conflicting demands. At the same time, when your own child is being bullied, it is normal for protective parents to want to fix the problem immediately—and maybe to punish the people who caused or allowed your child to be hurt, embarrassed, or scared.

When possible, try to find out about problems when they are still small. Tell children clearly, cheerfully, and often, "If someone is bothering you at school, if you see someone picking on another kid, or if you are having trouble acting safely yourself, your job is to tell me so that we can figure out what to do to make things better."

Pay attention to changes in your child's behavior. Help children to develop the habit of telling you about what happens at school each day by being interested, by staying calm, and by not lecturing. Ask specific questions in a cheerful way, such as "What was the best thing that happened today? What was the worst thing?" Remember that, if adults act anxious, children are less likely to share upsetting information. Volunteer even a couple of hours a week in the classroom or schoolyard so that you can help out, get to know teachers, and stay aware of potential problems at school.

If your child has a bullying problem at school, here are seven practical Kidpower People Safety solutions that can help parents to be effective in taking charge.

1. Stop your own knee-jerk reactions.

2. Get your facts right.

3. Pinpoint the cause.

4. Protect your child.

5. Prevent future problems.

6. Get help for your child.

7. Give kids skills to protect themselves in the future.

A detailed description of how to implement these solutions is on page 239.

Safety Checkup

✓ Remember that most parents, educators, and school administrators have the same goals—the safety and well-being of the young people in their care and the adults responsible for educating and supervising them.

✓ Support schools in developing and implementing prevention policies in mindful ways to accomplish the purpose of keeping kids safe.

✓ Stay connected with what is happening at school.

✓ Work in partnership with your child's school to prevent and solve problems pro-actively.

✓ Teach your children skills for taking charge of their own safety.

✓ Expect educational leaders to take responsibility for making sure that everyone at all levels of a school are supported in understanding and upholding these policies as well as for figuring out how to overcome obstacles that often get in the way of Putting Safety First.

✓ Provide extra safeguards for children with disabilities or other special needs by having personal safety skills and child protection practices incorporated into their educational plans.

✓ Make sure schools choose prevention programs that are positive, practical, truly experiential, emotionally safe, and adapted for different needs.

CHAPTER 7

The JOY of the Game:
Reclaiming Youth Sports

When Amy was a high-school lacrosse goalie, her father would walk right onto the field in the middle of a game to take pictures of her playing. At that time, lacrosse was played without marked sidelines, and without them he ran amok. Amy felt embarrassed and distracted and would try to shoo him back into place, as the play was rapidly advancing back toward her goal. Although he meant well, her father was so caught up in his own needs that he forgot about the needs of the kids on the field. Having to worry about her dad intruding to take photos hurt both Amy's performance as a goalie and her enjoyment of the game.

Unfortunately, adult egos can interfere with children getting the full benefits of participating in youth sports. Instead of getting caught up in the glory of having a child who is successful in sports or in the excitement of winning or the agony of losing, every parent, coach, and spectator needs to keep in mind what their true goals are for young athletes.

At a Kidpower workshop many years ago, a kind father, Ron, told Irene, "We need this kind of training for coaches too! At the children's soccer games that I coach, we do our best to keep our team members from bullying each other or kids from other teams. But sometimes the kids' parents will start screaming insults and threats at our coaches because they disagree with some decision. Even after they've signed pledges not to, some parents still believe that acting this way and booing players is part of sports. What should we do?"

"Why are you coaching children's soccer?" Irene asked. "This is a volunteer job, right? Is your goal to have children learn to win, or for some other reason?"

"I like to coach because team sports build character and discipline," Ron said.

"What are children learning about discipline and character when they see their adults losing control and behaving abusively?" Irene asked. "Perhaps the best learning that these children might gain is by seeing you and the other coaches modeling positive, respectful, firm leadership."

To role-play the problem, Ron pretended to be an upset parent and yelled at Irene, "How dare you do that! I'm going to report you."

She calmly replied, "I am following our rules. You are welcome to tell anyone you wish that you disagree! Now please sit down so we can continue the game!"

Ron mentioned that they also had many young teenagers who volunteer to coach. "It's awful," he explained, "when a 35-year-old man starts bellowing at a thirteen-year-old, 'What gives you the right to make this decision?'"

Irene pointed out that volunteering to be the coach *does* give someone the right to make decisions and that, as unfortunate as it is that a few people act this way, learning how to deal with upset people is an exceptional leadership skill.

Fortunately, in recent years, coaches and leagues have made efforts to reclaim healthier, realistic values for kids in sports and have found new ways to communicate and set boundaries. This sign from the Buffalo Grove Park District spells out values, helps keep everything in perspective, and importantly, sets ground rules that can be referred to if a parent's behavior goes off the rails.

The sign reads:

- This is a **game** being played by **children**.

- If they win or lose every game of the season, it will not impact what college they attend or their future income potential.

- Of the hundreds of thousands of children who have ever played youth sports in Buffalo Grove, very few have ever gone on to play professionally. It is highly unlikely that any college recruiters or professional scouts are watching these games; so let's keep it all about having fun and being pressure-free.

- Imagine how you would feel if you saw a parent or coach from the opposing team cheering for your child when they made a great play. Then envision what kind of person you would think they are for doing that. You can be that person.

- Referees, umpires and officials are human and make mistakes, just like players, coaches and you. No one shouts at you in front of other people when you make a mistake, so please don't yell at them. We do not have video replay; so, we will go with their calls.

- The only reason children want to play sports is because it is fun. Please don't let the behavior of adults ruin the fun.

Buffalo Grove [Illinois] Park District[1]

Supporting Each Other in Remembering "This is for FUN!"

If someone forgets, hopefully having the ground rules so clearly stated will help members of a parent community to feel empowered to do something to intervene to keep things positive. Depending on the situation and the relationship with the other person, possible interventions might include changing the subject, modeling supportive behavior by praising all the players, or gently reminding them of the rules.

For example, Marie went to watch her seven-year-old son and kids of other ages rehearse their martial arts demonstration.

While Marie was standing on the side of the room watching and waiting for her son's class to come on, another mother started coaching her daughter in a highly critical way. The volunteer martial arts teachers were dealing with too many kids and lots of chaos. When this mother turned to Marie and started making derogatory comments about her daughter's performance within earshot of the child, Marie could see that this little girl was starting to look upset.

Marie interrupted the other mother to say, "I know you mean well, and I think the best gift we can give our kids during this rehearsal is our positive support." The mother seemed open to Marie's comment and asked her to explain more, so Marie said, "I think the best way we can help our kids is to avoid giving them directions and just let them enjoy being in the demonstration, without wanting them to be perfect. This demonstration is for kids, and it is supposed to be fun, not perfect."

The mother was quiet for a while and then came close to Marie said, almost apologetically, "I just want the best for her."

With lots of sympathy, Marie replied, "Yes of course you do! Maybe the best for her right now is to see her mom just being proud of her daughter. I *know* you are proud. You wouldn't care so much if you weren't."

The other mother smiled and said, "I have some apologizing to do. Excuse me." She then left to go talk with her daughter, who started to smile.

The Damage to Young People of a "Win-at-All-Costs Mentality"

If you ask a group of parents about why they think playing in sports is good for their kids, they often say:

"It helps develop character."

"Kids learn to discipline themselves and how to work as part of a team."

"Being active helps keep kids fit."

"Kids find sports exciting and fun."

"I have wonderful memories of doing this myself."

If you ask kids about their experiences in youth sports, the stories are mixed. Many will describe great experiences with inspiring coaches. But others will say:

"I'm just a loser—I'll never be good enough."

"Everyone seems disappointed in me. My parents point out everything I did wrong after every game."

"I feel embarrassed by how my parents scream at the referees and boo at the other team."

"Some kids on the team keep calling me names, and the coach doesn't do anything to stop it."

"My coach is really smart but is always putting kids down. Instead of telling us to how to get better, he yells at us every time something goes wrong."

"I sprained my ankle and the injury got much worse because my coach kept pushing me to keep going and not wimp out and let the team down."

"My coach kept making sexual jokes, and I felt so embarrassed and uncomfortable that I quit playing even though I loved the game."

What do young people learn about character, persistence, and discipline if they see adults acting like poor sports? And, what does it teach children about values if they are being bullied, shamed, unnecessarily injured, or abused as part of their sports experience?

Jim Thompson and the Positive Coaching Alliance

Jim Thompson, visionary founder and CEO of Positive Coaching Alliance (PCA), is leading a movement that has made youth sports safer and more fun for millions of young people.[2]

The "Positive" part of PCA comes from a commitment to "relentless positivity" that Jim first learned at age 20, when he worked as a teacher's aide for emotionally disturbed youth, many of whom had been neglected and abused. Jim was inspired by how these very troubled kids flourished under a regime of clear limits and, within those limits, very specific behavior goals that were always framed as what TO DO instead of what NOT to do, with each step in a positive direction rewarded with attention and awards.

The "Coaching" part of PCA comes from Jim's many years of coaching youth sports. He first started as a sports father—and was motivated to change the climate after seeing that intense parents were putting pressure on their kids to win.

The "Alliance" happened after Jim joined a national task force on building character through sports and wrote the final report. "When I flew back to Washington, D.C. for the last meeting of the task force where the report was approved," he said, "I realized this report is going nowhere. It was going to sit on a shelf. This task force was going to go away. I realized that there needed to be an organized effort to change the way youth sports are done."

Thanks to Jim's intimate knowledge about using "relentless positivity" to coach youth sports, his business background, and his work on the task force, Jim knew what needed to change. He joined with the many people he'd worked with over the years to establish Positive Coaching Alliance in 1998 as a national non-profit dedicated to "developing 'Better Athletes, Better People' by working to provide all youth and high school athletes a positive, character-building youth sports experience."

PCA Models for Changing the "Win-At-All Costs" Mentality

In furthering PCA's vision to transform the culture of youth sports, Jim and PCA have distilled complex concepts of sports psychology into simple, easy-to-use ideas and methods that coaches, sports parents, and youth sports leaders can apply to their teams.

PCA teaches that, "Winning is not everything. It's not even half. Winning is one of the goals of a coach, but it's not the most important goal."

According to PCA's national spokesperson, legendary coach Phil Jackson, "There is more to life than basketball. And not only is there more to life than basketball, there's more to basketball than basketball."

Jim adds, "If all kids are learning in sports is that sport, that is a huge missed opportunity."

From these insights, Jim and PCA developed the following key models that PCA uses to educate coaches, sports parents, youth sports leaders, and youth athletes themselves.

The ELM Tree of Mastery™: Mastery = Effort + Learning + Mistakes

E for effort. Give your best Effort every time.

L for learning. Continue to Learn and improve no matter what happens.

M for mistakes. Develop the mental toughness to bounce back from Mistakes.

The Double-Goal Coach®. Coaches are encouraged to see their goals with their teams as both winning (important) and as teaching life lessons (much more important). Having these priorities clearly in mind prepares coaches to choose teaching life lessons over winning when necessary to help develop character and live and play with integrity.

Filling a Child's Emotional Tank. This concept was adapted from Ross Campbell's book, *How to Really Love Your Child.* PCA teaches that kids are more motivated to take on challenges and bounce back from losses when their emotional tanks are kept full by their coaches and parents are provided with techniques for being a "tank-filler instead of a tank-drainer."

The ROOTS of Honoring the Game™. Jim encourages coaches to tell athletes, "I don't want you to honor the game because I want you to. I want you to honor the game because it's important to you." This means respect for:

Rules. You never bend the rules even if you can get away with it.

Opponent. A worthy opponent is a gift. You can't play your best unless you're being challenged.

Officials. You show respect to the officials even when they make a mistake.

Teammates. You don't do anything that embarrasses your team on or off the field.

Self. Respect for yourself.

The Second-Goal Parent®. In PCA trainings, Jim asks parents, "There are two people whose job it is to win games. Who are they?"

Parents quickly realize that winning is "the job of the coaches and the kids. It's not me."

Jim explains that parents have a much more important job, which is to focus on the second goal of youth sports of *teaching life lessons and helping kids develop positive character traits such as resilience.* Suppose, for example, their child fails to make a winning shot with a penalty kick.

Instead of criticizing, a parent can use a PCA tool—"You're the Kind of Person Who…" statements. This means taking a positive approach and helping to fill their child's emotional tank by saying, "I'm sure you're disappointed you didn't make the winning shot, but you know what? One of the things I like about you is that *you're the kind of person* who doesn't give up easily."

The Triple-Impact Competitor™. At the request of PCA's high school partners, Jim developed this model as an antidote to the glamorization of the individual in professional and college sports, which is all about the star player. A Triple-Impact Competitor is someone who:

1. makes himself better, which leads to mastery,

2. makes her teammates better, and

3. makes the game better by competing in ways that honor the game.

Jim sums up PCA's vision by saying, "We don't want coaches, parents, and athletes just to be a little more positive. We want to change their identity. For a 'win-at-all costs' coach, we want to show that it's much more fulfilling, and you're actually going to win more if you are a Double-Goal Coach. If you are a Triple-Impact Competitor, it's much more fulfilling than just 'me, me, me, me, me' and your team is going to win more. And it also is a great framework for good citizenship.

"If we can create hundreds of thousands of youth who are each a Triple-Impact Competitor coming out of high school sports," says Jim, "they could really transform the way our whole country is because they're going to be the business leaders, the political leaders, the non-profit leaders, the education leaders, the union leaders in the future. That would be really exciting!"

Protecting Youth Athletes from Sexual Abuse

When sports leaders like PCA put safety and character development ahead of winning, they help create a culture where bullying and abuse become far less able to take root and grow.

After the deeply upsetting publicity about cases of child abuse in youth sports, PCA started collaborating with Kidpower to provide coaches, youth sports leaders, and parents with educational resources about how to protect their athletes.

PCAs National Advisory Board Member Mark Murphy, President and CEO of the Green Bay Packers, sponsored educational videos that have reached more than 150,000 people so far.

In the introduction to the *Protecting Youth Athletes from Sexual Abuse* video,[3] Mark Murphy says, "Our country's most important resource is our young people. It's up to all of us to do everything we can to keep them safe. A number of recent events have highlighted that more action is needed to protect youth athletes from child abuse!"

Jim Thompson adds, "All the good things that come from sports can be erased if a child is abused. Those who would abuse children tend to go where the kids are, places like youth sports. They also tend to stay away from organizations that have a visible and effective policy to protect kids and that report suspected abuse."

Key actions for all adults:

- Stay aware that you cannot identify a child predator by how he or she looks.

- Establish a league policy about child safety that everyone knows and understands.

- Avoid having coaches be alone with players in an isolated place. Instead, even for one-on-one training, be sure that what is happening can be seen by other adults.

- Where it is not practical to have another adult present all the time, parents or guardians might make an exception as long as they are aware that this situation requires Inner Circle level screening and oversight.

- Do background checks but know that these alone are not enough.

- Look for grooming behavior, such as singling a player out for special attention or keeping secrets.

- Pay attention and speak up about anything that makes you uncomfortable.

- Teach children how to recognize unsafe behavior, set boundaries, not keep problems or behavior against their safety rules a secret, and get help.

- Make sure kids know how much you care about their safety.

- Take action if a child comes to you for help or you suspect abuse or if you have any concerns.

The *Protecting Youth Athletes from Sexual Abuse* videos show adults how to take action respectfully and clearly. In one story, Jamie's father approaches his son's coach to thank him for giving Jamie a jacket when it was cold and to express concern because Jamie had told him that his coach had said to keep it a secret. The father models being questioning rather than accusing. Jamie's coach models being open and appreciative of hearing concerns. It turns out to have been a misunderstanding because, when Jamie had thanked him, his coach had said, "Don't mention it."

Uncomfortable conversations like these can help to increase safety without damaging important relationships. Jamie's coach was open to hearing concerns—and, if he had had bad intentions, he would now know that Jamie doesn't keep secrets and that Jamie's father is paying attention and will check things out.

Many of the actions for protecting kids from abuse are also relevant for addressing bullying. In the Recommended Policies developed by Kidpower and PCA, Prohibited Behaviors include "use of profane or degrading language or behavior. Coaches are also responsible for stopping disrespectful language or behavior between team members, including sexual jokes or harassment … Threatening or intentionally afflicting physical injury." A strong statement that makes disrespectful, threatening, or violent language or behavior against the rules, in person or online, is the first step in preventing and stopping these behaviors.

The Tremendous Good of Most Coaches— and the Risk of a "Pied Piper" Abusive Coach

The vast majority of coaches in youth sports are extremely caring people who do great things for kids. Many volunteer their time. As one mother wrote, "When I was a child, even though my father didn't know anything about sports, he studied soccer to become the coach for my team. He volunteered for years and made it possible for us to play. And more recently, one of my friends, who had never played a game herself, stepped in to become a coach when there was no coach for her kids' team."

Most of the time, harm to kids in youth sports is accidentally caused by well-meaning people who lack understanding and skills. They get triggered and upset, and then say and do hurtful things. They worry that losing will be damaging for their players. They confuse their own wish to win in the moment with what is best for the long run. As adults coaching at any level, we strengthen our leadership and our connection with our players when we acknowledge mistakes and, if we have caused harm, make amends. Sometimes, a simple but heartfelt, "I'm sorry. My words sounded hurtful. You are doing a great job on this team, and I am so happy to be your coach!" can be immensely healing.

For millions of young athletes, youth sports coaches provide important opportunities for healthy trust and positive connections—including positive connections that help us all learn how to fix everyday mistakes in meaningful relationships.

Unfortunately, as in any other activity with children, a small percentage of coaches are pedophiles, and they can harm a lot of children before they are caught unless safeguards are in place to stop them. As hundreds of cases have made compellingly clear, the sad truth is that those who want to molest children commonly put themselves in positions to be around children and teens for the purpose of building a sense of trust and connection with them and often with their families. Molesters can then use the trust and connections to create opportunities to hurt young people.

Whether the person is a family member, a neighbor, a teacher, a spiritual leader, an entertainment industry leader, or a coach, children can become very confused when the person who helps them is also the person who abuses them. Child molesters usually do not look or act creepy—they usually seem kind, honest, and charismatic.

Fortunately, like other youth-serving organizations, youth sports organizations now have far more safeguards in place than there used to be. And fortunately, we can keep kids safe most of the time if we pay attention to our intuition, don't let uncomfortable feelings get in the way of our speaking up about any concerns, and prepare our kids to recognize and set boundaries about unsafe behavior and to get help.

At the same time, because of the manipulative and pervasive nature of child abuse, it is important to understand what has happened in the past so that we can better protect young athletes from abuse in the present and the future.

People are especially shocked when they learn that well-known coaches with high prestige turn out to have molested some of their players. These are coaches who have helped a large number of young athletes to be very successful, usually including some of the children they have abused. Abusive coaches manipulate families by bestowing special attention, gifts, and travel on athletes in a grooming process. They say what they think parents and players want to hear in order to gain trust. When athletes are seeking the positive, honest attention from coaches, it can be very difficult to question the motives of a coach who is overstepping boundaries.

To take just one of far too many examples, UK soccer coach Barry Bennell is now serving a 16-year jail sentence after being convicted of serially abusing aspiring young soccer players through the 1970s and 1980s. His case exemplifies the pattern of a skilled, charismatic coach with a friendly public face who gained parents' trust and loyalty with sports skills, in order to have access to their kids. "He was the Pied Piper, he knew how to manipulate the environment to suit his needs and his desires and his horrible behavior," said Paul Lake, a former player who was abused by Bennell at ages 11 and 12. "He could gain trust from parents unwittingly under the guise of being this caring coach who could get your son to be a professional [player]."

Lake continued: "There were muted conversations around and suspicions around Barry Bennell even around that time. It was dismissed because there is no way that person—because he's a 'football man' and kids love him—would be an abuser of young men."[4]

It takes observation, courage, and persistence to stop an abusive coach. If reports of abuse are minimized or covered up, abusive coaches can continue to prey on young athletes for years. Although this pattern is more likely to be recognized and stopped into today's society, ongoing vigilance is required to protect young athletes because a "Pied Piper" coach might still find a way to seduce athletes and families with their skills and then abuse a few vulnerable kids in their power.

Some of the largest, most prestigious sports organizations have been wracked by abuse scandals and alleged cover-ups. Many teams, including US Olympic development programs have adopted new policies and added new "safe sports"[5] policies and training after years of serious abuse cases have finally received the attention they deserved. In many cases, it has taken multiple lawsuits and criminal charges to get real change.[6, 7]

The scandal of USA Gymnastics doctor Larry Nassar provides a shocking insight into how he was protected by the entire sports "system" that he worked for. Even though girls were reporting abuse for years, as early as 1997, there were multiple failures to address these serious issues. As a result, Nassar stayed in a position to continue abuse, disguised as medical treatment, of hundreds of girls for over 20 years. In 2017, Nassar pleaded guilty after being charged with molesting seven girls, most of whom were gymnasts. Since then, more than 265 women and girls have come forward to accuse Nassar of sexual abuse, including Olympic gold medalists Simone Biles, Aly Raisman, McKayla Maroney, Jordyn Wieber, and Gabby Douglas.[8]

The extent of Nassar's abusive behavior, and his revered position of trust within the gymnastics world, have spurred serious investigations into USA Gymnastics and Michigan State University to find out how this abuse could have been allowed to continue for so long.

It took a 2016 *Indianapolis Star* report, with gymnast Rachael Denhollander going on the record with her story, to generate serious investigations.[9] Even then, justice moved far too slowly. Nassar abused at least 40 more young women *after* the FBI became aware of abuse allegations and conducted a year-long investigation.[10] Ultimately, the President of Michigan State University and the entire board of USA Gymnastics were forced to retire after Nassar's guilty pleas.[11]

The question now is how all sports organizations are going to reform in the future to truly put the safety of their athletes ahead of anyone's reputation, fame, and fortune. Leadership from the top needs to change, and these leaders need to be held accountable by parents, coaches, and people in all levels of the sports organizations.

In addition, we need to make sure that young people have the skills they need to recognize and stop unsafe behavior and that their concerns are addressed swiftly and proactively.

When people of good will understand what's at stake and know what to do, they can further the true goals of youth sports—character, discipline, teamwork, fitness, and fun. The true win for young athletes is when we protect them from harmful experiences and foster their positive growth. And, of course, we also want them to have healthy, positive, life-altering experiences with coaches who prove to be important mentors!

How to Choose the Right Sport for Your Kids

At their best, youth sports teach children and teens how to work with other people, cope with failure, accept imperfection while striving for excellence, persevere in the face of obstacles, appreciate what you and others can do instead of mourning what you cannot, learn physical skills, control your temper even when frustrated, and many other life lessons.

As a self-defense leader, Irene often gets asked by parents how to choose what kind of martial art their child should take. Her answers would be relevant for any athletic or recreational activity.

- Choose something active that your child loves to do so they develop confidence in using their bodies physically and enjoy getting enough exercise to sleep well at night—be it hiking, dance, gymnastics, swimming, basketball or other sports, martial arts, music, or other activities.

- Look for coaches, teachers, or leaders who are enthusiastic, respectful, and knowledgeable; who manage the behavior of everyone involved so that there is a positive social climate in which to learn and practice; who are extremely safety-conscious; who address your concerns patiently and effectively; and who are consistently appropriate with children.

- Show up as a parent or guardian in a positive way by being present, by being encouraging without criticizing or correcting your child, addressing problems proactively, and by being a model audience.

- Remember that recreation for fun should be about the kids, not the adults. Allow your children to choose the activity rather than pressuring them to do something that you enjoyed when you were their age. Let them change activities if they wish.

Safety Checkup

✓ Remember that for most kids, youth sports is for fun and for personal growth rather than to become professional athletes.

✓ Use a program like the Positive Coaching Alliance to train both coaches and parents in how to support youth athletes and in how to set a good example by not getting so caught up in winning that they lose track of the social, emotional, and safety goals.

✓ Hold youth sports to the same standards as other youth-serving organizations by implementing safeguards, including conduct policies, training, and supervision.

CHAPTER 8

Spiritual Safety:
Places of Worship Should Be Safe for Kids

Once Irene was teaching a Kidpower parents' workshop with the help of an interpreter. When Irene got to the part about teaching children not to keep secrets about any kind of touch, her interpreter suddenly froze and couldn't go on. It turned out that this woman was going to have to testify the next day in court against her priest, who had molested her throughout her childhood. Her fear of facing him again was overwhelming—and the simple words "touch should not have to be a secret" reminded Irene's interpreter heartbreakingly of all the times she had had to keep the molestation a secret because she believed that her priest could do no wrong—and had thought that what was happening was her fault and not his.

Tremendous Good—and Tremendous Harm— Leading to Tremendous Change

Throughout history, tremendous good has been done by many people in organized religions, bringing people together in community, teaching important values, and connecting them with a higher power that brings purpose and hope into their lives. And throughout history, people in religious and other spiritual institutions have also done terrible harm—sometimes in the name of their faith through wars or prejudice—and sometimes by the actions of individual religious and spiritual leaders who have hidden their crimes behind their position of authority.

The drive to protect a religious institution's reputation at all costs and to avoid consequences has caused some places of worship to cover up terrible crimes against children and other vulnerable people for decades and even centuries. Instead of removing offenders from their positions, religious leaders have moved them to different locations and have often failed to make amends to those who were harmed.

The courage and determination to speak up by people who were victimized, and their families, have forced these stories to come to light—and are leading to change within many religious institutions and within the structure of many societies.

Instead of hiding crimes to avoid consequences for destructive behavior, abuse now has to be reported. Most large religious institutions now have training programs about abuse prevention and policies requiring safe and ethical behavior for their leaders and their members.

The courage and determination of believers who have been victimized by religions that had labeled them as unworthy or sinful have also led to changes, so that far more places of worship now welcome people of different cultures, races, sexual orientations, and gender identities.

Yes, there are still cover-ups and evasion of responsibility by both established and informal religious leaders—and wars are still fought in the name of religion. Manipulative cults still surface that attract young people who are searching for meaning. As tragic as these problems are, social change, including in religion, takes time. Most reforms have happened as a result of the grassroots activism of members rather than from the top leadership. Our goal here is to identify the issues where we can take action, some of the obstacles, and best practices for keeping places of worship safe for young people.

In the Name of God, Choose Love and Compassion

Irene was once on an airplane trip in very rough weather. As their airplane kept circling to find a safe time to land, she noticed that the woman next to her was sighing and reading the Bible. Thinking that this woman was afraid of crashing, Irene asked, "Are you okay?"

Her seatmate looked up gratefully and said, "A few months ago, my younger sister told me that 'she' is actually a 'he' and not my sister, but my brother. To support him, I have been staying with him and helping him recover from the surgery he chose as part of his transition. And this is against everything my parents and pastor have told me is right. And yet, I love this person who is now my brother and could not turn away. I am trying to find something in the Bible about this so that I won't feel as if I have committed a terrible sin."

Forgetting about the bumpy flight, Irene turned to the woman and said gently, "The Bible was written a long time ago. Our interpretation of many things written in there have changed with the times as we understand more about people."

When her seatmate nodded her head, Irene continued, "When most people talk about God, Jesus or a Higher Power, they talk about love. Sometimes terrible things are done in the name of love, so we have to look at who is hurt and who is helped by anything we do or let others do. It seems to me that supporting someone important to you through a challenging time was done out of love that helped him and didn't harm anyone. I am not an expert, but I don't see how it can be a sin."

A tragic reality is that young people sometimes commit suicide because they fear that their sexual orientation or gender identity is a sin. Another tragic reality is that accepting destructive behavior is sometimes tied to religious beliefs—so that, for example, abused wives have been told by their priests, pastors, rabbis, imams, and closest family members that speaking up against their husbands' violence would mean breaking their marriage vows.

Abusing children, rejecting family members, tolerating violence against innocent people, and hating yourself for something you truly cannot help are not practices condoned by most modern leaders of major religions.

If we blindly follow any religious or spiritual leader, we are giving our power away rather than using our ability to think for ourselves and to choose where, how, and whether to act on what someone else tells us is right or wrong.

As our understanding grows about how people's bodies and minds work, then it doesn't make sense to label people with different sexual orientations and gender identities as "sinful" or to think of people with different races, cultures, faiths, or abilities as being less worthy.

Even if we feel uncomfortable about some kinds of differences, we can still choose to love one another, which is at the core of most major religions. We can have the courage to put aside our discomfort or disagreement and treat people who are different than us with respect, compassion, and kindness.

Higher Power = Greater Vulnerability = Greater Responsibility

Longing to trust a leader who represents a faith that we cherish is normal. In positive and healthy religious and spiritual communities, leaders provide hope and healing. They inspire their members to get along with others, cope with problems in their lives, be generous to those in need, and join together for the greater good.

Unfortunately, the traps of blind faith, automatic obedience, or unconditional respect for an authority figure, especially if a revered leader is the head of a community of people who are important to us, can make it hard to see when this person is acting in harmful ways. And the fear of rejection and potentially breaking ties of family, tradition, and friendship can get in the way of speaking up about problems or concerns. When people are taught that agreeing to tolerate or hide abusive behavior is a requirement of their faith, it can create a moral dilemma that is hard to overcome.

Sadly, as cases of sexual abuse in different religious institutions become more and more public, we have to accept that someone being a beloved leader of a highly regarded faith community is not a guarantee that this individual will act safely toward children. We need to accept that religious leaders are human—and can have human failings as well as human strengths. The higher authority that comes with being the official representative of a religion must be used with great care to avoid misuse.

A dramatic example of unwavering grassroots pressure causing a powerful hierarchy to admit its mistakes is the story of abuse finally being acknowledged as a serious unacceptable problem by the Catholic church. The abuse was hidden for many years—and disbelieved for many more. Because of the secrecy surrounding the abuse, many caring and ethical members of the church did not know what was happening and were horrified when they found out that these stories were true.

After years of minimizing or covering up abuse by the priests involved and some higher members of the church hierarchy, the church as a whole finally had to admit its mistakes, make amends, and make a commitment to preventing and stopping abuse in the future.

Activist groups led by survivors and their families, lawyers, and journalists all played important roles in this effort, as reported by the *Boston Globe* newspaper's investigative team—as told later in the book and Oscar-winning film *Spotlight*.[1] It is clear that abuse can happen in any religion, but the struggle of the Catholic church that unfolded over decades was a major tipping point that caused immense cultural and policy change worldwide.

What has been heartening is that perpetuating or tolerating abusive behavior that used to be swept under the rug in our society is now considered to be a breaking of the values of most faiths. Through child abuse prevention policies and educational programs, most religious institutions, schools, and programs are taking steps toward change.

What to Look for in a Faith Community

Realize that you can choose which faith community to join—and that you can work to fix problems that concern you—and you can leave a specific community if the problems they create outweigh the benefits. Think about what is important to you. Considerations might include:

- Welcoming for everybody, even those who are not part of the faith

- Encouraging open communication, questioning, and exploring rather than being dogmatic

- Being family-oriented with involvement of parents and other family members strongly supported

- Actively inviting and welcoming people of all sexual orientations, genders and ethnicities, as well as welcoming of interfaith families

- Inclusion of people with disabilities

- Accessible and collaborative leadership rather than being solely top-down

- Services and community activities for all ages, from families with young children to elderly people

- Projects that add joy and meaning to your life

- Whether leaders are "walking their talk" in terms of upholding their values rather than only giving lip-service and doing something that conflicts with these values

- Background checks of staff, two-deep leadership, and other organizational safety practices described in Chapter 5

- Child abuse prevention training for staff and parents

- Personal safety training for children

If you choose to include someone from your place of worship in your inner circle of people with close access to your children, apply these standards rather than simply trusting someone because of the religious beliefs that they share with you.

What Makes Something a Poison Stew?

Deciding to leave a community of people who are connected by strong beliefs that you share can be very painful. Many years ago, Irene became a leader in a nonprofit organization with a group of amazing teachers who were deeply committed to the cause of teaching self-defense to women. After she had given her heart, her time, her trust, and her expertise to that organization for over two years, Irene learned that one of their trainers was systematically approaching former students to pursue sexual relationships with them.

Because this behavior was harmful to these vulnerable women and against the values of the organization, Irene set boundaries to try to stop this man from continuing to work with students. When these boundaries were not accepted by the other leaders, she felt as if her only choice was to leave. She was shocked by the failure of other leaders to take action to protect their students and heartbroken when her decision caused many people she had loved and respected to turn against her.

"Even after all this time," Irene reflects, "I still remember how sad I felt about the loss of friendships—and my worry that I would not be able to continue to do work that had become so important to me. Finally, I imagined that we had had a stew filled with the most tasty and nourishing of ingredients. And then someone dropped a poisonous mushroom into the pot. I realized that even if everything else was great about the recipe, it would still be a poison stew."

The good news is that, after recovering from the loss of this community that had been so important to her, Irene gathered with many other like-minded people who joined together to start Kidpower.

What Kids Need to Know About Their Faith and Their Safety

Once in a Kidpower workshop, Irene was teaching a group of young children the difference in their safety rules when they were together with their adults and when they were on their own. She asked, "Who is the only person who is with you all the time?"

Most of the children answered, "My mom. My dad. My grandpa. My teacher."

One little boy raised his hand and said, "God. Or Jesus."

"I mean really here with you in person right now," Irene tried to explain.

With utter conviction, this child said, "God or Jesus are really here with me in person right now and all the time."

"You are right!" Irene replied. "And we have talked with a lot of ministers and priests and they have told us that when it is just you and God or Jesus, you should follow the safety rules as if you are on your own. Rabbis and imams will also tell you that when you are alone with God or Allah, your job is to follow the safety rules as if you are on your own."

Respect for different faiths and spiritual beliefs is truly important. We want to honor each family's choices, as long as what they do is beneficial for their children. Children need people in their lives who they can count on, and we want to encourage respect for the deep commitment and ethics of most religious leaders, teachers, and other members of a religious or spiritual community.

At the same time, parents, educators, and other caring adults need to understand that most children are very literal. If we tell them to do what a religious leader says because this person knows best, they are likely to believe us, even if this person is harming them and tells them to keep what happened a secret. If we tell children to believe whatever a religious leader says, they might believe that what this person does is their own fault.

Here are ways to safeguard children while encouraging them to respect their faith:

- Don't force children to hug or kiss anyone they don't want to, even if this is the common practice in your place of worship, even if the person asking for affection is your faith's most respected leader. When kids are shy or reserved, don't force them to make a connection even by looking at someone. As they get older, let them connect in other ways, such as a wave, fist bump, smile, or handshake.

- Teach children not to keep secrets about anything that happens at your place of worship or about anything that anyone from your spiritual or religious community does.

- Teach children that if someone breaks the safety rules, this is against your beliefs and that this person is making a mistake.

- Make sure that people in positions of authority and trust in your faith follow the same child abuse prevention policies as everyone else—including avoiding special favors, not being alone with kids unless parents know each time, and other potentially risky behavior.

- Encourage people at your place of worship to teach and practice boundary-setting and help-seeking skills of the kinds taught by Kidpower.

- Pay attention to your intuition and ask questions if someone's behavior concerns you.

- Listen to your kids when they talk with you about their problems, even if it makes you uncomfortable or you think they are confused or being silly, and let them know that you are glad they told you.

You can also refer back to strategies covered in Chapter 5 to help make sure your place of worship is worthy of trust.

Keep your radar on. If someone's behavior seems to be failing to uphold the above safeguards, first notice what is happening so you can take action. Then, as described in Chapter 2, intervene to address the behavior and stop it from growing into a safety problem for your child or anyone else's child.

Safety Checkup

✓ Make a list of what is important to you in a religious or spiritual community—and remember that you have choices about whether to join or not, and to stay or go.

✓ Don't give your power away, even to someone who is representing what you believe to be a higher power. Remember that blind faith, automatic obedience, or unconditional respect for an authority figure can be dangerous.

✓ Be prepared to leave a religious or spiritual community if it is acting in conflict with your values. Although leaving a community that has been important in your life can be very painful, know that you can recover and go on to find or create other places to invest your heart, your time, and your faith.

✓ Encourage children to enjoy and respect your place of worship, while safeguarding them with age-appropriate knowledge and skills.

A Place to Spread Their Wings:
Safety on College Campuses

After moving her child into college, Amy has found the topic of campus safety to be very much on her mind. She says, "This has been such a bittersweet time. Nothing has been quite as exciting, full of pride, and nerve-wracking as sending my 18-year-old out into the world. I hope with all my heart that all the young adults who we so deeply cherish will be able to grow, explore, and spread their wings in college as they make new friends and immerse themselves in learning. And, with all the news about assaults on college campuses, I hope with all my heart that my own child will be safe!"

Facing Hard Issues About Campus Safety

Moving away from home is a vulnerable time of novelty and exploration, where young adults have more freedom and take more risks, with much less mature adult supervision, intervention, and support than they had in high school. Although statistics show that young people ages 18 to 24 who do *not* go to college are at greater risk of sexual assault or violence than those who do, parents trust that their kids will be safe when they are going to college—and, unfortunately, sometimes they are not.

This is no time to be taken in by the Illusion of Safety, no matter how beautiful the campus looks in a brochure, or real life. Campus safety should be an active, ongoing process involving both college leadership and personal vigilance from the students themselves.

There is no question that campus safety, particularly sexual assault, is a major concern. It seems obvious that sexual assault should not be accepted as part of the college experience. Unfortunately taking action to address this problem effectively has been challenging. The Campus Sexual Assault Study[1] was funded by the US National Institute of Justice in 2007 to research the prevalence, causes, and impact of sexual assaults on college campuses and to identify risk reduction interventions.

One of the findings was that about 1 in 4 women and 1 in 16 men had experienced an attempted or completed sexual assault during their college years. With today's greater awareness about sexual assault, there is a strong possibility that these numbers are actually much higher. Other findings from the study include:

- For 84% of women who reported sexually coercive experiences, it happened during the first four semesters on campus.

- Alcohol and assault of an incapacitated person are major components of completed sexual assaults, most commonly after the victim voluntarily consumed alcohol or drugs, as opposed to being slipped drugs without their knowledge or otherwise incapacitated, such as being asleep.

- Before college, women experienced physically forced sexual assaults and incapacitated sexual assaults happen at almost the same rate (experienced by 7.0 and 6.4% of women). During college, the rate of incapacitated assault increases dramatically, and physical assaults decrease. In the Campus CSA Survey, 11.1% of women surveyed had experienced incapacitated sexual assault and 4.7% had experienced physically forced sexual assault since entering college.

Highlighting the role of incapacitation and alcohol is not intended to blame survivors for being assaulted, but to look at the factors that go into assaults happening. Rather than focusing on just date-rape drugs that are slipped into a person's drink unknowingly, we need to realize that the most common date rape drug is alcohol being supplied out in the open at campus parties where excessive drinking is encouraged and often celebrated.

Make a Safety Plan About Using Alcohol and Other Drugs

Too many college administrators and faculty have seen the damage and heartbreak caused in lives full of promise, either because young people are harmed, accused of harm, or truly caused harm as the result of decisions made while under the influence of alcohol and drugs.

Here are a few recommendations for how to talk with young people who are headed to or enrolled in college or who are preparing to live away from home.

Research shows that parents matter in influencing their child's attitudes and behaviors around alcohol and other drugs.

The Maryland Collaborative to Reduce College Drinking and Related Problems encourages parents and family members to engage in conversations early and often with their students. Tips, scripts, and information can be found on the Maryland Collaborative website, "College Parents Matter." The website shares seven different communication tips and eight high-risk drinking situations.[2] Each situation has a conversation script that parents can utilize. Unfortunately, even with the "best" parenting practices, there is no guarantee that students will refrain from starting to use alcohol or drugs, developing a drug or alcohol problem, or, even worse, experiencing serious drug or alcohol-related problems. Conversely, the worst of circumstances does not necessarily predispose one to a life of addiction.

Other general safety tips that are important to consider when a college student chooses to be with people who use or abuse alcohol or other drugs include:

- How am I going to get safely to and from my destination?

- How can I make sure that at least one other trustworthy person knows where I am and who I am with?

- What will I say and do to make sure that I am only drinking, swallowing, or taking substances that I really want?

- Which person that I really trust can I bring with me so we can look out for each other?

- Does that person know what to do and how to get help if we have trouble?

- What is our agreement if one of us wants to leave and the other doesn't?

- How will I get home if the person I am riding with seems to be drunk or under the influence?

- When I get to my destination, do I know where and to whom I would go to safely get help if I need it?

Seeking "Justice with Fairness" to Address Sexual Misconduct—One University's Story

"Title IX" is a US federal civil rights law that protects everyone's right to have an education from kindergarten through college. In order to learn, people are entitled to a learning environment that is free of gender-based discrimination or harassment. This means that schools are responsible for addressing problems that come up in their community, including sexual harassment and assault.

From 2010 to 2016, there was a growing awareness that colleges in the United States were not doing a good job of handling sexual assaults on campus, leading to a period of intense activity and reform. Grassroots activists representing survivors of sexual assault protested campus policies that were inadequate and sometimes led to blaming the assaulted students for what had happened to them.[3]

Many colleges' systems for handling sexual assault complaints were inadequate, and some had huge structural flaws. For example, an undergraduate peer Honors Court that had been originally set up to handle academic cheating was also tasked with making judgments about sexual assault allegations. These cases needed to be handled by trained adult professionals, not student peers.[4]

Taking effective action when there are charges of sexual assault or harassment is complicated in an educational setting. In a criminal legal process, District Attorneys can look at a case and decide whether there is enough evidence to move forward with a prosecution. In contrast, colleges and other educational institutions have the obligation to help students and remain fair to all parties involved, no matter what.

Grassroots pressure from their own students and top-down guidance from the Department of Education led to a wave of change and reform on campuses across the country.[5] In 2013, Amy was appointed to the University of North Carolina's Title IX Task Force at UNC Chapel Hill, giving her a seat at the table with this important group that was convened to recommend changes to the university's policies on how it handled sexual assault, harassment, domestic violence, and more.

Over the next 16 months, this group of two dozen people representing constituents from across the campus worked to thoroughly revamp and improve the university's policies.[6] Amy says, "Being on the Title IX Task Force was a difficult, yet ultimately rewarding and inspiring experience. The best part of the Task Force was that it involved people from so many parts of the university, including the student body President, who was a male fraternity member, student activists, professors, counselors, lawyers, Vice Chancellors, the head of the LGBTQIA+ center, and more. I was appointed as the one 'community representative' who was not a UNC student, faculty or staff member. That put me in the position of coming in fresh into a group where a lot of members initially intensely mistrusted each other.

"For the first few meetings, at times it felt like the group might fall apart in conflict. But thanks to excellent facilitation by Christi Hurt, then the head of the Women's Center, and a truly inclusive and open process, this group became very functional and made major improvements to the policies on how the university handled sexual assault and related issues. We were able to make almost all of our recommendations by unanimous consensus. We worked with nationally renowned legal experts Gina Maisto Smith and Leslie Gomez to create new processes that were fair to everyone involved, as well as compassionate to those who reported sexual assault, harassment or domestic violence. No system is perfect, but I really felt like our recommendations were vast improvements."

Task Force Insights

Handling sexual assault cases fairly is a difficult challenge for any educational institution to take on, but there are compelling reasons to do so. The UNC Title IX Task Force experience gave Amy the following insights:

- Due process for all people involved is crucial. A system will fail if it is not fair to both complainants reporting assault, and respondents.

- Treat everybody well. Compassion is always called for. Student activists responded to universities' poor responses in addition to the trauma of assault itself. Rape myths and victim-blaming cause needless additional suffering.

- In parallel to the official disciplinary or criminal process, universities should ask themselves what they can possibly do to make students' lives better. "Interim measures," such as changing class schedules or dorm assignments, can be done without disturbing due process. This is not a substitute for other policies and processes, but it should be added in.

- Offer counseling and support, including confidential counseling in addition to making it clear how to report complaints through official channels for university action, as well as the option of reporting to the police.

- All staff involved in investigating and deciding cases must be appropriately trained professionals.

- The process and policy for handling even very difficult issues can truly improve when people with different perspectives work together with respect and commitment.

- The implementation of a consent-based conduct policy on campuses across the country has been a revolutionary change.

Consent-Based Sexual Conduct Policies

In recent years, many institutions have adopted consent-based sexual conduct policies, which means that both people have to actively agree to sexual activity, for it to be allowed. For too long, a huge proportion of disadvantages and burdens in the system have fallen on the victims of sexual assault. This goes back to the very definition of forcible rape, which from 1927 to 2012 was defined as forced sexual intercourse—"the carnal knowledge of a female, forcibly and against her will."[7] The definition of rape has now been expanded to include non-consensual penetration, no matter how slight, with any body part or object and can apply to any gender.[8]

In some college policies, outdated provisions required complainants to present evidence that they tried to physically resist an attack. For example, in 2013 a Harvard student said she was assaulted, but decided not to press charges because the University said there was little hope they could launch an investigation and charge her assailant because he "may not have technically violated the school's policy in the student handbook."[9]

At that time, Harvard's policy, more than 20 years old, defined "indecent assault and battery" to be anything involving "unwanted touching or fondling of a sexual nature that is accompanied by physical force or threat of bodily injury." Unfortunately, this definition did not include someone being incapacitated or emotionally intimidated, which can make consent impossible, even without physical force or threat. For this reason, the student was unable to press charges.[10] In 2014, Harvard updated its polices, but did not adopt an affirmative consent requirement.[11]

Consent-based policies mean that the person who wants to initiate sexual contact is responsible for being sure that their potential partner is giving affirmative consent to proceed with intimate activity. Affirmative consent policies also stress that someone who has been incapacitated due to alcohol or other drugs cannot give consent. Students must take seriously their obligation NOT to sexually assault or exploit a drunk or drugged person.

The concept of consent can and should be taught in age-appropriate ways throughout childhood and adolescence. Strong boundaries and the demonstrated skill and commitment to not only set them but also to respect them can help people be safe from violence—as well as safe from accusations resulting from their own behavior.

Even preschoolers can learn rules such as "any kind of touch should not be a secret." If young people had these kinds of discussions throughout their lives, including discussions of healthy relationships, and how to respect other people's boundaries, the concept of consent would be very familiar by the time they stepped onto a college campus or entered the workforce.

Talking to Our Sons as Well as Our Daughters

As we struggle to ensure that everyone's rights are protected in today's polarized social climate, many parents are also deeply afraid that their sons will have their lives derailed and even destroyed by assault allegations. Instead of just worrying, we can have open conversations and make sure that our children have the knowledge and skills they need to make safe and wise choices.

As one mother said: "Growing up in our family with the values we have, and being upset by the times when he saw the harassment experienced by his older sister, my son has always shown a tremendous respect for women. Even so, I was very worried about the safety of my young adult son when he started college. I did not think he would assault anyone, but I did worry that he might have a communication problem and do something that might leave a woman feeling that he had crossed her boundaries, especially when he was experimenting with drinking.

"For my peace of mind, I asked my son to keep upholding at college the values and skills he'd been learning most of his life. Although he was somewhat annoyed by my conversation, my son agreed to think first and avoid driving, sexual behavior, or other risky activities when he or others were using alcohol or drugs. He promised to check first and make sure that the other person would also want anything they did sexually and use protection. Later my son told me how he kept speaking up when anyone was disrespectful to any woman—and how he had taken the car keys away from a drunk friend."

Bystander Intervention

Another major positive change in campus culture has been a new emphasis on bystander intervention. This has been done informally for years, with friends using the "buddy system" and committing to looking out for each other at parties, not leaving anyone alone, or letting a drunk friend be taken away into a private room where they could be assaulted. In recent years, new programs have been developed that realized that with training and encouragement, bystanders can become part of the solution rather than part of the problem. Dr. Dorothy Edwards developed the Green Dot Bystander Intervention Program—in which a "green dot" represents any behavior or choice that promotes safety for all of us and communicates utter intolerance for any form of violence.[12]

The Green Dot program teaches students skills and tools that help them overcome obstacles, such as being embarrassed to step in, not knowing what to do, and overcoming a diffusion of responsibility. The training sets new social norms that make it expected that more students will look out for each other and step in to defuse problems as they develop, whether it is a fight brewing or a sexually coercive situation developing. Equally importantly, Green Dot gives bystanders tools for how to intervene, including *directly* confronting a situation, *distracting* by changing the conversation and the energy of the interaction or by distracting the individuals, or *delegating* by finding someone who will be more successful in fixing the problem such as a bartender, other friends, or a police officer.

For example, one young woman was out with friends and noticed another young woman nearly passed out on the bar, while a man who was clearly a stranger circled furtively around her. He eventually helped the woman out of the bar. The female bystander, who'd been watching the scene unfold and growing increasingly concerned, followed them out. On the sidewalk, she told the man that if he tried to leave with the woman, she'd call the police. The guy walked off, leaving the woman on the sidewalk, oblivious to the assault she might have just escaped.[13]

The program encourages students to share their actions on social media using #WhatsYourGreenDot, and colleges can even post campus maps describing all the green dots submitted by community members, to show that specific actions are being taken.[14] Bystander education researcher Dr. Elizabeth Miller compares the Green Dot program to "designated driver" interventions. "It's not saying, 'You are the problem.'" Instead, "It taps into a sense of generosity and sense of connectedness."[15]

Initial research into the effectiveness of Green Dot has shown remarkable results. A 2014 evaluation study found a greater than 50% reduction in the self-reported frequency of sexual violence perpetration by students at schools that received Green Dot training, and a 40% reduction in self-reported frequency of total violence perpetration including: sexual violence, sexual harassment, stalking, and dating violence.[16]

Changing Traditions to Ensure a Campus Culture of Safety

Rather than handling complaints, the ideal solution would be to prevent assaults from occurring. This creates cultural challenges within a college community, as some of the risk factors for assault are intertwined with campus traditions that are valued by students and alumni alike. Parties— as evidenced by annual "Top 20 Party School" lists—fraternities and sororities, athletic events, and social drinking are entrenched aspects of life on many campuses.

Since the highest risk for sexual assault is during the first four semesters on campuses, and even the first month of school, safety education should start during orientation and continue as ongoing education. College leaders should look out for and minimize inherently dangerous situations, such as parties during orientation thrown by upperclassmen that single out or target first-year female students as guests.

To take another example, hazing is a complex problem that intertwines traditions and creating a strong group bond with practices that are unsafe and sometimes deadly. Byron Hurt is a filmmaker and proud member of Omega Psi Phi Fraternity, who says he has experienced hazing and has hazed other young men.

At first Hurt was reluctant to take on such a sensitive and controversial topic. However, he was profoundly moved by the story of Robert Champion, a band member at the Florida A&M University, who was killed by his fellow band members in a violent, clandestine hazing ritual. Bryon Hurt's upcoming documentary is titled *Hazing: How Badly Do You Want In?*[17]

Hazing expert Dr. Susan Lipkins describes the cyclical "Blueprint of Hazing" as part of her effort to understand and stop it:[18]

The blueprint of hazing states that the newcomer, or victim, is hazed. Once accepted by the group, the victim becomes a bystander, and watches as others get hazed. Eventually, the bystander achieves senior status and power, and becomes a perpetrator.

They do onto others what was done to them, and they feel as though they have the right and duty to pass on the tradition. High school students pack up this blueprint and stuff it into their backpack, in order to take their hazing experience with them to college, the military and the workplace. Each hazing brings with it the possibility of a new twist. Perpetrators want to leave their mark on the tradition, and therefore they may add or change the tradition, slightly.

Ultimately, change will come when we establish new traditions of building community through positive connections rather than through manipulation, prejudice, and enduring assaults. At the University of Idaho, for example, during pledge week, all of the fraternities and sororities had large signs with handprints from every member saying, "These hands don't haze!"

Talking to Young Adults About Hazing

Hazing has caused humiliation, trauma, injuries, and deaths, damaging and destroying too many young lives.

Although hazing rituals are intended to create a sense of belonging within a group, silly pranks can escalate into ritualized bullying, assault, and abuse, often fueled by alcohol and drugs. The desire to belong and the pressure of emotional coercion can drive young people to endure or inflict harmful behavior that can quickly get out of control. Others agree to inflict harm on themselves through binge eating or drinking, pill-popping, or using laxatives.

Even though states, colleges, fraternities, sororities, and sports organizations are making hazing against the rules, laws and policies are clearly not enough. You have to be prepared to protect yourself—or students or athletes you know—from being harmed—and from being sucked in to causing harm.

Here are some suggestions that provide a framework for discussing hazing with college students.

1. Ask questions up front. Learn what new members or pledges are expected to do, and be clear about your boundaries. Avoid groups where secrecy about how people treat each other is required. If you believe that hazing is part of an initiation, consider whether the benefits of belonging are worth the risk of legal consequences, serious injury, or death.

2. Don't make yourself an easy target. You're far more vulnerable to harm from hazing or other unsafe behavior if you're not able to think clearly. Accept that drugs and alcohol affect thinking and judgement. Limit your use. Make sure that people who care about you know where you are, what you are doing, and who is with you.

3. Pay attention! Humiliating activities are a red flag. Telling someone that they have to do something miserable in order to belong is emotional coercion. Being forced to take off one's clothes, being tied up, being hurt physically, being pressured to swallow anything unsafe or unknown—or being taken to an isolated place and dumped—are all forms of assault and abuse, not harmless pranks. Joining in or "just watching" are ways of participating in destructive behavior.

4. Resist the pressure to belong. Stand up for yourself and others. Remember you have the right to be treated with safety and respect—and the responsibility to act safely and respectfully toward others. Even if others are pressuring you to do differently, you have the power to choose your words and your actions. You could say, "That's not safe!" You could walk away. You could leave quietly if speaking up feels too dangerous. If necessary to be safe, you could lie to get out of it—and then, get help.

5. Shine a light on dangerous behavior. Problems should not be secrets and dangerous behavior is a problem. It's OK to lie or to break a promise in order to be safe and get help. Even if you promised not to say anything, find trusted people in positions of authority who can protect you from retaliation, and report what happened. Even if you made a mistake that led to your being harmed, and even if you feel very embarrassed, what happened is the fault of the person who did this to you. You deserve to have support. Although speaking up can be very uncomfortable, remember that you might be protecting another person from even greater harm.

Leadership from the Top

As with any other organization, a university policy is only as good as the implementation and leadership that supports it.

At Elon University's convocation in August 2017, speaking under the elms on a bright August morning in North Carolina, President Leo Lambert gave what he knew would be his final address to a new crop of students before retiring. He wove his expectations for the community throughout his speech: treat each other well, respect differences and actively reject prejudice, and stop sexual assault and gender-based violence. He spoke from years of experience when he said that alcohol use is associated with almost every college tragedy, and that students with repeated alcohol problems would be invited to leave campus to receive treatment and reconsider their priorities.[19]

President Lambert's address to more than 1500 new students set a powerful tone, and reinforced the university's expectations with the faculty, parents and older students in attendance. Convocation is one of the revered traditions at Elon and it was powerful to hear these specific, clear, compassionate messages from the school's leader on day one.

Assault prevention can take many forms, and an "all-of-the-above" approach is useful if a college can find programs that work for their community in empowerment self-defense, bystander intervention, alcohol harm reduction, and more. An overall training plan should involve all genders, the LGBTQIA+ community, Greek system chapters for fraternities and sororities, sports teams and marching bands, and incoming students.

Safety Checkup

✓ Continue to insist that colleges keep improving their policies, prevention programs, and responses to sexual assault.

✓ Ensure that alcohol and drug harm reduction efforts are actively upheld on all college campuses.

✓ Keep implementing consent-based policies and education to help prevent rape on college campuses.

✓ Replace harmful campus traditions such as hazing with positive ways of building community.

✓ Insist that boundary-setting and consent skills are taught to young people of all genders so that they can prevent harmful behavior from growing.

PART III

Creating
Safer Societies

CHAPTER 10

Overcoming Harmful Prejudice with Understanding, Determination, and Courage

Being treated as worthless because of prejudice can feel dehumanizing and can become life-threatening. In the early 1970s, when Irene was 23 years old, she served as a VISTA Volunteer. One of her projects was to set up a sheltered workshop for people with developmental disabilities in a small Midwestern town. What none of her supervisors had realized is that sending an olive-skinned, brown-haired, brown-eyed young woman to create change in a community with mostly blond-haired, blue-eyed, fair-skinned people was a recipe for disaster.

The day she arrived, Irene was startled when asked by two county officials, "Are you Injun or are you Jewish?" She sometimes waited for an hour in the one grocery store because the clerk would not serve her until every other customer had left. By night, she would get anonymous phone calls with terrifying messages like, "It's too bad that Hitler didn't do a better job." By day, she would visit families of people who were called "retards" and often chained onto tables in back bedrooms to keep them from wandering off and getting into trouble.

After six hellish weeks of rejection everywhere she turned, Irene started feeling as if she had transformed into a dark-covered shell instead of a real person. She persisted because, in spite of everything, she did not want to abandon the very vulnerable people waiting in those back bedrooms for something to do and somewhere to go. Finally, Irene realized that her life was in danger when some teens driving by threw a bottle at her as she was walking mid-day on the town square. She stopped before the bottle hit her head so that it crashed onto the ground at her feet. After Irene had moved away, she was able to find two blond-haired blue-eyed VISTA Volunteers to take her place and set up the sheltered workshop, which eventually became a great success.

This experience left Irene with a fierce determination to stand up for people who are being victimized by prejudice for any reason. As traumatic as those six hard weeks were for her personally, she realized that most people facing this kind of prejudice live with it constantly, from birth, reducing their opportunities, putting them at greater risk of harm, and causing long-term stress that has major lasting health impacts.

Times have changed, and the widely accepted prejudice faced by Irene—and the people with developmental disabilities who she wanted to help—would be considered wrong by most people today. We have come a long way—and we still have a long way to go.

Not a Perfect World

In a perfect world, no one would care if people were different, as long as they weren't being hurtful to anyone.

In a perfect world, people would not be bothered or harmed by others because they are of different races, sexual orientations, gender identities, appearances, incomes, religious beliefs, abilities, political beliefs, or cultures. Different colors of skin and shapes of faces and bodies would be celebrated rather than judged. It would not matter whether children have married parents, divorced parents, two moms, single dads, grandparents, or guardians. If children's families have problems, this would not be a reason for other people to think less of them.

But we don't have to tell you that this is not a perfect world. Harmful prejudice because of differences can lead to bullying, social injustice, and hate crimes. Negative assumptions about young men of color being dangerous have led to innocent people being shot by law enforcement officials who said later that they believed that their lives were at risk. Negative assumptions about different religious beliefs and cultures have too often led to violence instead of to peace.

Sadly, most of these injustices are the result of what is called "institutionalized oppression," which means that beliefs and practices that harm certain groups have been developed and supported, often over hundreds of years, by social systems and institutions. In this context, individuals from these groups are at far greater risk of having their rights to safety and fairness limited or lost. We will explore institutionalized oppression further, including the Black Lives Matter "Campaign Zero" movement, in Chapter 11.

"It's Not Fair!"

Young people have a strong sense of justice, and they are usually outraged when they are picked on because of their identity. With different groups, the negative assumptions that they encounter might be different, but the feelings are the same: shame, hurt, sadness, wanting to be accepted, fury, fear, wanting to hide, and wanting to get even.

In Teenpower workshops, we have teens or pre-teens practice de-escalating and walking away instead of getting into fights or arguments. Often they protest, saying, "It's not fair! I should be able to go down the street without some creep harassing me. You just said that I have the right to be proud of who I am, and now you are telling me to shut up and take it."

And of course, we agree with our students because they are right—it's *not* fair!

We try to provide perspective by saying, "Our goal is to help you to be as safe as possible in an unfair world. What other people believe or say is not as important as your safety. You can be proud while being realistic about the dangers caused by prejudice. This means that you need to make wise choices about when you show the world what you think and who you are—and when you focus on being aware and getting away from potential trouble. We believe that when you are under attack, your first priority is to get away safely. When you are back in a safe space, that is the time to work to make the world fairer in the future.

Some of the most effective leaders of social change have chosen, calmly and intentionally, to stay in dangerous situations. However, these actions usually turn out to be most powerful when they are taken as conscious, centered choices solidly grounded in principles and with clear awareness of the benefits and risks of action versus inaction."

Reactive behavior that is fueled by triggered emotions—such as righteousness, indignation, anger, or offense—is likely not only to be dangerous but also much less effective in furthering justice, fairness, or equality.

When we all make our personal safety a priority on an everyday basis, we can strengthen our skills, deepen our knowledge, become more effective leaders and advocates, and make more intentional choices about how we assess risk in our efforts to work toward social justice for ourselves and others.

Sick and Tired of Walking Away

In a workshop Irene led with a high school special education class, her teaching partner Mark was pretending to be a drunken man on the street. Irene coached the students to walk away assertively as Mark shouted insults like, "YOU RETARD!"

When it was his turn, fifteen-year-old Ross turned around and threatened to punch Mark instead of walking away. Suddenly Ross started yelling, "From the time I can remember, people have been telling me that I'm dumb. Retard. Freak. Poor thing. Stupid. Special Ed. For years and years. I am sick and tired of walking away, and I'm not going to!"

Both Mark and Irene explained that Ross had a right to his feelings, but that they couldn't let him practice physical self-defense fighting skills unless he first showed that he could walk away from insults without acting as if he wanted to fight.

Mark modeled looking powerful while walking away. Ross sat and thought about it while he watched the other students practice. Finally, he asked if he could say everything he wanted to say out loud to Mark, who was pretending to be an attacker. He got permission from his teacher as long as he didn't use foul language.

Mark stood calmly and sadly, while Ross shouted at him, "I HATE YOU! YOU ARE HORRIBLE! I WANT TO HURT YOU THE WAY THAT YOU HURT ME! F*** YOU!"

When he was done, Ross said he was now ready to practice walking away with calmness, awareness, respect, and confidence from Mark pretending to be horrible. He did a great job, and everyone clapped for him.

As this story shows, it can be very hard to walk away—and very empowering to address the feelings that make it hard and then to be successful and cheered for leaving a potentially dangerous situation.

Any Word but THAT One

Because so much devastating harm has become associated with certain words, these words can assume an enormous amount of power for young people. In fact, many adults, in describing these words, will have a hard time saying them aloud and will use initials instead. The "N" word. The "B" word. The "C" word. Of course, in a great many situations, this method of referring to a word by its first letter is considered the only appropriate way to refer to the word—and doing otherwise can be experienced as deeply offensive and triggering.

Hurtful words about aspects of our identity including race, gender, ethnicity, sexuality, body size, and religion are "identity attacks." Identity attack language is commonly used on purpose to demean others or to cause intentional harm. It often causes harm when harm was not intended—for example, this can happen when children repeat things they have heard without a true understanding of its meaning and impact. Identity attack language communicates bias and prejudice in addition to disrespect and devaluation.

"I can walk away from any word but that one," young people who have faced identity attack language will tell us. "If someone uses *that* word, I have to fight to defend my honor!"

What the actual words are will be different for different people and different groups, but the issue of being triggered by identity attack language is the same. After a community had had three funerals for boys who had been killed within a few months in fights that started over insults, the local youth group asked for a Teenpower workshop. Kidpower Program Co-Founder Timothy Dunphy got permission from the youth group leaders to use the most offensive words possible, so the boys could practice staying calm, walking assertively away from trouble, and going to safety.

Because peer approval was so important for this group, Timothy got the other boys to cheer their friends as they walked away from the insults, saying things like, "That's cool, man! I want you to live! Those are just sounds, man!"

Hard-Won PRIDE

The acronym "LGBTQIA+" refers to people who are lesbian, gay, bisexual, transgender, queer or questioning, intersexual, asexual, and people who have other expansive sexual orientations or gender identities.

LGBTQIA+ young people are highly vulnerable to being physically and emotionally targeted simply because of who they are. Awareness of the intense prejudice LGBTQIA+ people and their loved ones experience can make self-acceptance much more of a struggle. Many understandably fear harassment, threats, and isolation. They worry not only about themselves but also the harm and the rejection their loved ones, such as parents and siblings, may face as a result of the young person's identity. Understandably, such major potential consequences can make the pathway to acceptance much more painful and difficult.

By the time they get to a self-defense workshop, many young people who identify as LGBTQIA+ have already reported being bullied, harassed, threatened, sexually assaulted, or beaten up. When they turn to trusted adults for help, many not only do not get the help they need but are also told by that they "deserved" it or that they were "asking for it."

Practicing how to handle different types of insulting or threatening behavior makes a big difference in our ability to respond in real life, which is why we include these kinds of practices in Teenpower. The types of situations young people might face as a result of prejudice about sexual orientation or gender identity include:

- "I am holding hands with my girlfriend walking home after school and this guy starts following us, saying that we need to have sex with real men."

- "A guy starts to approach me in an isolated place, making threatening comments about the 'Gay Pride' sign on my (T-shirt, wheelchair, car, etc.)."

- "I am walking with my boyfriend and these guys start to threaten us, saying that they don't want fags in their town."

- "I am at a party, and someone starts shouting, 'Hey, are you a guy or a girl or a what?'"

Teenpower uses similar role plays to also help young people stay calm and centered so they can make wise choices in the face of cruel words and actions because of sexism, racism, anti-Semitism, Islamophobia, ableism, ageism, or other kinds of prejudice. Again, the purpose is to help them increase their ability to manage their normal, absolutely justified emotional reactions so that they can make safe and wise decisions for themselves, even when confronted with verbal attacks like these.

Regardless of the reason for the prejudice, the underlying safety principles and skills are the same. While it is important to be proud of who we are no matter what anyone else thinks or says, it can be dangerous to let pride get in the way of choosing to Put Safety First. The best strategy will depend on the situation and might be to:

- Leave quietly and quickly and get to a safe place.

- Set strong boundaries.

- Yell for help.

- Use physical self-defense to escape.

With practice, young people can become prepared to stay calm, clear, respectful, and persistent when setting boundaries about prejudice with people they know. They will be most effective if they use assertive body language so that they project confidence and if they use neutral language instead of being sarcastic or provocative. Rehearsing how to manage their emotional triggers prepares young people—and adults—to stay in charge of what they say and do even when they are upset, and to Think First before engaging in hurtful behavior of any kind themselves.

Creating an Inclusive Environment From #Day1

Imagine how great if it would be if young people knew from the *first* day of their school, camp, team, or job that their community was going to be as supportive as possible of every person, and would not tolerate cruelty of any kind!

The Tyler Clementi Foundation's #Day1 Campaign aims to do just that by providing adult leaders with a two-minute orientation speech that states clearly the unacceptability of bullying, harassment, and other forms of prejudice. They also provide an Upstander Pledge for students and staff to sign and Kidpower intervention tools for how to address problems when they happen.[1]

Tyler Clementi was a freshman at Rutgers University who killed himself in despair after his roommate publicly broadcast a webcam video of Tyler in an intimate moment with another man. This incident represents a cruel example of cyberbullying, homophobia, and an utter violation of an innocent person's feelings and privacy. Tyler's roommate Dharun Ravi was convicted of a bias crime and invasion of privacy and was sentenced to 30 days in jail.[2]

While nothing can bring Tyler back, the Clementi family has established their foundation in Tyler's memory with the purpose of taking action to prevent what happened to their son from happening to others.

People in positions of authority in schools, organizations, businesses, and communities can use the #Day1 script and Upstander Pledge to be clear about expectations from Day One with their new students, staff, volunteers, and other participants—and to reaffirm their personal commitment to create a safe and respectful place for all their members. It is so powerful for leaders to set a positive expectation that everyone will be welcome and that no one will be bullied or harassed about their race, culture, size, sexual orientation, gender identify, appearance, faith, political beliefs, class, or mental or physical disabilities.

Making Wise Choices When Being Unfairly Targeted by Public Officials

We deeply wish that our society would live up to the promise of equal protection for all; a society where people do not feel the need to coach their children and teens about exactly how to behave if they are stopped by police, in a best effort to ensure their own personal safety. We need to continue to work together to reach this goal. Chilling statistics show that young men of color in the U.S. are far more likely to be stopped for questioning, treated with suspicion, and killed by police officers.[3] And any innocent person of any age, race, or gender can be harmed just by being perceived as a threat, which is more likely to happen if you escalate a confrontation with law enforcement officials, even if "*they* started it."

Being targeted unfairly is wrong and deeply upsetting. Until things change, many families coach their children and teens in what to do if they are stopped by police, because they cannot control what others do—but they can increase their own children's skill level to do all they can to increase the chance of a positive outcome. By having a clear plan of action, young people will be better able to make safe and wise choices in the heat of the moment.

We recommend that people prepare themselves, their children, and their loved ones to handle these types of situations by reviewing resources from civil justice organizations such as the American Civil Liberties Union (ACLU), the Council on American-Islamic Relations (CAIR); the Mexican American Legal Defense and Educational Fund; Asian Americans Advancing Justice (AAJC); the Equal Justice Initiative (EJI); and the Southern Poverty Law Center. The ACLU made a YouTube video with English and Spanish titles that shows what to do to protect your rights if you are stopped by immigration officials or are arrested.[4]

Knowing your rights in advance and practicing these skills before you need to use them is very useful in being prepared to avoid making a bad situation worse and to increase the likelihood you can get away safely.

What Young People Need to Know and Do If Stopped by the Police

The following skills and strategies are important to discuss practice with young people when they start going out into the world:

- Stay calm and respectful, especially if officers are rude, demanding, or threatening.
- Limit speech to phrases recommended by civil rights organizations such as, "Am I free to go?" "I do not consent to a search," and "I want to remain silent."
- Keep your hands relaxed, free, and visible so officers can see that you do not have a weapon.
- Avoid sudden aggressive moves or language.
- Try to defuse the conflict by being very polite.
- Recognize that alcohol or drugs can impair your ability to stay calm and make safe choices—and might harm your credibility if you file a complaint.

- If possible, document what is happening by turning on the video camera of your phone or by using the ACLU's Mobile Justice app that allows people to record any concerning incidents and share them immediately with the ACLU.

- Ask bystanders to witness what is happening and to record it if they can.

- Leave calmly if you are allowed to do so.

True Allies

Even with the best of intentions, we will make mistakes with each other, and it is important not to let those mistakes stop us from continuing to work toward greater understanding and acceptance. From early childhood on, we are immersed with mixed messages about different groups in our society, and we will sometimes say or do something that perpetuates prejudice instead of stopping it. Acknowledging when we make mistakes that reveal our bias or prejudice is difficult, and doing so opens doors for dialogue and greater mutual respect and understanding.

Lillian Roybal Rose is a cross-cultural communications trainer and longtime Kidpower advisor. Her approach is wise and inspiring because, while educating people about the harm done by prejudice and institutionalized oppression, she also views each individual with respect and compassion. According to Lillian, "The field of cross-cultural communication starts with the working assumption of the goodness of all human beings and helps people to become true allies to each other in making a more just society. A true ally is not someone who helps another person. A true ally is someone who takes a stand based on her or his own values with no strings attached. We will make mistakes with each other out of fear or out of misunderstanding. We have to stop blaming and shaming each other for these mistakes. A true ally is not someone who never makes mistakes. A true ally is someone who never goes away."

Diversity training like Lillian's can be a great help in creating a common ground between people with very different life situations. Young people from privileged backgrounds sometimes feel so guilty about the harm done to others who are less fortunate that they tend to minimize their own pain or to treat people who are more likely to suffer from prejudice as "poor things." They need to learn that pity is another way of treating others as less powerful than oneself and can become another form of oppression. In addition, minimizing our own pain doesn't make it go away and is a form of oppressing ourselves.

Lillian tells a story of a young white man who said in one of her workshops, "I come from a wealthy family and never wanted for anything. All that has ever happened to me was that my father hit me. Compared to what these people have suffered, I don't have the right to feel bad about anything. It wasn't that bad."

Lillian turned to this young man and said, "Pain is pain. It *was* that bad. Until you can accept and acknowledge your own pain, you will never be able to treat others as peers or to be an effective ally. Pity can come out as a form of paternalism that is very condescending, even though I know that is not what you want."

Instead of showing pity, we can be true allies by speaking up clearly about the importance of treating people with respect regardless of their differences. We can take leadership in creating an inclusive community by setting clear expectations with a path for follow-through if things go wrong.

When people in positions of power or prestige label others in degrading ways or use language that seems to condone any kind of destructive prejudice, we can state our strong disapproval of this behavior, even if we appreciate their sports victories, enjoy their music or films, or agree with their politics.

Educating the Educators

Often, ongoing guidance and advocacy is needed to create an inclusive community, even among well-intentioned people. A child with any kind of difference—such as being highly sensitive, being on the autism spectrum, being a high achiever, having any kind of disability, or carrying extra weight—might face prejudice and discrimination. As the following story shows, choosing to set aside frustration to advocate for a child with relentless, cheerful persistence is sometimes necessary to reach people who want to do the right thing but don't know how.

One Kidpower mother has a seven-year-old child, Kai, who identifies as non-binary—neither a girl nor a boy—and who uses the pronouns they/them/their. Although they attended a very progressive school, educators were having trouble recognizing and addressing the kinds of teasing and hurtful comments that Kai was experiencing at school.

Kai's family was proactive, emailing and speaking with teachers before school started to offer support and help in making the classroom welcoming for their child. They were assured that the teachers were well prepared to offer a safe and welcoming learning environment, such as by offering a gender-neutral bathroom. Ultimately, though, Kai's family learned that they needed to be persistent advocates for their child, because it took time and repeated parental intervention for the educators to understand the extent of the problems that Kai was experiencing.

The family used Kidpower skills to help prepare Kai to deal with family, teachers, and kids accidentally mis-gendering them by using the wrong pronoun, both individually and in groups, such as by calling out, "Hey boys and girls, come to the carpet now," instead of "Hey kids, come to the carpet now."

Unfortunately, the educators were not prepared to notice and address repeated mistakes, or to respond effectively to the teasing and taunting that made Kai feel progressively unwelcome and like they had no real friends at school.

Once, when Kai gently reminded a long-time teacher about their pronouns, the teacher said, "You're just going to have to learn to get over that," rather than apologizing and offering to do better. In this atmosphere, it was also common for Kai to be challenged on a near-daily basis with comments from other children who really didn't understand gender diversity at all and were not being offered good guidance by teachers. This lack of understanding led to repeated hurtful comments like, "If you're not a girl, why are you wearing pink?" Or, "You must be a boy, you're wearing boy clothes." Kai felt worn down and unsupported by having to repeatedly explain their gender identity.

Then, one classmate told Kai, "If you aren't a boy or a girl, then you are *nobody*!" Sadly, although the teachers witnessed this happening in the moment and talked with both kids to calm down the situation, the educators did not take this cue to finally have a larger discussion about welcoming people of all differences, including gender diversity, in their school. Worse, "you're nobody" became a regular taunt by several children and was used repeatedly.

As a result, Kai's mom again insisted that her child needed more protection and support and that the school needed to go beyond passive tolerance and move toward proactive welcoming for not only this child, but also all of the students and staff, in understanding and supporting people with non-binary gender identities.

After many meetings and persistent advocacy, Kai's mom was able to have the classroom and supporting teachers spend an hour together with her, where she facilitated a discussion and educated them about this kind of prejudice looks like and provided recommendations of books and resources that they could use in creating a more inclusive school environment.

The school also agreed to send a letter to parents, that Kai's mom helped them write, to introduce the topics of her child's non-binary gender identity and open the lines of communication to help everyone understand and welcome gender diversity in the school community.

Kai's mother stayed clear on her goals for her child to be in a supportive learning environment and, as hard as it was, did not give up in the face of prejudice, discomfort, and resistance to change.

Educating the Public

At a Kidpower workshop for parents of children with special needs, Sonia's mother told us, "Sonia has severe cerebral palsy. She uses a wheelchair and needs a speech board to communicate. She has to struggle to move her hand or to sit up. When we go out in public, people don't realize how intrusive we find their stares, well-meaning comments that feel patronizing, and assumptions that she can't hear and understand what they are saying. I get so upset that I want to yell at them, even though I know that Sonia really doesn't want me to make a scene."

Children with disabilities often seem different and are more vulnerable to being bothered, bullied, or even attacked because of prejudice or because they seem like easy targets. Here are some ways of educating the public:

- Treat innocent questions from children as an important opportunity to build awareness and understanding. Suppose a child asks, "Why does she use that wheelchair?" We can give a simple answer, such as, "She uses a wheelchair because her legs don't work so well."

- If kids are asked questions that feel overly personal or intrusive about their own bodies and they are capable of answering for themselves, then practice possible responses, such as, "Bodies are different. I am proud of who I am."

- Respond to the respectful concern of another adult by being clear about what you want and don't want without acting triggered. For example, "No, thank you. I appreciate your offer, and we are fine." Or, "Thank you. That would be great."

- Set boundaries firmly and respectfully if someone is disrespectful in public, as long as it is safe to do so and consistent with your own values and priorities. Rehearse responses like, "Excuse me. Pointing at others and talking about their bodies can feel hurtful, even if you don't intend it that way."

- Make a plan with your child about how you will respond if people act or speak as if your child is not there. Your confident actions can show people how to interact respectfully and can be more effective than explaining the problem. Practice how to change the subject, as well. For example, suppose you and your child Sonia are outside and another parent starts complaining to you about the weather and not even greeting or looking at Sonia. Or worse yet, suppose this parent starts talking to you about Sonia, saying, "Poor thing. This weather must be terrible for her." You can interrupt by saying, "Excuse me. I'm interested in Sonia's opinion." You can then turn to the child who is being ignored and say something about what is going on, such as, "What do you think, Sonia? Is it too hot or, just right?"

- Be prepared to leave calmly and get help if you are not in a safe place or if someone's behavior seems unsafe. Imagine yourself feeling deeply offended—and choosing to leave calmly and respectfully anyway in a safety situation.

- Report any unsafe behavior to the people in charge of those places. This could mean contacting the head of a youth sports league, or a restaurant manager, or a school principal, or a camp director, or the security department at an amusement park, or the leaders of your local transit system. Ask them how they can make sure that everyone who visits their place is treated with respect.

"Are they going to like my skin?"

During a Kidpower group phone-coaching session, one mother asked, "My four-year-old was playing with her preschool classmates, and the other girls said she could not play because of the color of her skin. She told me about it after school, and the teachers did a great job of addressing it, including adding some diversity lessons. But my daughter is still confused and worried. Now, when we go to see new people or family we have not seen in a while, she asks, 'Are they going to like my skin?' How can we help her?"

Irene's suggestions to the mother included:

- Tell your child, "Sometimes kids say hurtful things about our differences, like hair styles, skin color, glasses, or by making fun of our name, or by always bringing up our mistakes in a way that hurts our feelings. We all need to learn how to protect our feelings and learn how to feel good about ourselves. This can be hard to do even for grown-ups. I am so proud that you told me, and I am proud of the great things the school did to help educate the other children on how to celebrate differences. Let's practice ways we could respond to the things that are worrying you."

- Practice using the 'Kidpower Trash Can' technique, maybe with puppets or dolls at this age, to take the power out of the words, "You can't play with us because of the color of your skin." The puppet could say the mean words, and your daughter can practice throwing them away and saying, "I love my color! I will find another friend." You can also write the words on a piece of paper and let your daughter scribble them out, crumple the paper up, and throw it in the trash.

- Remember that the Trash Can is a "taking charge" skill to protect feelings. It does NOT erase the problem. Exclusion based on skin color or other aspects of identity is dangerous and hurtful. Young children are likely to engage in this behavior without knowing how truly destructive it is, and adults are absolutely responsible for taking charge with clarity, caring, compassion, and boundaries so that the behavior stops. Children who know the Trash Can and other filtering techniques are more prepared to protect themselves in the moment, leave safely, and tell adults they trust about the problem.

- Let your daughter know that "If anyone says something hurtful, I want you to protect your feelings and then get adult help. This kind of behavior is unsafe, but sometimes other kids don't know that. Telling adults who can help can help other kids grow too, and learn to be kind and understanding to others."

- Practice how to decide which adult to go to and how to interrupt a busy adult to get help. Practice how to persist until the adult listens. Practice how to move away and go to another adult if the adult you chose listens to you but responds in a way that is not helpful, such as by saying, "That's just how kids are. You need to learn to deal with it on your own."

- Practice how to speak up by saying, "That is a hurtful thing to say. Please stop."

- Practice how to stay silent and move away from kids acting unsafely so your child has this choice as well. In some situations, speaking up might be an effective way to address the problem. In other situations, such as in spaces with children who are not being well-supervised and who you are not likely to see again, quietly leaving to play another game might be a better fit. Teach your child both choices—and other skills you want them to have—so they are empowered to choose in the moment.

Teenpower Lessons About Prejudice— a Workshop Story from Irene

In a Teenpower workshop for boys from 12 to 15 years old at a Jewish Community Center, parents had asked Irene to prepare students to deal with verbal bullying. With parental permission, the teen boys wrote down the actual words that others might use against them as emotional attacks. The students then chose the words that would be likely to upset them so they would be able to use these words in practices for protecting their feelings and staying centered.

As they sat together in a circle, Irene asked each student to read his list aloud to help take the power out of these hurtful words. The insults included words like: "Beanpole, Ugly Jew, Dirty Faggot, Fatso, Wimp, Dummy, Jewing People, Wetback, Creepy Homo, and Whitey."

One boy said, "I hate it most of all when anyone insults people by saying that they are gay or lesbian or trans." All the other boys nodded their heads in agreement about what a terrible insult that was, including one boy who Irene thought might possibly be deciding he was gay.

Irene smiled at the boy who had made the comment and said, "Thank you so much for bringing this up. I have been thinking about how important someone's intention to hurt is in whether or not something is an insult. For example, my background is Jewish. Suppose someone comes up to me and says in a nice way, 'Hey, aren't you Jewish?'" Since, even though I'm not a practicing Jew, I'm proud of my Jewish heritage, I might decide to say, 'Why, yes I am. Thank you!!'"

Irene made eye contact with the boys who were Jewish who smiled back at her. Then she went on, "Suppose someone says to me, 'You have curly hair!' Even though as a girl I longed to have the smooth, straight hair that was fashionable then, I can decide that this is a compliment. But suppose someone jokes to someone else, 'I hate those ugly greedy curly-haired Jews!' Of course, I wouldn't like that. This person's way of speaking is insulting, even if they think they were just joking or were talking about someone else and not me."

Irene went on, "Most people want to believe that they are tolerant of differences. However, there are many beliefs that people don't even realize actually come from prejudice. For example, assuming that most Jewish people are greedy is a prejudice. Regardless of their culture, most people care a lot about having enough money. In fact, Jewish people have a culture of being very generous and charitable. Another prejudice is that being thinner is better than being heavier or that being tan is better than being pale. A hundred years ago, people who were pale and had plump bodies would be considered good-looking. What we now call beautiful, people in those times would have called emaciated."

The boy who had "Fatso and Whitey" on his list looked up at Irene and grinned. She grinned back and continued. "There are many great ways to look, and many great ways to be. Being tolerant means understanding that being different does not mean being bad. Many people think that referring to someone who has identified as being gay, lesbian, or transgender by their identity is automatically an insult. Of course, if someone wants to be rude, *anything* this person says can be an insult. However, it is a prejudice to assume that being gay, lesbian, or transgender is bad. This is just a part of who someone is, no different than having curly hair or being Jewish.

"You can feel very alone if everyone around you says that being different is automatically bad. Personally, I am lucky enough to know many powerful, courageous, brilliant people who have different sexual orientations and gender identities. And, although we are different, we are each proud of who we are, and we are proud to know each other."

In order to show understanding about what her students might have done in the past while inspiring them to do differently in the future, Irene said, "Joining in when other people are teasing someone in a mean way is normal. Agreeing with prejudiced remarks about a certain group of people can make us feel like part of the group we are with. Just watching and saying nothing is also normal. Speaking up can be scary, and you want to choose when and how you do it. What we need to keep in mind is that something can be normal and still be incredibly hurtful and dangerous, even if that was not our intention. Standing by doing nothing makes it look like we agree with what's happening. Having who you are be used as an insult can feel awful, so we want to do our best not to be part of doing this to anyone. If you can't speak up in the moment, you can leave to get help from an adult. You can also reach out to the person who was attacked later. We may have joined in or stayed silent in the past because we didn't understand or know what to do. Now that we *do* understand, we can take responsibility for practicing and using responses that support safety for everyone."

Even though Teenpower workshops normally don't include this much talking, the boys listened with total respect and silence the whole time Irene was speaking. She finished up by saying enthusiastically, "I don't know about you, but I'm tired of sitting here talking. Let's get up and practice!"

So, that's what they did. Irene and her teaching partner coached each of their students to be successful in practicing how to:

- Protect themselves emotionally and walk peacefully and confidently away from an instructor shouting the hurtful words on their lists at them, while saying to themselves, "I am proud of who I am."

- Set boundaries about prejudice by saying, "I understand that you were joking, and I feel uncomfortable when you label a group of people in a negative way. Let's talk about something else," and to persist with their boundaries even if the other person gets upset.

- Speak up in the moment if someone is insulting someone else by saying, "Please stop. Remarks like that are just not cool"—supporting each boy in adjusting the wording so that he could communicate this message using the language of his own peer group.

- Get the attention of a busy, impatient adult and be persistent in asking for help.

One boy asked to be called "gay." He walked away saying out loud, "Even though I am not gay, if I was, I would be proud of it!"

And finally, as a last resort, the boys in the class practiced how to escape from an attack in case of an emergency when they couldn't leave or get help. Of course, that practice meant learning self-defense moves for hitting and kicking the head-to-toe padded Full Force instructor and they liked *that* a lot!

In the workshop described above, Irene used examples that were relevant for these young teens and that were okay with their parents. There are many other ways of addressing this issue that can also work, while staying within the boundaries of different kinds of beliefs.

Managing Our Own Prejudices

As humans, it is normal for our minds to make shortcuts that lead to "pre-judging," or prejudice. We need to become more aware of these unconscious tendencies and biases, which become harmful when we treat someone as less worthy because of our assumptions. Staying aware of our own prejudices can help us to make better decisions about our actions and provide an important role model for our children.

We can assess when our prejudices are based on reality by asking ourselves questions. Is this person just looking or acting in a way that I don't understand or find upsetting—or is this person acting in a way that is truly potentially dangerous? Am I blaming a whole group of people because of trouble caused by a few people from that group? Am I trusting and liking this person just because of familiarity, position, appearance, or charisma—or is my trust based on what this person is actually doing? By understanding when our perceptions are biased and treating people as being of value even when their differences make us uncomfortable, and by committing to reflect about this and make changes in an ongoing way, we can reduce the likelihood of our prejudices contributing to oppression.

Finding Your Common Ground

As adults, our responsibility is to ensure the emotional and physical safety of all of the young people in our lives. We cannot take a strong stand against bullying, prejudice, and other kinds of destructive behavior by trying to stop some kinds of attacks and insults and ignoring others. Racism is wrong. Sexism is wrong. Ableism is wrong. Classism is wrong. Ageism is wrong. And, even though these kinds of prejudice don't have an "ism" attached, attacks on someone's belief, culture, religion, gender identity, gender expression, sexual orientation, body size, appearance, or other identities are also wrong.

Kidpower welcomes a diverse group of people of all backgrounds with many different perspectives and often-conflicting religious and political beliefs. Our shared common ground is that we are all deeply committed to safety and respect for everyone. Staying in charge of what we say and do, getting involved, setting boundaries, upholding values of fairness and integrity, moving away from trouble, getting help, and practicing instead of worrying are all tools to address prejudice and to help keep people emotionally and physically safe.

Every person has the power to speak up clearly about the importance of treating all people with respect. For example, one of our Kidpower values is to be inclusive, with a boundary: *We welcome people of any age, culture, religion, race, gender, political belief, nationality, sexual orientation or gender identity, marital status, any kind of disability, or level of income who share our commitment to integrity and safety for everyone and who can join us in upholding our values.*

With compassion and self-awareness, we can overcome destructive beliefs inside ourselves through getting to know people who are different than ourselves. Together, we can teach our children to treat themselves and others with respect and understanding instead of fear and hate. And we can work together to face prejudice with compassion and determination in order to create greater justice and safety for everyone in our society.

Safety Checkup

✓ Recognize the role that institutionalized oppression plays in affecting our beliefs and in giving some people fewer rights, privileges, and freedoms than others.

✓ Accept that our starting point is an imperfect world. Acknowledge that harmful prejudice is very unfair, and prepare yourself and the young people in your life to recognize harmful prejudice and to make safe choices.

✓ Set a good example by modeling respect for differences and by acknowledging your mistakes when you haven't responded as your best self toward others.

✓ Set a good example by apologizing and making amends when, even as your best self, your own lack of knowledge or understanding has resulted in actions—including uses of power—that are experienced as harmful or disrespectful to people whose life experiences are different from your own.

✓ Accept that we all have prejudices that can sometimes be hurtful to others—and that this does not make us or anyone else bad people—it just means that we have to pay attention, put ourselves in the shoes of others, and do our best to be open-minded and inclusive.

✓ Instead of blaming people for having hurtful prejudices or not stopping unsafe behavior, educate them when it is safe to do so.

✓ Prepare young people with skills so that they know how to protect themselves and advocate for others. Rehearse how to Put Safety First using examples relevant to them.

✓ Take leadership in agreeing on a common ground of safety and respect in schools, workplaces, organizations, and community.

CHAPTER 11

Giving Our Kids a Better World to Live In

"Peace in every home, every street, every village, every country—this is my dream. Education for every boy and every girl in the world. To sit down on a chair and read my books with all my friends at school is my right. To see each and every human being with a smile of happiness is my wish."

—From *I Am Malala* by Nobel laureate Malala Yousafsai, the brave Pakistani woman who survived an attack by the Taliban at age 15. Malala's unstoppable education advocacy has sparked a global movement benefiting all youth.

Is the Glass Half Empty—or Half Full?

As we look at the world that our kids will inherit, there are lots of reasons to worry—climate change, mass shootings, political unrest, terrorism, global epidemics, massive extinctions of different species, poverty, starvation, and war. Age-old injustices such as domestic violence, violence against women, and sex trafficking are still rampant, even when outlawed in most countries.

Yet, there are lots of reasons to have hope. In 1989, the same year that Kidpower started, the Berlin Wall came down and Germany was reunified.

Nelson Mandala walked free in 1990 after 27 years in prison in South Africa. The Americans With Disabilities Act passed in 1990. The right to same-sex marriages was upheld by the US Supreme Court in 2013. The air and water are cleaner in more and more communities—and there is less trash. Thanks to better knowledge, information sharing between countries, and talented and committed people, we are far better able to recognize and stop epidemics.

Communication and information sharing are becoming amazingly efficient, bringing great benefits as well as new challenges like fake news, cyberbullying, and online addiction. It is hard to imagine that in 1989, we didn't have the Internet, smartphones, or laptop computers to help us or to harm us.

Sometimes people ask, "Are things worse than they used to be?" It is terrifying when disasters and violence destroy and disrupt so many lives. It can be frustrating when some battles that seem to have been won go backwards.

The pendulum toward positive social change often swings backwards and forwards.

What gives us hope is that the center of the pendulum itself is set over a different landscape than 100, 50, and even 20 years ago.

Today, we have better tools than ever for joining forces with like-minded people to work toward positive change. Today, most people do not believe that children or women should be property. We have far more awareness about the lasting harm done by prejudice, bullying, abuse, violence—as well as littering and pollution. Far more people in almost every country recognize the need to protect their kids and to have violence-free families—and to teach respect and kindness instead of hate and fear.

Agreeing to Agree—and to Disagree, While Still Working Together

In 1989, Irene's hometown of Santa Cruz was heavily damaged by the Loma Prieta earthquake. After the dust settled and the rubble cleared, the city learned that the damage was so severe that half the downtown had to be condemned. The City Council appointed a task force to make recommendations about how to rebuild it that included liberal politicians, conservative business leaders, and others with widely different viewpoints.

The group quickly became mired in disagreement because they were trying to reach a consensus on issues where a minority of members had profoundly different wishes. Finally, Irene was hired as the facilitator so that they could get their report done within the time limit.

Realizing that she had to start somewhere, Irene announced in her introduction, "I have to admit that I have a strong bias. *I want our downtown to be rebuilt!*" As the committee members laughed and nodded their heads, Irene added, "I think you feel the same way. So let's agree to agree on *that* as our common ground."

Irene also got the group to agree on ground rules about respectful communication and time limits. From there, the Task Force was able to find many ideas where they all agreed—and some ideas where they needed to agree to disagree. Their report included recommendations where there was consensus and recommendations that had passed with a majority vote with the viewpoint of those in disagreement recorded.

In the US, polarization about how to address concerns like gun violence, immigration, police shootings, health care, and environmental protection seem to have paralyzed our ability to make decisions. The prevailing viewpoint seems to be, "If you are not with us, you are against us." If we just keep shouting at each other, we will never be able to figure things out. Instead, we need to seek out common ground, develop trust by respecting each other's perspectives, and find practical solutions.

Community Policing

For example, we can learn best practices from communities that are being successful in reducing violence—and these practices all seem to come back to better communication and greater connections between police officers and members of the communities they serve, as well as safer ways of responding to suspicious or dangerous behavior.

In the NPR Code Switch blog post, "Civil Rights Attorney on How She Built Trust With Police,"[1] attorney Constance Rice described the fear that many police officers were facing daily in Los Angeles—and how she worked together with Police Chief Charlie Beck to train them to develop trust. "The first thing I tell these cops is that you are not in the arrest business; you are in the trust business. We are going to train you in Public Trust Policing. It goes beyond community policing. What it does is it puts police in a position of helping a community solve its problems."

In Richmond, a California community with high poverty and crime rates, rates of violence have dropped after officers got out of their patrol cars and started walking the streets, going to community meetings, and asking people how they can help with concerns. A headline in the September 6, 2014 *Contra Costa Times* announced, "Use of Deadly Force By Police Officers Disappears on Richmond Streets."[2] The article described how, in addition to closer connections with community members, Police Chief Chris Magnus has implemented a number of reforms to prepare officers to handle crisis situations and use alternatives to deadly force.

Citizen Involvement

Citizen involvement in police departments and the legal system is essential in ensuring that public safety officers are held accountable for their actions and supported in doing their jobs. As citizens, we can:

- Thank our law enforcement officers for putting their lives on the line for our safety. Police officers face injury and death in the line of duty, not only because their jobs require them to move closer to danger— rather than farther away, which is generally the safest choice—but also, sometimes, because they are targeted because of their role.

- Invite police officers to community meetings to discuss concerns.

- Establish advisory committees to provide oversight in order to prevent problems or to address them early.

- Ask to ride along with a patrol officer to learn what their jobs are really like.

- Be prepared to take action if we can do so safely when we witness abuses of power or other unsafe behavior, such as by taking videos, leaving and writing down notes about exactly what we saw, and reporting.

- Call 911 to report an emergency if we fear someone might get hurt. We don't have to judge what is happening—or who is right or wrong— just describe what we are seeing or just saw.

- Ask elected officials to provide funding for diversity training, implicit bias training, body cameras, and other resources that can increase understanding and accountability and reduce injury or death.

- Ask questions about the legal systems that are in place both for police and for the public—and, if they seem inequitable, lobby for changes in the law or the implementation of the law.

- Vote for people and policies that best represent our values.

- Accept that people have different levels of comfort with police that grow from different life experiences. To deepen your understanding of these differences and consider how we might find common ground, ask non-judgmental questions about the experiences and perceptions of people whose life experiences seem very different from your own. Listen to their words without arguing. Listening is not the same as agreeing. Attempt to understand how they have come to their position.

- You may have strong negative reactions to police from past experiences. Being aware of those deep feelings can help you "think before you react"—a Kidpower skill—so that the feelings do not control your behavior or decision-making.

Black Lives Matter's Campaign Zero Plan

Addressing a problem as complex as institutionalized oppression requires a systematic response. The Black Lives Matter movement was initially sparked by the outrage caused when 17-year-old Trayvon Martin was shot dead by neighborhood watch volunteer George Zimmerman, who was later acquitted of a crime for his actions.[3] Since then, Black Lives Matter has grown from an online hashtag, #BlackLivesMatter, to organized protests in Ferguson, MO, Baltimore, MD, and many other cities around the US; to the creation of a comprehensive plan for ending police violence. Their Campaign Zero plan has a vision that, "We can live in a world where the police don't kill people—by limiting police interventions, improving community interactions and ensuring accountability. We can live in a world where structures and systems do good, not harm."[4]

Campaign Zero integrated recommendations from communities, research organizations and the President Obama's Task Force on 21st Century Policing to create detailed recommendations in ten policy areas, aiming to protect and preserve life. The campaign's policy solution categories are: end "broken windows" policing of minor infractions, increase community oversight, limit use of force, independently investigate and prosecute suspected police misconduct, increase community representation, use body cams and film the police, training, end "for-profit policing," demilitarize police forces, and implement fair police union contracts.[5]

Looking at People Through a Lens of Compassion Instead of Fear

Cross-Cultural Communications expert Lillian Roybal Rose provides a framework for developing understanding.[6]

> In any relationship, whether it is individual or social, it is important to understand the experience and therefore the perspective of the other person. Understanding is *not* the same as excusing. Instead, knowing why someone does what they do helps us be effective in setting boundaries about unacceptable behavior and in working toward change.
>
> In other words, understanding someone's perspective does not necessarily change *what* you do but *how* you do it. If you need to set boundaries, it will work far better if you do this in a way that communicates compassion rather than blame.

When people are from a culture or race that has been dehumanized for generations over hundreds of years, we should be able to respect their right to be angry. Yes, we can set boundaries to stop them from expressing that anger in destructive ways. We can do our best to redirect their anger into constructive action.

We all participate, often unknowingly, in allowing different kinds of oppression. For example, when I tried to take my mother for a walk in her neighborhood in her wheelchair after she had had a stroke, I was angry when I found that the curbs had not been made wheelchair accessible. But before this time, I had never noticed how the curbs made accessibility so much harder for people using wheelchairs and had unintentionally colluded with a system that did not make this a priority by doing nothing about it.

My blaming anyone for being angry about being harmed by prejudice is as if I beat you with a bat and then blamed you for bleeding on my carpet.

I believe that all people are basically good and want to do the right thing. Some of our life experiences injure us and can create patterns that trigger fear and oppressive policies and actions. Vilifying each other for taking harmful actions out of fear does not lead to change. Again, instead of blame, we must work together toward a greater understanding and set effective boundaries that lead toward a fair, compassionate, and just society.

In order to create better understanding, we need to be careful of what we label as 'violent.' It is important to remember that blocking a road or building might be massively inconvenient and illegal—but this is an act of peaceful civil disobedience, not of violence. Destroying property, threatening physical harm, or assaulting others are violent acts—and it has been heartening to see how many of the thousands of protestors, who are peacefully demanding change, have spoken up or acted physically to stop those in their midst who started to act violently.

No matter who you are and who "they" are, looking at people
through a lens of fear alters perceptions in ways that makes dangerous
reactions more likely.

Trying to Get Unstuck

On October 1, 2017, the deadliest mass shooting by a lone attacker in modern US history happened in Las Vegas. The entire country was horrified that a man with a cache of modified automatic weapons could spray bullets into a crowd of 22,000 defenseless country music fans, killing 58 people and injuring 489 more, in just a few minutes.[7] Just a few months later, as we were working together to finalize the manuscript for this book, another mass shooting shocked the nation. This time, 17 teens and educators were killed and 17 more injured in the shooting at Marjory Stoneman Douglas High School in Parkland, Florida.[8]

Both of us are strong advocates of stronger gun safety laws to help prevent horrible tragedies like the ones mentioned above—and both of us have people in our lives that we respect and trust who are strong advocates of protecting our Constitutional right to bear arms. Both of us have beloved friends and family who are gun owners.

Compared to all other advanced countries, the number of mass shootings in the United States is shockingly high. The US has six times as many firearm homicides per capita as Canada, and nearly 16 times as many as Germany.[9]

The Pew Research Center reports that US citizens "… have shown broad and consistent support for expanded background checks for gun purchasers. In a July, 2016 poll, 85% of the public—including large majorities of both Republicans (79%) and Democrats (88%)—favored making private gun sales at gun shows subject to background checks. There also was substantial bipartisan support for laws to prevent people with mental illness from purchasing guns."[10]

Other countries including Canada and Switzerland also struggle with these issues, going back and forth between the rights of gun owners and the risks of mass shootings from angry individuals intent on killing as many people as possible.[11, 12]

So why has it been so hard to enact legislation? And what are other countries, even those with high gun ownership, doing that leads to such a lower number of violent shootings? Why do some caring, ethical gun advocates have such a great suspicion of what seems, to other people, like reasonable requirements for owning and selling guns? Why is it so much harder to get agreement on requiring licensing, mental health checks, and training for the ownership of guns than it was on licensing and putting restrictions on the ownership and driving of cars?

If our society is ever going to get unstuck on this issue, we need to find common ground between people who fear the misuse of gun control and people who fear the misuse of guns. We need to listen to each other rather than demonizing, threatening, or ridiculing each other.

In conversations with people whose views are different than our own, we have heard many views including:

- "We all want the same things—to be safer and to keep our freedom."
- "We don't have a lot of trust in our government, and fear that all our rights as citizens will be taken away if we accept any restrictions."
- "Our officials need to properly and equitably enforce the gun laws that we already have."
- "We don't want irrational people owning guns either, including criminals. It undermines trust when people who have committed armed robbery end up back on the streets."
- "We have had bad experiences of registering our guns according to the law and then suddenly being told that these same guns are now illegal in our state."

Irene asked a dear friend and life-long NRA member, who is very smart, rational, and deeply committed to preventing violence, "If you were in charge of the world, what would you consider to be reasonable restrictions? And what safeguards would you need in order to trust that agreeing to some requirements would not lead to all of your rights being threatened?"

"That's a good question," her friend said. "I need to think about it—and will get back to you."

Irene's friend says that his support of the NRA has become increasingly reluctant, as the leadership has responded with such a lack of compassion for innocent people harmed by mass shootings. He continues his NRA support for now, explaining, "It's the only game in town" for effectively protecting gun-owner's rights and is exploring more moderate groups that support responsible gun owner's rights along with gun safety laws.

It's hard to find solutions when people are so divided. But conversations like these, where people listen to each other respectfully and start seeking answers together, are at least the way to begin.

Turning Tragedy into Advocacy

One hopeful phenomenon is that the outpouring of grief from the Parkland High shooting is currently being channeled into activism by the young survivors themselves. These social-media savvy, articulate, angry teenagers have become their own spokespeople. They are holding the adults in charge accountable for failing to protect them from a disturbed 19-year old with an assault weapon.

These student activists know that they don't leave their rights behind when they are at school. They are staging Constitutionally-protected walkouts, and travel to state capitols and Washington, D. C. to press their leaders for change. It is going to be hard to ignore their voices.[13]

Many adults had become numb and resigned, seeing that so little progress has been made during the two decades since the Columbine High School shooting in 1999. But we see a new glimmer of hope that this time, something really is different, and fair and safe gun laws and implementation of those laws will finally become a reality as this new generation rises to power.

The Courage to Change the Things We Can

Thinking, texting, posting on social media, obsessively following the news, and worrying about problems can feel as we are doing something—but are not the same as actually taking action. Instead of getting overwhelmed, we can remember the Serenity Prayer[14] that has helped countless people, regardless of their religious beliefs, to keep things in perspective.

Based on a sermon written by theologian Reinhold Niebuhr in 1934, the most common form says: "God grant me the serenity to accept the things I cannot change, the courage to change the things I can, and the wisdom to know the difference."

Having serenity does not mean giving up—it means being realistic about what is and is not in your power instead of wasting energy in being frustrated and stressed—so that you can use your power to keep advocating for ways to make things better.

Like the ripples of a pebble thrown into a pond, the results of even small actions can go much further than we might imagine. Find something that works for you: give a donation, send a letter, give an endorsement, make a phone call, buy a book, go to a meeting, make an introduction, reach out to help a neighbor in need, post a sign stating your values, or listen to someone whose views are different with compassion and respect. If we each do what we can, together we can truly make a difference.

In addition to courage, positive change takes knowledge and skills— and the ability to join with others for the greater good. We hope that this book has provided you with some insights and tools that you can use in your own life and share with others.

kidpower®

Kidpower Skills and Action Plans

Kidpower Skills and Action Plans

As readers ourselves, we authors appreciate not having to go hunting other places for core information that is referred to in a book. For this reason, we are pleased to be able to offer some of Kidpower's most important skills, strategies, and actions plans as a bonus to readers of *Doing Right by Our Kids*.

These tools can be adapted to help people of all ages and abilities, in a wide variety of situations, to create a positive social climate in their families, schools, workplaces, and communities. You can learn a lot by reading the skills and implementing them yourself. In addition, when evaluating a personal safety program, it is important to know what that program will be teaching.

At Kidpower, we are deeply committed to bringing these core ideas to life by teaching with our Positive Practice Method™, where each person is coached to be successful in rehearsing a skill or strategy in a context that is relevant to their lives. In our three decades of providing services, we have seen again and again that ongoing practice is essential to developing strong 'People Safety' skills.

In this Toolkit, you will find:

- *10 Core Kidpower People Safety Skills*
- *Preparing Children for More Independence: Six Steps from Kidpower*
- *Make SURE! Kidpower Action Plans for Adult Leaders*
- *My Child is Being Bullied at School! Kidpower Action Plan for Parents and Guardians*
- *How to Prevent and Stop Cyberbullying*
- *How to Pick a Good Self-Defense Program*

Since 1989, Kidpower Teenpower Fullpower International® has prepared millions of people of all ages, abilities, cultures, beliefs, genders, and identities worldwide to take charge of their safety—and to protect the well-being of those in their care. Visit **www.Kidpower.org** to learn more about the Kidpower curriculum, workshops offered in your area, potential partnerships, and the long-distance training and consulting via videoconferencing that can serve any location with Internet access.

10 Core Kidpower People Safety Skills

As discussed throughout this book, countless children, teens, and adults, including those with special needs, have used the following skills to prevent and solve problems with people, including themselves. These skills help individuals stay safe from most bullying, abuse, harassment, assault, and other emotional and physical violence—and to develop safe and strong relationships that add joy and meaning to their lives.

The description for each skill below includes an explanation of why it is important, how to practice, the safety rules that apply, and how to use this skill in daily life for adults, as well as children and teens. Most of these skills are relevant to use with people we know—and people we don't know. We have included some specific stranger safety rules in Skill #4.

1. Stay Aware and Act Confident

People will bother you less and listen to you more if you seem alert and communicate an attitude of calm, respectful confidence.

By staying aware, you can notice potential trouble—be it an escalating argument between two people, or a car coming the wrong way down the street—and can take protective action to avoid or stop the problem sooner rather than later. You are much less likely to be selected as a target by an attacker when you appear to be alert to your surroundings.

Staying aware often requires splitting your attention. Most of us have occasional bouts of tunnel vision where we become so focused on what we are doing—talking to someone, texting, cleaning something up—that we lose track of what is happening around us. When we are in a private, quiet, familiar place where we have a history of being safe, this is usually just fine. When we are out in public, or in a place where a lot is going on, or when we notice that something is starting to change, we are safest if we stay aware and act alert.

To practice acting with awareness, look around. Turn your head and shoulders calmly so that you can see in different directions. Be sure that you are really registering what you are looking toward by telling yourself what you just saw. Even if you have something else you need to get done, split your attention so that you go from focusing on this activity to scanning your environment.

Staying calm means that you seem peaceful and fully present. Projecting a calm attitude will give you more credibility with others and is less likely to provoke a confrontation. Feeling worried or angry when someone is acting in a way that concerns you is normal. To clear your mind and help yourself act calm even though you may feel upset, get yourself centered.

A good way to do this quickly is to first, take a deep breath in and let it out quietly and slowly. Next, gently press your palms together or against something else, such as your legs or a table. Now, press your toes down so you can feel your feet in your shoes or on the floor. Straighten your back. Finally, focus on what you want to accomplish.

Showing respectful confidence means that you act as if you believe in yourself and as if you see others as worthy of respect. Acting passive and having a timid attitude will often result in your being ignored, overlooked, or forgotten. Acting aggressive and approaching others in a rude way is likely to result in your being avoided, resented, or in a fight.

Instead of engaging with a potentially troublesome person who is trying to approach you, you can leave in a calm and respectful way, while staying aware, conveying the message, "I see you. I don't want to connect with you or fight with you. I notice you are there and I'm moving along."

As you are walking away, you might briefly acknowledge the person with a polite but disengaging comment such as, "Sorry, no … Have a nice day … No, thank you."

If you need help from someone who seems distracted or unhelpful, it's normal to feel frustrated or discouraged. Instead of becoming demanding or giving up, you can project an assertive attitude that gives the message, "Of course, you are going to care about what I want, once you understand what it is. What I have to say is important to me, and you are such a good person that I believe it will be important to you, too."

To communicate an attitude of respectful confidence, check your body language, facial expressions, tone of voice, and choice of words. Make sure your body is upright rather than leaning forward into someone else's space or cowering backwards. Instead of glowering or wincing, do your best to smile or look neutral and calm. Instead of jabbing the air or wringing your hands, put your hands down and stand or sit tall. If your voice sounds whiny or angry, change your tone to be firm and polite. Instead of using insulting or apologetic language, state clearly—and with determined persistence— what you want or don't want. Avoid sarcasm since this is likely to escalate any potential conflict. If you can sincerely act cheerful, this is likely to be disarming to most people.

2. Protect Your Feelings from Hurtful Words or Behavior

Too often, people feel terrible about themselves, or get into fights, as a reaction to what someone else said or did. At any age, hurtful words and insulting behavior can get stuck in your heart or your head and stay there for a really long time. Think of all the misery and conflict that could be avoided if everyone knew how to keep this from happening!

Your feelings are important, and you have the right to these feelings. Although it can be hard to remember in the heat of the moment, logically you know that you are much more than these upset feelings. Fortunately, you can learn how to take care of your feelings so that they do not rule your life, or cause you to make unsafe choices, or act destructively toward others.

The Kidpower Trash Can Technique for protecting yourself from hurtful words has been used by people as young as two and as old as 102, from around the world. Trying to "just ignore it" when someone says something unkind to you usually doesn't work. However, using your body to physically throw away hurtful words can help you remember to do it with your mind in the moment.

Suppose someone tells you that you are paranoid for caring about child safety. To practice using the Kidpower Trash Can, ask someone to call you "paranoid" or say it to yourself in the mirror.

Now, take one hand and put it on your hip. Imagine that the hole made by your arm is your personal trash can. With the other hand, grab some air, imagining that you are grabbing the word "paranoid." Next, throw that word into your personal trash can. Finally, put your hand on your heart and say something positive to replace those words, announcing out loud, "I am proud of my commitment to safety!"

Hurtful words are like trash. If someone throws real trash at you, it would be unsafe to stand there helplessly and let it land on you. Instead, you can grab the trash before it hits you, throw it away, and take care of yourself by washing your hands. Using positive self-talk to replace the hurtful words is like washing your hands after touching trash.

You can also use your personal trash can to throw away negative self-talk, which undermines your joy in life and sets a terrible example for your children. Suppose you are constantly telling yourself, "I didn't get enough done!" Imagine throwing those words away and saying out loud, "I do a lot! And enjoying myself and resting is also doing something important."

Using these gestures and saying affirmations out loud can feel silly; but people of all ages, from the schoolyard to the boardroom to the senior center, have found this practice to be amazingly effective. And of course, you and your children can imagine a trash can if you are with people where acting it out physically would not be a good idea.

3. Stay in Charge of What You Say and Do by Managing Emotional Triggers

Have you ever found yourself unreasonably upset over something very minor? Or gotten so excited about something that you made a fool of yourself? Very likely this happened because you were caught up in an emotional trigger. Just as a small gesture of pressing a needle to a balloon can cause it to explode loudly, emotional triggers can seem very small or unimportant to one person and completely overwhelming to someone else.

Emotional triggers are thoughts, words, gestures, smells, songs, or other things that cause people to explode with feelings. When your mind is exploding with feelings, it is hard to think clearly or make wise choices for yourself and your loved ones.

Some triggers cause a flood of positive feelings instead of negative ones. People who are triggered might like something so much, admire someone so much, or believe in someone or something so strongly, that they go overboard in a way that might be harmful to themselves or others. When people are flooded with triggered positive feelings, they might react by:

- Falling helplessly in love with someone whose behavior is harmful

- Showering a beloved child with unwelcome attention

- Blindly trusting and following someone in a position of power or prestige

- Wanting to please others and be liked so much that you don't take care of yourself.

Other triggers cause a flood of negative feelings, leading to people getting so upset by how someone looks, or what someone says or does, that they act in a way that is likely to make the interaction worse rather than better. When people are flooded with triggered negative feelings, they might react by:

- Becoming heartbroken and feeling as if life is not worth living

- Becoming fearful and feeling helpless

- Becoming furious and wanting to get even by making the other person feel bad

- Disconnecting emotionally and feeling as if nothing matters

- Flailing, by going on automatic pilot and trying way too hard to do something even if it makes no sense.

You can learn how to understand and manage your emotional triggers so that you are in charge of them, instead of them being in charge of you. Words, gestures, and facial expressions are all symbols of communication that can have different meanings to different people. If the meaning you make of what others say or do is making you miserable, you can take the power out of these triggers by finding ways to minimize their impact. One way is to write down a list of all the things that others say or do that cause you to explode with feelings. Say them out loud over and over as you visualize them, alternating with your favorite foods or vacation spots, or something silly that makes you laugh. Now, tear the list into bits and throw it away.

Once you are no longer so triggered, you can think about your options and make conscious decisions about how you can respond, rather than being on automatic pilot. You can consider the pros and cons of different responses, including their potential long-term effects on your relationships and life goals.

As one father told us, "I used to get furious when my son would throw tantrums. I was so afraid of doing the wrong thing that I would disconnect and act if I didn't care—or yell at him to stop. Of course, these reactions just made the problem worse. Learning how to manage my triggers around anger has helped me to calm down, take a step back, and see that he is just a little boy who gets overwhelmed sometimes. This has helped me to set limits in a calm and loving way, instead of either rejecting my child or frightening him into obedience."

Children learn more from the examples we set than from what we tell them. Teachers sometimes say that they can predict how their students will behave with other kids by noticing what their students' parents do. The parent who gets triggered by wanting to please everyone, who can't say no and gets over committed and overwhelmed, often has kids who let friends walk all over them. The parent who gets belligerent and rude every time something doesn't go their way often has a child who bullies other kids.

When you can stop the flood of emotions that comes from triggers and make wise choices about what you say and do, the benefits to your relationships will be remarkable!

4. Recognize What is Safe and What is Not

Think of how many children have been harmed because their adults did not recognize or teach them to recognize when someone's behavior might be dangerous! You cannot take protective action if you don't recognize potential risks. We would not call it "paranoid" to be aware of the risks caused by not washing our hands—and we need to treat potential problems with people with the same level of awareness. Instead of being fearful, we can focus on the simple things—like washing our hands—that each of us can do, and teach our kids, to take charge of their well-being.

Often, people are blinded by the 'Illusion of Safety,' which happens when people automatically assume that a familiar or seemingly harmless situation or person will be safe. For example:

- A swimmer who dives into a peaceful blue lake without checking the depth of the water risks crashing into the bottom.

- A religious community that assumes that a spiritual leader will act safely toward children, simply because of their position, risks having kids be abused.

- A caregiver who leaves a child at a pool party for even a few minutes, assuming that others will take care of this child, risks having the child drown.

- A parent who assumes that a young child will know better than to do something unsafe risks having a visit to urgent care.

- A woman who assumes that a charming man is safe risks being assaulted.

- A lonely person who assumes that the nice lady calling on the phone is telling the truth risks getting scammed.

- A man who answers a text while walking into a crosswalk, assuming that drivers will see him, risks getting hit by a car.

To avoid the Illusion of Safety when deciding whom to trust with our kids, we need to keep in mind that we cannot accurately judge safety from superficial appearances. Instead of making assumptions, make assessments by asking yourself the following questions:

- What do I really know about this person?

- What do people I trust tell me about this person?

- Has anyone ever expressed concerns about this person?

- Does this person really listen and respond to my concerns?

- Can I drop by anytime this person is caring for my kids?

- Have my kids shown any discomfort about this person?

- How well does this person show respect for boundaries?

- Is this person trying to pressure, charm, or trick me into doing something I don't think is right or wouldn't normally do?

- If I am trusting this person with my children, does this person seem fully present, all of the time?

When children are harmed, most of the time it is due to the actions of people they know, rather than strangers. They get injured, ill, or lost because their adults are distracted or lack awareness. They are bullied by other kids, often right under the noses of the adults in charge. They might suffer sexual abuse from someone they love and trust. They might be assaulted or even kidnapped by an acquaintance, family member, or friend.

Even though kidnapping and violence from strangers are statistically less likely than other risks, "stranger danger" fears loom large in the minds of both parents and kids. Adults go back and forth between saying nothing because they don't want to scare their kids and believe it will never happen where they live—to flooding children with deeply upsetting information when there is an abduction attempt that happens too close to home or is publicized in the media.

Not teaching children how to be safe with strangers leaves them vulnerable. However, teaching children to be scared of people they don't know does not make them safer—it just makes them anxious and less able to get help from strangers when they need it. In fact, some children who have been kidnapped got to know their abductor and were then afraid to run to other people for help because *those* people were strangers. There have also been some tragic cases of children lost in the woods who hid from rescue parties full of strangers.

Until children have enough life experience to make their own sound judgments, they need simple, clear knowledge and rules. At Kidpower, we teach children the following rules and guidelines for Stranger Safety:

- Most people are good. This means that most strangers are good. Just like you cannot always tell from the outside whether or not an animal is safe to be close to, you cannot tell from the outside whether or not a person is safe. You don't need to worry—you just need to follow the safety rules.

- A stranger is someone you don't know well and can look like anybody.

- The rules are different when you are together with your adults than when you are on your own. Being together means that your adults are talking with you and seeing you—or holding your hand.

- If you are on your own, away from your adults, move away and 'Check First' before you let a stranger get close to you, talk to you, take anything from you, or give anything to you.

- Check First before you go anywhere with anyone, even people you know, unless that was the plan.

- If you are old enough to be out without an adult, you might be in a place with lots of strangers, most of whom are probably kind people. If someone you don't know tries to approach you, Think First. Is this person approaching only you or everyone? Are there people close by in case there is a safety problem? Whether you are online or out in public, don't give personal information to people you don't know well unless your adults have said that this is okay.

- The rules are different when you are having an emergency where you cannot Check First. Perhaps you are out on your own without your adult and someone starts bothering you. Or you have gotten lost. If this happens, you might need to get help from a stranger. Make a safety plan for everywhere you go for how to get help when you are having a safety problem.

In addition to knowledge and skill, young people need life experience in order to judge the safety of different situations both with strangers, and with people they know who are more likely to be the ones causing harm to them. Until they have enough life experience to use their knowledge and skills in different situations on their own, they need our protection and guidance. As Kidpower Instructor Erika Leonard says, "At age 11, my son could have passed the driver's test. And he understood the mechanics of driving a car better than I did. But none of us would have wanted him driving on the freeway with us!"

5. Move Away from Trouble and Toward Safety

Once you have used your awareness and understanding to notice a possible safety problem, you need to take some kind of action quickly—before the problem grows bigger:

- Suppose that you are waiting in line in a large shopping center. Two people ahead of you in line start having a heated argument, making threats and shoving each other. Do you think it safer to stay near these upset people, or to move away and get help?

- Suppose that a teen boy is leaving a football game. A couple of fans from the opposing team block his path. They have clearly been drinking and are shouting accusations and waving their fists. Is it safer for him to argue with these furious fans or, instead, to move around them or, if this is not possible, to go back into the stadium? Is it safer to ignore their behavior or to inform a security guard?

- Suppose a teen girl is at a party where there are guys drinking and making increasingly graphic sexual jokes—and the friend she came with seems confused and somewhat drunk. Is it safer for this young woman to stay at the party, or to take her friend with her and call for a ride home?

- Suppose that that a child is playing at a park and is approached by an overly friendly squirrel. Is it safer to play with the squirrel, or to move away and Check First with the adults in charge?

Most people will agree that, in the above situations, it is obviously safer to leave and get help. Too often, though, people get hurt because they stay where they are, or keep doing what they are doing, rather than changing their plan, even though someone is acting very aggressively or suggestively.

When you leave a threatening situation, don't hang out nearby. Instead, get yourself all the way to where people can help you. One of our students told us this story about what happened to a friend of hers. As her friend Sophie was driving home alone one night, she noticed a group of drunken young men in her way on the street. Instead of driving away, Sophie stopped to see what was going on. After one of these men jumped onto the hood of her car and thumped her windshield, Sophie drove about 30 feet away and stopped again, feeling somewhat shaken up. One of the men ran over to her car and pulled off a windshield wiper. At this point, Sophie realized that she should have driven away long ago—and did so.

"Target Denial" is a martial arts term that means denying yourself as a target to someone who might hurt you—or, in other words, "don't be there!" Don't be there with your body if a place seems unsafe or person starts acting in a way that is potentially dangerous, even if you need to cross the street.

Don't be there with your feelings if someone's behavior or words are emotionally abusive. If you cannot distance yourself emotionally, you might need to leave physically.

Don't let your child be there if the adults in charge cannot do a good job of keeping them safe, even if this means changing where they are learning or playing. Don't let your loved ones, including yourself, be there for the activities of your family, friends, organization, faith community, or school if they are not upholding your values and safety standards, even if this means upsetting someone by pointing problems out.

Often, Kidpower gets requests for help from parents who are upset because their child has been bullied, harassed, or emotionally coerced by other kids—or even by a teacher. We coach parents in how to speak up effectively and respectfully to find solutions to the problem, and if need be, to go up the chain of command to get help.

In the previous chapters, we have described how to advocate for your children to resolve problems at school and in other activities. If the leaders in a school or recreational program are not responsive to your expressed concerns, sometimes the best solution is to change the plan and move your child to a different school, team, dance class, or social group. Making changes like this is often not easy, but getting away from an emotionally damaging situation that cannot be resolved teaches your child that you are walking your talk about putting safety first.

Overcoming the Bystander Effect

Whether something is happening to ourselves or someone nearby, people of all ages can get caught up or stuck in watching a problem rather than taking action by helping or leaving. This tendency to watch the troubles of others instead of doing something useful is called "the bystander effect."

Rescue workers are hampered in their efforts when bystanders wanting to have a good look get in the way. People at a party or game where a fight breaks out can get punched, or worse, when they watch and end up getting drawn in instead of moving away. Teens, and adults, get caught up with taking videos of someone getting bullied or sexually assaulted and post them to social media, instead of doing something to stop the attack like yelling, intervening, getting help, or calling 911. Everyone in an organization or school knows that some of the activities going on are not up to safety standards, but no one does something about it until there is an accident causing harm that was preventable.

The bystander effect can be caused by curiosity, boredom, denial, fear, overwhelm, lack of confidence about what to do, or shock— and can be overcome when we are prepared to Put Safety First, leave or stop an unsafe situation, and get help by changing our plan.

6. Check First and Think First

When everyone in a family, school, or group remembers to Check and Think First before changing their plan or making decisions, lots of problems can be avoided. In Kidpower, we use the Pizza Story to teach this point. Irene first heard the story from a California police chief who described how a father had gotten off work early and picked up his son on the way home from school to go get pizza. Unfortunately, this father forgot to call the mother to tell her that they had done this. As you can imagine, when her son didn't come home, the mother got worried. She called everyone she could think of—including the father—but no one answered, so she called the police. The police searched the town until the boy and his father got home, full of pizza, to be met by a relieved, but furious, mother.

We tell children, "Safety for kids lies in their grown-ups knowing where they are—and emotional safety for grown-ups lies in the same thing. The safety rule is to Check First before you change your plan about who is with you, what you are doing, and where you are going." We apply the Check First rule to opening the door, cooking something on the stove, using electricity, eating something you find, getting close to an animal or person you don't know well, posing for a picture, doing something online that you don't normally do, or going anywhere with anyone, even people you know, unless that was the plan.

Even as an adult, you are safer when the people who care most about you know where you are and how you are doing, which means that it is important to let them know. Checking first before making changes or decisions that involve other people will also prevent conflict in relationships and reduce the risk of mistakes.

For adults and for children who are on their own and can't Check First right away with a grown-up, the safety rule is to Think First before you change your plan; let someone you don't know well get close to you; or do something unfamiliar. Make being nice, asking for something, interacting with others, or using technology a conscious decision rather than an automatic habit. Ask yourself questions like the following and teach more independent children and teens to do the same:

- Is it safe to open the door without knowing who is there, or to someone I was not expecting?

- Is it safe to answer that text when I am driving or crossing the street?

- Is it a wise choice to give money to this person, in this place, for this cause?

- Is it a wise choice to enter personal information on that website?

- Is it kind to post that embarrassing photo of your classmate to social media?

- Is it kind to click "like" on a post that is personally attacking a peer, even if you dislike that person?

- Is it respectful to keep commenting on how cute a child looks or to whistle or stare at someone?

Most of all, Think First before you entrust anyone with the well-being of your child. As repeated stories on the news and from survivors of child abuse have made painfully clear, you cannot assume that someone is safe because this individual is famous, popular, kind, charismatic, in a position of authority, or very familiar.

7. Set Powerful and Respectful Boundaries

To teach about boundaries in our workshops, we begin by asking, "How many of you are ever annoyed or offended by other people?" Children and adults alike will raise their hands. Then we ask, "And how many of you are ever annoying or offensive to other people?" Our students laugh and raise their hands again.

Next, the instructor demonstrates the Wishing Technique by putting a hand on a student's shoulder and saying, "Imagine that you don't like my hand on your shoulder and wish, without doing or saying anything, that I will take my hand away." As the student sits silently wishing, the instructor keeps touching the student's shoulder and says, "Hmm. Wishing doesn't seem to be working. Maybe you should wish harder. Everybody here wish together. Wish, without saying or doing anything, that I would take my hand away." Of course, even when hundreds of people just wish, this doesn't work!

Finally, the instructor asks the group, "Do any of you ever wish that someone would change their behavior—do something differently or stop saying or doing something—without saying anything?" Most of our students sheepishly nod their heads. The instructor then coaches the student to "Look me in the eyes. Move my hand off your shoulder. And say, 'Please stop touching my shoulder.'"

In relationships, offending or bothering each other sometimes is normal. In order to enjoy these relationships and avoid unnecessary conflict, we need to speak up instead of just wishing that the other person would know what we do and don't want.

Learning to use boundary-setting skills with people they know can protect children and adults alike from potential harm—and can help them develop better relationships with those people.

Kidpower has four principles for setting personal boundaries:

1. *We each belong to ourselves.* This means not just our bodies, but also our time, our space, our thoughts, and our feelings.

2. *Some things are not a choice.* Other people have boundaries too, which we need to understand and accept unless they are conflicting with our own values and needs. Negotiating between the boundaries of others and the boundaries of ourselves is complicated for adults, let alone kids, which is why we deal with these issues as specifically as possible. We should follow the rules of our school, workplace, social group, or family—as long as these rules are safe, respectful, in keeping with our agreements about values, and everybody knows about them. For children, accepting what needs to be done for health and safety is usually not their choice.

3. *Problems should not be secrets.* For children, any kind of touch, games, presents someone gives them, photos, videos, friendships, and activities should not be secret.

4. *Keep telling until you get help.* Tell children: "If you have a problem, your job is to find an adult you trust who has the power to help you, and to be persistent until you get the help you need. It is never too late to tell. If one person does not help you, find another."

Real life is more complicated than any set of rules. This is why we coach our students through role-plays to rehearse boundary-setting skills using situations that are relevant to their lives. We encourage parents to practice these skills at home with their children, and teachers to practice at school.

For older children, teens, and adults, we use the following boundary-setting model to prepare individual practices for speaking up:

1. *Make a Bridge* by saying one sentence that shows a caring connection to the other person's reality: "I am sorry that I forgot to do something that was my job."

2. *Use an "I" statement* about your feelings or an objective non-attacking statement of the situation: "I feel upset..." or, "It's harder for me to understand what the problem is..."

3. *State the problem* or missing behavior in specific terms with no negative assumptions about the other person's character or intentions: "…when you raise your voice and call me names like 'lazy.'"

4. *State the desired outcome* in clear, specific, positive language: "Please remind me or tell me you are unhappy in a regular voice without calling me names."

We simplify the practice to make it age-appropriate for younger children. For example, "I see you want to play with this. It's my turn now. Please wait until I'm done." Or just, "My turn. Please wait."

How you set boundaries makes a big difference in how well they will work, so we practice having students use an assertive attitude when they speak up for themselves or others. Even verbal two-year-olds can learn how to use an assertive body language, tone of voice, and words when they are setting boundaries.

Suppose a little girl is aggressively shouting, "MINE!" and grabbing to get her teddy bear away from another child. You can coach her to go over to the other child and say firmly and kindly, "That's mine. Please give it back." Suppose a little boy is passively and unhappily standing frozen when another child pulls his new book out of his hands. You can coach him in the moment to speak up in a firm and kind manner, hang onto his book, and say, "This is my book. Please stop."

Because many people react negatively when told they need to change their behavior, we coach students to persist in setting boundaries by using positive responses to common negative responses. If someone says an insulting remark is just a joke, you can say, "It's not a joke to me. Please stop." If someone says, "But I did you a favor," you say, "I appreciate that. But doing this right now for you still won't work for me."

Often the person we most need to set boundaries with is our self! We will make wiser choices for ourselves and others, reduce stress, and increase happiness when we can set internal boundaries such as:

- Coping with disappointment without getting horribly upset

- Listening to another person's point of view respectfully even when we feel very annoyed

- Not letting uncomfortable feelings stop us from doing something important

- Delaying gratification even when we want something urgently and remembering that "wants" are different than "needs."

Healthy boundaries help to create positive relationships that enrich our lives. A fabric of positive relationships is essential in creating a positive society, in which our children can play, learn, grow, and live. When we notice and pay attention to the boundaries of others, we can build their trust and find win-win solutions to potentially conflicting wishes or needs.

When children experiment with negative uses of their power, or define their boundaries by pushing against them, they need help from adults in using their internal boundaries to act safely and respectfully rather than trampling over the boundaries of others.

Knowing how and when to speak up, and when and how to listen, is useful throughout our lives. As one woman said after a Fullpower workshop that included many older adults, "I am 94 years old, and no one ever taught me this. I am so glad to have learned about boundaries now!"

8. Follow the Safety Rules about Touch, Teasing, and Play

Touch, teasing, and play are activities that can create boundary problems in relationships. The Kidpower safety rule is that touch, teasing, or play for affection and fun should be:

- Safe

- The choice of each person

- Allowed by the adults in charge

- Not a secret, which means that others can know.

Often parents and other caregivers worry about how to explain to children about the private parts of their body. They don't want to raise sexual images that are not appropriate for kids; they don't want to say so much that kids are afraid to touch their own bodies; and they don't want to confuse children. Unfortunately, saying nothing might leave kids more vulnerable to sexual abuse.

In Kidpower, with the help of many parents, educators, and mental health experts, we have developed and field-tested language that seems to work well for different ages and different cultures. We tell children, "Your private areas are the parts of your body that can be covered by a bathing suit. For play or teasing, other people should not touch your private areas, ask you to touch their private areas, or take or show videos or pictures about people's private areas. For health or safety, such as if you're sick, your parents or doctor might need to touch your private areas—and anything about people and their private areas should never be a secret."

Between consenting adults, touch, teasing, and play might be private but they should not have to keep what they are doing a secret if either of them feels there is a problem and wants help. And the other safety rules apply—this behavior should still be safe, the choice of each person involved in witnessing the behavior, and allowed by the adults in charge. Rules about touch in your own home, where you are the adult in charge, are often different than the rules about touch in the workplace, in a restaurant, or at school.

We teach students how to say no with their bodies and their voices by moving someone's hand off their bodies, putting their hands up like a fence or wall between themselves and the other person, stepping back, or walking away powerfully and respectfully.

Whether someone is being abusive or just thoughtless, the continuum of intrusion often follows a progression where the other person:

1. Doesn't seem to notice that their behavior is not okay with you.

2. Doesn't listen to the boundary when you speak up.

3. Uses emotional coercion by making you feel wrong for setting a boundary.

4. Crosses the line by offering a bribe, misusing power, repeating the behavior, or breaking the safety rules about private areas.

5. Makes you promise not to tell anyone.

We practice setting boundaries for these different levels of intrusion by using very un-intrusive friendly touch. Set up the role-play by asking the child if you can touch their shoulder to practice. They might prefer their hand, knee, shoe, or hat, or even just have a hand almost touching for the practice. Here's how you can lead a role-play based on these levels:

1. Doesn't notice

Start by putting a hand on the child's shoulder and saying, "Suppose I am a family friend, and I keep leaning on your shoulder. Maybe you liked it at first, but now you've changed your mind." Coach the child to pick up and move your hand away, look you in the eyes, and say, "Please stop touching my shoulder."

2. Doesn't listen

Now put your hand back and say, "But I like touching your shoulder." Coach the child to move your hand away again, stand up, take a couple of steps back, make a fence with their hands between you and say firmly, "I said stop!"

3. Uses emotional coercion

Act sad and say in a very sorrowful voice, "I thought you liked me. If you were my friend, you'd let me touch your shoulder." Coach the child to say, "I do like you, and I want you to stop."

4. Crosses the line

Say cheerfully, "I'll tell you what! If you'll just be more friendly and let me touch your shoulder, I'll give you all the sweets you want." Coach the child to keep standing with their fence up, and back up further if they can, and say, "Stop or I'll tell!"

5. Demands a promise not to tell

If this is an older child, you can explain, "Most of the time we want you to tell the truth and keep your promises, but you can lie and break a promise if you are doing it to be safe and are going to tell a grown-up you trust as quickly as you can." Then, acting like the family friend again, say in a slightly grumpy—not a super threatening—voice, "You had better not tell. Something bad will happen if you tell!" (We do not ever get explicit about what will happen.) Coach the child to say, "I won't tell if you stop." Finally, make sure the child understands that, even if the person stops, it is still important to get to adults they trust as soon as possible and to tell.

For a less verbal child, the responses in this role-play can be simplified to: "Please stop! I said stop! Sorry and stop! And, Stop or I'll tell!" We wait until they are older and understand the concept of a safety lie before practicing how to respond if someone demands a promise not to tell.

Because emotional pressure and relationships are major reasons why children won't tell, we have developed a careful way in Kidpower to tell children what they need to know without giving too much information. We tell children in our workshops: "Sometimes the people kids care about have problems, and sometimes those problems are so big that they do things to hurt kids or make them feel uncomfortable. If this happens to you, or to a kid you know, it is not your fault. It means that everyone needs help. Your job is to tell an adult you trust, and to keep telling until someone does something about it. It is never too late to tell and get help!"

9. Persist Until You Get the Help You Need

Thirteen-year-old Cecilia came to a Teenpower workshop after having this frightening experience: "I was walking home from school when a man drove next to me in a car and started to stare at me and ask me questions. I got scared and ran into a shopping center nearby. The man got out of his car and followed me, calling out that he just wanted to talk with me. I ran through the store, looking for a salesperson to help me, but all of them were busy with other customers. Finally, I hid in the dressing room and waited until the man went away."

Although she was safe, thankfully, the experience of feeling so helpless and alone left Cecilia full of anxiety. We practiced with her how to go to the front of the line, interrupt impatient adults she doesn't know, and be persistent in explaining what the problem was by saying, "Excuse me. I need help! A man is following me."

Cecilia's story shows how incredibly important it is that young people have a safety plan, so that they know how to get help everywhere they go. Whether they are lost, bothered, or have some other kind of safety problem, they need to know what to do—and they need the opportunity to practice the skill before they need to use it. Since children's perspectives and under-standings are constantly changing, it is important to review their safety plan each time they go somewhere they haven't been for a while. Older children can be asked to tell you their safety plan, just for your peace of mind.

Children also need to know how to persist in asking for help from adults they do know, including parents and teachers. Teach children that they may need to wait if they just want something, but to interrupt and keep asking if they have a Safety Problem. Practice with them how to keep asking even if the adult is oblivious, gets annoyed about being interrupted, or doesn't understand the problem at first. Remind them that if one adult doesn't help them, their job is to find someone who will.

If we want kids to ask for help, we need to make it as easy as possible for them. One of Kidpower's core child protection strategies is to make sure kids know you care. Don't assume that a child knows. As stated in Chapter 3, if all young people were confident that they could go to their adults for help, many problems could be avoided or stopped.

We encourage all caring adults to regularly discuss the following Kidpower Protection Promise™ with the young people in their lives:

"You are VERY important to me. If you have a safety problem, I want to know—even if I seem too busy, even if someone we care about will be upset, even if it is embarrassing, even if you promised not to tell, and even if you made a mistake. Please tell me, and I will do everything in my power to help you!"

You can also ask occasionally in an interested and non-anxious way, "Is there anything you've been wondering or worrying about that you haven't told me?" Stay calm and caring when kids talk with you about problems, so they can feel safe coming to you and won't worry about upsetting you.

10. Finally, Be Prepared to Use Your Voice and Body to Escape from an Attack

If someone is threatening to harm you and you cannot leave or get help, you have the right to fight to protect yourself and your loved ones. We teach children as young as six, and seniors as old as 96, physical self-defense skills for escaping from an attack. We don't teach these skills until children have learned the other 9 Kidpower People Safety Skills above. Before we start teaching physical self-defense skills, we require young people to promise only to fight if they are in danger and cannot leave or get help.

Younger kids just need to know what to do in an emergency, without a lot of explanation about why someone might try to cause them harm. Teens and adults often want to understand the logic behind the skills we teach so we explain that predatory attacks usually follow a fairly predictable pattern.

Most attackers will:

1. *Select a vulnerable target.* Size does not matter nearly as much as whether someone is projecting an attitude of awareness, calm, and respectful confidence.

2. *Create a Position of Advantage to increase privacy and control.* Most of the time, attackers want privacy and control, so that others don't see what they are doing and intervene or report it. Giving someone who has the intention of harming you more privacy and control is like giving oxygen and fuel to a fire—it will get bigger.

3. *Dominate the person being targeted through humiliating, hurting, or stealing from this individual.*

4. *Escape to avoid getting caught.* Unfortunately, if police officers or other responsible adults are going to help us, it is usually in the escape part of the pattern, which is after the attack has already happened.

In self-defense, our goal is to interrupt this 'Pattern of Attack' sooner rather than later. We can deprive an attacker of both privacy and control by being and acting aware, taking charge, and getting help. Act aware to avoid being selected as a target. Stay aware to notice problems sooner rather than later. Take charge by moving away from trouble, setting boundaries, yelling in a threatening situation, or if need be, using physical self-defense skills to escape. And get help by reporting what happened, to prevent this person from harming others, and by getting emotional support, because being threatened or attacked is upsetting.

Children and women are more likely to face predatory attacks. We teach them to yell, fight to escape, and get help. Men, especially young men and teens, may also face competitive attacks, where someone is challenging them and trying to start a fight. We teach them to try to de-escalate the situation by using "false surrender" techniques: pretending that they are at fault and are sorry—and to leave as soon as they can. If de-escalating doesn't work, we of course also teach them to yell, fight to escape, and get help.

The good news is that one strong move can stop most attacks and even young children can learn these moves. Moving someone's hand away confidently and saying firmly, "Stop or I'll tell!" will discourage most pedophiles or harassers. Going quickly to safety as soon as you notice someone is acting in an unsafe way will put you out of the reach of danger most of the time. If someone is threatening you and you cannot leave, yelling, "STOP! LEAVE! HELP!" will usually cause that person to run away. Finally, if all else fails, knowing how to hit, kick, jab, and keep shouting can give you—and your children—the opportunity to get away and get to safety most of the time.

Preparing Children for More Independence:
6 Steps from Kidpower

Parents and guardians often struggle with the question, "How can I prepare my children for more independence while still keeping them safe?" Instead of taking an "all or nothing" approach to allowing children to do different things without adult supervision, Kidpower recommends following a six-step process:

1. Make realistic assessments about the situation and the child.

2. Teach about safety in ways that build confidence, not fear.

3. Learn, practice, and coach the use of People Safety skills at every opportunity.

4. Co-Pilot with your child to field-test their use of safety skills in the real world.

5. Conduct Trial Runs to rehearse independence in controlled doses with adult backup.

6. Keep communications open with listening, ongoing check-ins, and reviews of skills and safety plans.

1. Make Realistic Assessments

Parents often ask Kidpower instructors some variation of the question, "How will I know when my children are old enough to do something on their own?" For example:

- When can he play alone in the front yard?

- Is she ready to walk to school by herself?

- When can he stay overnight with friends?

- Is she old enough to ride the city bus?

The answer is that it depends. There is no magic age when children are ready for certain activities. It depends on the specific situation and on the skills of the particular child.

For example:

Suppose your daughter wants to go to a friend's house for an overnight birthday party. Assessment questions about the situation might include: How well do I know this friend's parents? If I don't know them well, can I arrange to meet them and make sure that I feel comfortable letting my daughter go? What activities are planned? What level of supervision will be provided? Who else will be at home?

Assessment questions about your daughter's skills include: Does my daughter know what our safety rules are and how to follow them? Can she speak up if she feels uncomfortable? Can she say no to her friends if they start to do something unsafe even if she feels embarrassed? Does she know how to call me anytime, even in the middle of the night, if she needs help?

Suppose your son wants to walk to school by himself. Assessment questions about the situation might include: What is the route to school like? What hazards are along the way? What is the traffic like? Are there crossing guards, crosswalks, and stoplights? Are there interesting, but potentially dangerous, things that might tempt my son into changing his plan, such as ponds, animals, or construction? What kinds of people, such as strangers, gangs, or bullies, might cause a Safety Problem for him? Are there stores, neighbors, or other places he could get help if he needs to?

Assessment questions about your son's skills include: How aware and careful is my son? Does he get lost in daydreaming, or can he pay attention to the traffic and people around him? Does my son understand and know how to follow our safety rules? Can he remember to check with me first before he changes his plan, even if something looks very interesting or his friends start pressuring him? If someone challenges him in a rude way, can my son walk away from trouble and get help, or will he feel the need to prove himself? Can he interrupt a busy adult to get help if he needs to? Can my son yell and run to safety if he's scared?

By making realistic assessments, we can determine whether a specific child is ready to handle a specific situation independently and, if not, what this child would need to know and be able to do in order to become ready. We need to remember that children develop skills at different paces and have different personalities. What is safe for one child at a given age in a given situation might take longer or require extra precautions to be safe for another child.

If you are unsure or concerned that your child might not make the safest choice, or if you feel that your child isn't ready to do something independently, take the time to review skills with them or make different plans that provide more supervision and support.

2. Teach About Safety in Ways That Build Confidence, Not Fear

Many times parents don't want to discuss personal safety issues with their children because they are afraid of damaging their children's trust in the world as being a safe and happy place. Or, when something frightening happens in the news or in their community, some parents will try to make themselves feel safer by discussing their fears with their children in a way that upsets their children without protecting them.

First of all, we need to separate our adult fears from our children's needs. We can discuss our worries with other caring adults, but our children do not need our anxiety. They need our faith that they can learn to protect themselves and our help and wisdom in learning how.

If something bad happens, managing our children's information diet is every bit as important as managing their food diet. Hearing vivid details over and over and seeing their adults acting upset can be emotionally damaging for children. As parents and guardians, our job is to stay aware of what our children are hearing from adults, their friends, and the news— and to be careful about what we are saying where they can overhear us even if they don't seem to be paying attention. In a calm, reassuring way, we can address any questions they might have about what they've heard without providing upsetting details.

Instead of focusing on the bad things that have happened, we can give children tools for keeping themselves safe most of the time.

For example, we think it is very unfortunate that in English "stranger" rhymes with "danger." Children are not served by believing that the world is full of dangerous people they don't know. Instead, at Kidpower we talk about 'Stranger Safety.' We teach children that most people are "good" and that this means that most strangers are good. Rather than focusing on the bad things that sometimes happen, we encourage parents and caregivers to focus on teaching and practicing the skills and behaviors children can use to stay safe with strangers.

3. Learn, Practice, and Coach the Use of People Safety Skills

Kidpower uses the term 'People Safety' to mean people being safe with people, including others and themselves. Just talking about problems can cause children to become more worried without making them safer. Successful practice of how to take charge of their emotional and physical safety can increase children's competence and reduce their anxiety.

Instead of dwelling on the bad things that sometimes happen, parents can empower children by giving them opportunities for successful practice of the following People Safety skills in contexts that are relevant to their own lives:

• Walking and acting with awareness, calm, respect, and confidence

- Checking first with their adults before they change their plan about what they are doing, where they are going, and who is with them, including people they know

- Moving away and checking first with their adults if they are on their own before they let a person or an animal they don't know well get close to them (or thinking first if they don't have an adult to check with)

- Moving out of reach if something or someone might be unsafe

- Setting strong, respectful boundaries with people they know

- Protecting their feelings from hurtful words

- Staying in charge of what they say and do in order to make their safest choices

- Making a safety plan for how to get help everywhere they go

- Being persistent in getting help from busy adults

- Understanding that the safety rules are different in emergencies where they cannot Check First and need to get help from a stranger

- Yelling and running to safety if they are scared

- Using self-defense skills to escape and get to safety if someone is acting dangerous and they cannot just leave and get help.

4. Co-pilot to Field-Test Skills in the Real World

Once children have been successful in practicing People Safety skills through role-plays, the next challenge is for them to learn how to generalize the use of these skills to different kinds of real-life situations. Co-piloting is a technique that can be very effective in helping you see how well your child can stay safe out in the real world.

This is how co-piloting works: before you let your child do an activity alone, you tag along on that activity with your child, letting your child lead the way. This gives your child the opportunity to show you what they can do, and it gives you the opportunity to notice any unexpected problems and ask questions to check on your child's understanding.

Walk a short distance behind your child on the way to school or a store, noticing potential hazards the whole way to the destination. Stay close enough to hear and see what is going on. Don't intervene unless something unsafe happens, and your child does not seem to know what to do. If your child takes public transit, follow your child onto and off of the bus, train, or subway. After the journey is over, ask your child questions about how they would handle different kinds of situations, including the potential hazards you noticed. For example:

- What will you do if someone you know offers to give you a ride?

- What will you do if there is construction, and you can't go this way?

- What will you do if a nice woman asks for help in finding a lost puppy?

- What will you do if you take a wrong turn?

- Where will you get help if you have a safety problem in the block that is more isolated?

- What if an older kid tries to bully you? What will you do?

- What if the bus doesn't show up?

- What if you get off at the wrong stop?

Repeat the co-piloting process a few times, staying further away each time and discussing what happened afterwards with your child.

Another kind of co-piloting can help keep kids safe online. The Internet, smartphones, video games, and other technology put children out onto digital public places where they can easily come in contact with strangers of all ages and walks of life, even when they are sitting right next to us. To keep our kids safe, we must stay aware of what is happening with them in the online as well as the physical world. Many children are ahead of their adults when it comes to technology, and parents or guardians often feel unsure about how to set boundaries for, and keep track of, their children's digital activities. We suggest that adults and children co-pilot social media and websites together, exploring what is out there, side by side.

5. Conduct Trial Runs with Adult Backup

Rather than giving blanket permission for activities requiring more independence, we can let children develop their skills and understanding by having trial runs with our backup. That way, they have the opportunity to do things on their own while having easy access to adult support in case they need help.

Irene's friend Marsha asked for her help because Marsha's young teenagers wanted to camp with their friends without adult supervision. They had lots of experience camping with their families and scout troops, but never by themselves. Since these teens were already walking and riding the bus in their community independently, Irene suggested that Marsha use the "trial-run" strategy by letting them camp on their own, but being close enough to reach adult help very quickly. Marsha took a campsite in the next loop from theirs so that her kids didn't need to see her, and she could be accessible just in case they needed her. Her children found out that camping on their own was a lot of fun—and a lot of work!

6. Keep Communications Open with Listening, Ongoing Checking in, and Review

Children are safest when they know that the adults in their lives are paying attention to what they are doing and are helpful people to come to with problems. Even after children are used to doing an activity on their own, it is important to continue to check in and review safety plans and skills. People can change. Situations can change. Problems can develop that were not there before.

In one Kidpower workshop, after Irene told the students not to keep problems a secret, a ten-year-old girl named Stacy tearfully raised her hand and said, "Since we were little kids, I used to love to go on sleepovers with my best friend. But now her parents are getting a divorce. They keep drinking and fighting in loud, angry voices. My parents don't know so they keep setting up times because they think I am still happy spending the night at my friend's house, but I feel scared for me and for my friend." Irene helped

Stacy and her classroom teacher make a plan for how she could talk with her parents and get their help, perhaps arranging for her friend to stay at their house rather than trading back and forth.

Remind children that problems should not be secrets and that you want to know what's happening in their lives. Be a helpful adult to come to by listening without judgment and not lecturing.

Make SURE!

Kidpower Action Plan for School and Organization Leaders

Note: Although the following is written for schools, the same concepts apply to any organizations responsible for the well-being of young people.

People in positions of leadership in a school can apply specific actions and provide important information to support parents and guardians in knowing what to ask of their principals, heads of school, directors, and other administrators to ensure a safe, respectful, and kind learning environment for their children.

Just like a stool needs at least three legs to be stable, so does change in human behavior. Best-selling authors Chip and Dan Heath describe these three strategies in their exceptional book, *Switch: How to Change Things When Change is Hard:* "Direct the Rider, Motivate the Elephant, and Shape the Path." The Rider is our intellectual mind. The Elephant is our emotional being. And the Path is what defines how we can get where we need to go.

In order to create school cultures of respect and safety, the Rider requires awareness so that people understand how big the problem is and what it looks like, the Elephant requires motivation so most people will feel strongly that what happens with kids is important for everyone, and the Path requires skills so that people will know what to do to intervene in the moment, persist in the face of resistance, make valid assessments, and provide support to others in speaking up, even when all of these actions are uncomfortable. Awareness, motivation, *and* skills are all necessary for concerns in schools to be addressed consistently, effectively, and practically.

Whether you are a school administrator, teacher, counselor, yard duty supervisor, or parent volunteer, here are six actions recommended by Kidpower that you, as a leader, can take to *Make SURE* that your school becomes an environment where bullying, violence, and abuse will have trouble taking root and growing, while leaving ample room for respect, kindness, and safety for all to become the main crop.

1. Make SURE everyone sees your personal commitment to safety, dignity, kindness, and respect.

2. Make SURE you know what is going on.

3. Make SURE safety is truly your priority in how you use time and resources.

4. Make SURE people who report safety problems are understood and appreciated.

5. Make SURE you support your staff through the process of working out problems.

6. Make SURE that you and others take meaningful action.

1. Make SURE everyone sees your personal commitment to safety, dignity, kindness, and respect.

Assess:

- Do you have well-written and comprehensive policies that are read and understood by all staff and parents?

- Do people see you and other school leaders constantly mentioning and upholding these policies in ways large and small so that they become a living, daily reality and *"rules to live by?"*

- Are you and others scrupulous about following safety rules yourselves?

When leaders are unclear about the rules, there are likely to be problems. Speaking up takes courage, creates discomfort, and requires persistence.

From a school counselor: "At the beginning of the school year, I heard that a few guys on our high school football team were shoving freshmen, joking about them being gay, and making crude remarks about girls. Instead of saying that this behavior was against their school's bullying and harassment prevention policies, their coach laughed and didn't do anything about it. As the school counselor, I told him that not stopping this behavior was undermining our school's commitment to respect. At first, the coach told me that I was making a big fuss over nothing. I gave him a choice—either he could tell his players that this behavior was unacceptable, or I would ask the principal to do it. He told them, and I heard that the behavior had stopped."

From a parent on a school committee: "Our principal was so sure she was right and seemed so frazzled that she was snapping at people and cutting them off in the middle of their trying to talk with her. I realized that I was not doing what we teach our students, which is to speak up. Finally, I worked up the courage to set a boundary by saying, 'I know you care a lot about our school and are really busy. I am finding it hard to give you important information or to get your help with problems when you seem impatient and interrupt. Please try to slow down a little and really listen.' At first, she was annoyed, so then I added, 'Our school policies say that we are committed to respect. This way of acting doesn't seem respectful.'" She apologized, and things have been better ever since.

As a school leader, in order to ensure the emotional and physical safety of the young people in your care, you need to have a common agreement with everyone in a leadership role about what the rules are—and an understanding among your staff, parents, and kids about what the rules mean.

Review your *Bullying, Harassment, Abuse, and Violence Prevention Policies* at least once a year. Discuss them with your staff so you can update them and discuss common problems in upholding these rules. If you wish, you can use Kidpower's online template in the resource section as a checklist.

Send your policies out each year to parents. Discuss and update these policies at an annual meeting or through an online forum.

The more clear, specific, and consistent we can be, the more likely people will be to follow these rules. Conversations about safety should be ongoing in the context of your daily activities rather than one-time or annual lectures.

Remember that people need reminders about what to do rather than just what not to do. For example, "No crashing" signs on the highway would be interesting but would not be particularly useful. Instead, we have signs like "Slippery When Wet" and "Slow Down. School Zone Ahead."

When children reach age four or five, start reminding them on a regular basis that, "You have the right to be safe and respected here—and the responsibility to act safely and respectfully toward yourself and others." Tell a story at an age-appropriate level to show how this rule applies to a problem that might come up in your regular activities. Show that you are interested and willing to address small problems—because getting everyone in the habit of thinking this way helps to develop understanding and to prevent bigger problems.

In addition to having ongoing conversations, as soon as children are about ten, discuss your actual policies to help them understand both their rights and their responsibilities. For example, Kidpower's recommended policy for schools starts out with this statement:

> *Our commitment is to ensure an emotionally and physically safe environment in our school community. We will do our best to stop threatening, harassing, bullying, cyberbullying, or other dangerous behavior both in-person and online. If any student, parent, or staff member feels threatened, upset, or endangered by someone's behavior, that person has both the right and the responsibility to speak up.*

You can ask students for examples of what behaviors are and are not safe, and where and how different kinds of behavior occurs at school. You can acknowledge what makes it hard to speak up and get help—and practice how to do this safely.

Although clear policies are important, rules by themselves are not enough. You have to keep reminding people of what the rules are—and keep taking visible action to show how you are upholding those policies in ways large and small to turn them into a living daily reality.

2. Make SURE you know what is going on.
Assess:

- What lines of communication do you have so that you will know right away if any of your parents, staff, or children has a concern about emotional or physical safety?

- What are you doing to overcome the resistance from people who want to protect your time, avoid discomfort, believe that everything is wonderful, deny that there is a problem, or ward off your disapproval?

No leader wants to have to be the one to say with terrible regret, "If ONLY I had known much sooner! I would NEVER have let this happen!"

Try to make it easier for people to tell you about their concerns than for them to not say anything, or to complain to each other. Integrate Kidpower rules such as "Problems should not be secrets," and "Tell someone who has the power to help" into the culture of your group.

Make it easy for people to email you, leave you a phone or text message, and make an appointment about any safety concerns—or have someone whose activities you supervise carefully and who you trust to act as your designated Safety Leader.

On a regular basis, walk around and look at what is happening at different locations, with different people, and at different times of the day. If you hear the hint of a safety problem, take a look and ask questions for yourself instead of depending only on the reports of other people.

Split your attention so that you see not just where you are going—but also what is happening around and behind you. Irene can remember watching a teacher lead a group of children on a walk. Although she stopped and supervised them when crossing the street, the rest of the time she was so focused on where they were headed that she never once looked back to see whether or not they were pushing each other, staying on the sidewalk, or picking the neighbor's flowers. What message does it send to children when their adults seem oblivious to what they are doing?

Put clear guidelines for how to communicate safety concerns into your policies. At least once a year, tell parents directly, both in person and in writing, "There is nothing more important than being worthy of the trust you have placed in us to educate your children and keep them safe from harm while in our care. If you become aware of a safety problem or even the possibility of a safety concern, I want to know. Please tell me right away even if I seem too busy, even if someone important will be upset or embarrassed, and even if you might be wrong. We will work together to find solutions rather than blaming people as much as possible, and we cannot address problems if we don't know about them."

An open-door policy does not work for many leaders, who have heavy demands on their schedule. If you have someone who is the gatekeeper to your time, make sure that you tell this person, "Please interrupt me if an issue comes up involving safety. I want to know."

Tell your staff, "Please do NOT try to protect me from bad news! If you think I am acting unsafely or not addressing a concern adequately, please tell me directly instead of talking to each other, or worrying about it silently. If you make a mistake that results in a child getting upset or hurt, I want to know right away! I will do my best to support you in fixing the problem. I will be far more upset if you don't tell me, and I end up finding out some other way. If you see someone else being unsafe or disrespectful with children, ask me for a private time to talk rather than just hoping the problem will go away. Remember that problems should not be secrets!"

Have adults make the Kidpower Protection Promise to all of the young people at your school on a regular basis: "You are *very* important to me! If you have or know about a safety problem, I want to know! Please tell me even if I seem too busy, even if someone we care about will be upset, even if it is embarrassing, even if you promised not to tell, and even if you made a mistake. I will do everything in my power to help you."

By paying attention, you are far more likely to notice problems when they are small and address them before they have the chance to grow. By showing that you want and expect to know, people are far more likely to tell you about their concerns.

3. Make SURE safety is truly your priority in how you use time and resources.

Assess:

- What process do you have for putting true safety concerns ahead of other issues?

- Are people spending more time on discussing what color to repaint the walls than on what to do to help a child being bullied within those walls?

- Are they putting more energy into figuring out how to raise money for new uniforms than on how to fix delayed maintenance of the playing field that is causing a tripping hazard?

In the *First Things First* chapter of his classic book, *The 7 Habits of Highly Effective People*, author Stephen Covey points out that issues that seem urgent can keep us from taking action on issues that are truly important. He suggests using these categories to set priorities about how we use our time and money:

- Important and Urgent

- Important and Not Urgent

- Urgent and Not Important

- Not Urgent and Not Important

Important safety concerns often don't seem urgent until problems get to the breaking point—or something bad has happened. Bullying, harassment, abuse, lack of adequate supervision of children, and emotionally or physically abusive adult leadership are all important safety concerns. So are unsafe driving, vehicles, buildings, grounds, equipment, or activities. Effective, proactive, responsible leadership means taking care of these important priorities before an accident or emergency occurs.

Discussing and thinking about these safety issues can *feel* as if you are doing something, but talking and worrying are not the same as doing something. The most effective way to prevent and solve most problems is to dedicate enough time and resources to find and implement solutions.

One school that was notorious for playground bullying transformed overnight when the new principal decided to make safety his highest priority. He decreed, "As of today, we will provide better supervision everywhere on the school grounds—and we will intervene on the spot when kids act unsafely and acknowledge when kids are being respectful."

Although he was tremendously busy, this principal made the time to go out into the schoolyard during recess, at lunch, and before and after school. He supported his staff in noticing and stepping in as soon as problems started—and in telling kids what a great job they were doing in playing together when things were going well. He enlisted parents to help with supervision. He arranged to get funding for a school counselor who could work with kids who were struggling with their peer relationships.

When children saw their adults acting in ways that really showed their caring, and they had adult help close by rather than trying to solve problems on their own, the school went from having the worst reputation for bullying in their community to having the best reputation for safety.

By realizing that safety concerns are both urgent and important, even if they are not yet an emergency, leaders can let interesting but less pressing issues wait—or delegate them to be handled by someone else.

4. Make SURE people who report safety problems are understood and appreciated.

Assess:

- When someone comes to you with an issue, do you ask caring questions, listen to the answers, manage the conversation so it stays focused and productive, and thank this person?

- How do you train your staff to make sure they understand and follow-up no matter how annoying someone is?

People usually wait until they are really upset before they speak up about safety concerns—and when people are upset, they often speak and act very disrespectfully. Leaders are often flooded with many different demands. When this happens, it is normal even though ineffective to wish that people like this would go away, try to placate them, hope that what they are saying isn't true, or simply dismiss their concerns because of the source or the way they were reported.

And some people become upset easily because they feel so anxious or are afraid that no one will pay attention to them unless they are very forceful. For someone who is constantly complaining and takes a lot of time, it can be hard not to think, "Oh, no! Here he comes *again!*"

No matter how good our communication skills are, staying calm and figuring out the real issue can be very challenging when someone has a lot of negative energy, repeats the same things over and over without getting to the point, makes insulting remarks, yells, sobs, whines, or sneers.

We need to remember that, at any age, feeling unsafe or disrespected is a huge trigger—and, for most parents, any threat to their children's well-being is an enormous trigger. When people are triggered, they are often not acting as their best selves. Instead of being irritated, we can respond with compassion while redirecting the conversation toward solutions.

People who are stuck in expressing their feelings over and over usually don't feel heard or know what to do. Allowing people to vent endlessly wastes everyone's time, builds up resentment, undermines this person's credibility, and does not solve problems. Instead of suffering in silence, hiding from this person, or trying to get someone off your back, redirect the conversation. Here's how to redirect a conversation that has gotten off track:

1. *Interrupt.* Jump in at a pause or stop the person mid-flow if there is no pause by saying politely and firmly, "Excuse me!" or "I need to interrupt."

2. *Restate the person's concern succinctly, factually, and with empathy.* For example, "My understanding is that you are concerned about Mr. Green's texting while driving on the last field trip." Or, "My understanding is that you are upset because you overhead Ms. Violet calling your daughter 'lazy.'"

3. *Acknowledge the person's feelings about this issue with compassion and no assumptions.* "I can imagine that you felt really worried when your son told you this and that you don't want this to happen on a field trip again." Or, "I can imagine that you might have felt angry when you overhead what sounded like a demeaning remark made to your daughter."

4. *Apologize.* "I am sorry that this happened."

5. *Express appreciation for speaking up.* "Thank you for telling me. Texting while driving is really unsafe and against our policies." Or, "I am so glad you said something to me directly so that we can find a good solution. Thank you!"

6. *State what you are planning to do.* "I will remind everyone about our requirements for drivers going on field trips. If Mr. Green volunteers again, I will make sure that his child's teachers know that we will not be able to use him until he has a discussion with me so we can be confident that this will not happen again. Or, "I will talk with Ms. Violet about what you heard her say and make a time where you can talk with each other directly with my support."

Conversations like these show how to demonstrate positive leadership skills when dealing with a problem or following up on a report of a problem. Set a good example by responding positively when someone tells you about something you did that might have caused hurt feelings or seemed unsafe. You don't have to believe everyone about everything they say or let people use up your time by venting for hours—but you do need to make sure you understand what the true concern was and are prepared to act on this concern.

5. Make SURE you support your staff through the process of working out problems.

Assess:

- Do your staff tell you when they make mistakes or when someone is upset with them?

- If they don't tell you, do you know what is stopping them from doing so?

- Is anyone at any level allowed to get away with disrespectful or unsafe behavior for any reason?

- What process do you follow when you become aware of a problem in supervising children?

- Do you model positive communication skills consistently?

- Do you provide teamwork training and positive problem-solving communication skills for your staff?

The people who are caring for our children are doing the most important job in the world. Too often, they feel isolated, frustrated, and criticized rather than supported and appreciated, especially when there is a complaint about something they have done or not done. Stories like those that follow are all too common.

From the teacher of six-year-olds from families struggling with many challenges: "I feel that high standards for their behavior and performance are essential in their being successful at school. Most children seem to love being in my class, and most parents seem appreciative. One day our principal handed me a letter from a mother whose child has required a lot of supervision, where she called me 'demanding and condescending.' He told me to work it out with her. I invest so much of my heart into my teaching that I felt devastated."

From an elementary school teacher: "One of the other teachers is constantly putting me down, rolling his eyes when I speak in staff meetings and either making rude remarks about my ideas or taking credit for them. If kids did this to each other, we would call it bullying. But when I speak to the Head of school, she says, 'Our kids and parents love him, and he doesn't mean any harm. I think you are overreacting. Just ignore him.'"

From a former high school math teacher: "I had to deal with many aggressive students on my own. There were no consequences for a student using insulting or threatening behavior or words. When I tried to set limits, the principal refused to back me up."

People need guidance and support from their leaders to help resolve problems with parents, kids, or each other. Meaningful support requires that a leader:

- Set up an effective process for managing disruptive behavior from children and teens with clear guidelines for how to respond to different kinds and degrees of behavior.

- Train staff supervising children in how to set limits powerfully and respectfully, and in how and when to get help.

- Establish and uphold best practices for positive communication and teamwork between paid and volunteer staff with no excuses and no one being "above the law."

- Ask open-ended questions when you become aware of a concern rather than making judgments or asking closed-ended or leading questions that can feel judgmental or presumptive.

- Take the time to observe what is actually happening during activities where the problem occurred.

- Give compliments about what is going well and suggestions about how to do something differently.

- Use care in sharing negative feedback and facilitating direct communication between different parties to help them work issues out.

- Follow-up to see how things are going and to make sure that agreements are kept.

6. Make SURE that you and others take meaningful action.

Assess:

- Do you go to look at the problem and ask detailed questions in a way that is caring of everyone involved?

- Do you make decisions quickly to fix potential hazards?

- Do you investigate thoroughly and have clear consequences for any cruel, abusive, or neglectful behavior?

- Even if you feel that a concern was inaccurate or caused by a misunderstanding, do you get back to the person who came to you about this problem to explain the steps you took and to express gratitude for caring?

Have you ever called a company that has trained their staff in sounding very supportive while doing nothing? The customer service representative will listen sympathetically and say, "I apologize and will make sure someone will get back to you to fix this." And then no one calls back and the problem does not get fixed!

Do you remember when Toyota's President apologized for the company's failure to act promptly on reports of brakes getting stuck and not working, leading to several deaths and costing millions of dollars?

Parents become outraged when a safety issue threatens their child and "no one does anything." For example, one mother contacted Kidpower because some girls were writing cruel things about her daughter on a social networking site. Even though all of the girls involved were students, the school officials said that "there's nothing we can do" because there was no overt threat, and that "this is not our responsibility" because it did not happen on school computers or during the school day.

Instead of having to deal with an immensely frustrated mother, the school could have gained credibility and saved time by doing what was possible, through meaningful actions such as:

- Listening to and supporting the girl

- Providing training to the school community about cyberbullying and online safety

- Talking separately with the students who had participated in the cyberbullying, and their parents, and helping them to find ways to make amends

- Helping the mother of the girl who was targeted file a complaint with the social networking site

- Encouraging the mother to file a police report

- Helping the girl find other students to connect with

- Referring the family to a program such as Teenpower where she could practice setting boundaries, protecting her feelings, and defending herself

- If her daughter was still traumatized by this experience, helping the mother to find a therapist.

The reality is that people make mistakes and cross each other's boundaries all the time. Meaningful actions to address unsafe behavior can help everyone to grow.

Here are the steps for taking meaningful action toward resolving a safety concern:

1. Figure out what happened and do what needs to be done to address the situation.

2. Make and implement a plan to prevent this problem from happening again.

3. Report, investigate, and have clear consequences for any abusive or neglectful behavior.

Even if you feel that the concern was inaccurate or the result of a misunderstanding, respond to the person who raised the problem with you, to explain what was done and to express appreciation for the fact that they spoke up.

My Child is Being Bullied at School!

Kidpower Action Plan for Parents and Guardians

Kidpower hears countless stories from parents, grandparents, aunts, and uncles who are upset because a child or teen in their life is being bullied, teased, or harassed at school—and because the school seems unable to take action.

School is a big part of kids' lives, and it is usually parents who make the decisions about how and where their children get an education. This means that most young people have no choice about where they go to school.

As a parent, you have the right to expect schools to provide an environment that is emotionally and physically safe for your children. It's normal to feel terrified and enraged about any kind of threat to your child's well-being, especially in a place where they are required to be.

We need to remember that most schools are working valiantly to meet an overwhelming array of conflicting demands. At the same time, when your own child is being bullied, it is normal for protective parents to want to fix the problem immediately—and maybe to punish the people who caused or allowed your child to be hurt, embarrassed, or scared.

When possible, try to find out about problems when they are still small. Tell children clearly, cheerfully, and often, "If someone is bothering you at school, if you see someone picking on another kid, or if you are having trouble acting safely yourself, your job is to tell me so that we can figure out what to do to make things better."

Pay attention to changes in your child's behavior. Help children to develop the habit of telling you about what happens at school each day by being interested, staying calm, and not lecturing. Ask specific questions in a cheerful way such as, "What was the best thing that happened today? What was the worst thing?" Remember that, if adults act anxious, children are less likely to share upsetting information. Volunteer even a couple of hours a week in the classroom or schoolyard so that you can help out, get to know teachers, and stay aware of potential problems at school.

If your child has a bullying problem at school, here are seven practical Kidpower 'People Safety' solutions that can help parents be effective in taking charge.

1. Stop Your Own Knee-Jerk Reactions

2. Get Your Facts Right

3. Pinpoint the Cause

4. Protect Your Child

5. Prevent Future Problems

6. Get Help for Your Child

7. Give Kids Skills to Protect Themselves in the Future

1. Stop Your Own Knee-Jerk Reactions

If your child tells you about being bullied at school, this is an important opportunity for you to model for your child how to be powerful and respectful in solving problems. As hard as it is likely to be, your first job is to stay calm. Take a big breath and say, in a quiet and matter-of fact voice, "I'm so glad you're telling me this. I'm sorry this happened to you—please tell me more about exactly what happened so we can figure out what to do. You deserve to feel safe and respected at school."

If your child didn't tell you, and you found out some other way, say calmly, "I saw this happen/heard about this happening. It looked/sounded like it might be unpleasant for you. Can you tell me more about it?"

Make a point of acting calm, even if you feel upset inside. If you act upset, your child is likely to get upset too. Kids often say that adults make the problem bigger by reacting in an unhelpful way. If you do this, your child might not tell you about problems in the future or might deny that anything is wrong. The older children are, the more important it is that they be able to feel some control about any follow-up actions you might take with the school.

In addition, if you act upset when you're approaching teachers, school officials, or the parents of children who are bothering your child, they're likely to become defensive. Nowadays, teachers and school administrators are often fearful of lawsuits, both from the parents of the child who was victimized and from the parents of the child who was accused of causing the problem. This is a real fear because a lawsuit can seriously drain a school's already limited resources.

At the same time, most teachers and school administrators are deeply dedicated to the well-being of their students and want them to feel safe and happy at school. They're far more likely to respond positively to parents who are approaching them in a calm and respectful way. However, no matter how good a job you do, some people will react badly when they're first told about a problem. Don't let that stop you; stay calm and be persistent about explaining what the issue is and what you want to see happen and how you can work together to do so.

2. Get Your Facts Right

Instead of jumping to conclusions or making assumptions, take time to get the whole story. Ask open-ended, non-leading questions of your child in a calm, reassuring way and listen to the answers.

Ask questions of other people who might be involved, making it clear that your goal is to understand and figure out how to address the problem rather than to get even with anybody.

Once you understand the situation, it works best to look for solutions, not for blame. Try to assume that overwhelmed teachers and school administrators deserve support and acknowledgment for what they're doing right as well as to be told what's wrong. Try to assume that children behave in hurtful ways do so because they don't have a better way of meeting their needs or because they have problems in their own lives.

Be your child's advocate, but accept the possibility that your child might have partially provoked or escalated the interaction. You might say, "It's not your fault when someone hurts or makes fun of you, but I am wondering if you can think of another way you might have handled this problem?"

3. Pinpoint the Cause

Is the problem caused because the school needs more resources in order to supervise children properly during recess and lunch, or before and after school? Does your child need to learn skills for self-protection and boundary setting by making and practicing a plan with you or by taking a class such as Kidpower? Does the school need help formulating a clear policy that makes behavior that threatens, hurts, scares, or embarrasses others against the rules with appropriate, balanced, and consistent consequences? Do the children who harmed your child need to learn about empathy and to develop skills for using their power in positive ways instead of negative ones? Does a child who is bullying need help because of emotional problems?

4. Protect Your Child

Your highest priority is, of course, to protect your child as best you can. Try to step back for perspective and keep the big picture in mind as well as the immediate problem. What protecting your child means will vary depending on the ability of the school to resolve the problem, the nature of the problem, and the specific needs of your child.

Through programs such as Kidpower, make sure your child has the chance to practice skills in order to walk away from people who are being rude or threatening, to protect themselves emotionally and physically, and to ask for help sooner rather than later.

In some cases, protecting your child might mean that their teacher and school principal, the parents of the other child, and you all work on a plan together to stop the problem. In other cases, the solution for your child might be that you work solely with the school staff to make a plan that changes the access the other child has to your child during school hours. And in yet other cases, the best solution for your child might be to change schools.

In extreme cases, you might want to explore legal action. Different countries and states have different laws about children's rights. If need be, explore the resources available in your community.

5. Prevent Future Problems

You also want to prevent future problems. All children deserve to be in an environment that is emotionally and physically safe. Dealing with ongoing harassment is like living with pollution—eventually, coping with the constant hurt can undermine your child's health.

In some situations, the solution might be to join together with other concerned adults to make lasting changes for the future.

Concerned parents can help schools find and implement age-appropriate programs that create a culture of respect, caring, and safety between young people rather than of competition, harassment, and disregard.

6. Get Help for Your Child

Finally, you want to get help for your child and for yourself to deal with the feelings that result from having had an upsetting experience or having dealt with ongoing social pollution like bullying behavior. Sometimes bullying can remind you about bad experiences in your own past. Parents often have to deal with guilt for not preventing the problem, and sometimes struggle with rage.

Getting help might mean talking issues over with other supportive adults who can listen to you and your child with perspective and compassion. Getting help might mean going to a therapist or talking with counselors provided by the school or by other agencies.

7. Give kids skills to protect themselves in the future

It's normal for parents to want to protect children from all harm. However, if we monitor their lives so closely that they never fall, never fail, and never get hurt or sad, then we'd be depriving our children of having the room to grow.

Instead, we want to give kids skills for taking charge of their safety while ensuring that the adults, who we entrust with their care, provide adequate supervision, intervention, and support.

Most upsetting experiences don't have to lead to long-term damage if children are listened to respectfully, if the problem is resolved, and if their feelings are supported. Young people can learn how to take charge of their safety by developing skills for preventing and stopping harassment themselves, by setting boundaries, avoiding people whose behavior is problematic, and getting help when they need it.

How to Prevent and Stop Cyberbullying

Cyberbullying or "electronic aggression" means deliberately using technology such as smartphones, the Internet, social media, or gaming environments to harass, humiliate, badmouth, or threaten someone. Like any form of bullying, cyberbullying can poison someone's joy in life, reputation, and well-being.

Acts of cyberbullying and other electronic aggression have caused a great deal of suffering that can and must be prevented. Our jobs as parents, educators, and other caring adults are to teach the young people in our care how to be good digital citizens, to model being positive digital citizens ourselves, and to insist that everyone demonstrate an ongoing commitment to using technology wisely and safely.

Here are 10 actions that we can take to protect young people from cyberbullying:

1. Set a good example

Remember that the actions of young people's close adults have a powerful influence on what they will do. As one teacher told me, "At our small private school, parents were gossiping, online and offline, about the troubles of one family. It is not surprising that their children started posting insults about a boy in that family who was having a hard time."

Let the children and teens in your life see you choosing to stay respectful even when you are upset. Let them see you reaching out to communicate in person directly and respectfully with someone with whom you have a problem rather than complaining behind this individual's back. Or, if this doesn't work, let them know that you will go in person to someone who is in a position to do something about the issue. Let them see you state disagreements objectively and politely, without name-calling or sarcasm. Let them see you choosing NOT to "like" or share a post or photo that is hurtful or disrespectful, even if it seems amusing. If you make a mistake, say so—and show how you are going to make amends.

State your disapproval when people in positions of power and prestige act in harmful or disrespectful ways, even if you appreciate their sports victories, enjoy their music or films, or agree with their politics. Model balance by turning your technology off and doing something together out in nature or with other people without being connected electronically.

2. Stay connected with your children's worlds online and everywhere else

Fifteen-year-old Audrie Pott committed suicide after she was sexually assaulted and a video of the assault was shared online with cruel comments. Her parents didn't know about the assault, the video, or the comments until it was too late.[1]

Spend time with your children and teens so that you know what they are doing. Explain that their activities on text messages, social media such as Facebook, email, chat groups, and use of computers can easily become public to the world and insist that these activities be public to you as well. If you don't understand exactly what your child is doing with technology, then have this young person teach you by leading the way and letting you be a co-pilot. If you are busy with technology yourself, remember to stop what you are doing and pay attention to your kids! Otherwise, you can be sitting side by side, each looking at your own smartphones or computers, and not notice what your child is seeing or writing.

Protect and supervise kids until they are truly prepared to make safe and wise choices themselves. Kids are safest when their adults know who is with them, what they are doing, and where they are going. Remember that with technology, even if you are side by side with a child, you won't necessarily know what online content they are consuming unless you are looking at the same screen. Discuss the Kidpower Protection Promise with all the young people in your care: "You are very important to me. If you have a safety problem, I want to know—even if I seem too busy, even someone we care about will be upset, even if it is embarrassing, even if you promised not to tell, and even if you made a mistake. Please tell me, and I will do everything in my power to help you." Point out that cyberbullying is a safety problem.

3. Make a commitment with young people to be good digital citizens

An antidote is a substance that can counteract a form of poisoning, and teaching digital citizenship can be a powerful antidote to cyberbullying. A citizen is an inhabitant of a place—and the online world is a place where most young people live a great deal of the time. According to Mike Ribble, author of *Digital Citizenship in Schools* and *Raising a Digital Child*, parents and educators are often like immigrants to the online world, while their children are like digital natives.[2]

Many adults are intimidated because technology changes constantly and rapidly, and it can be hard to keep up with it unless you grew up with it. Fortunately, the values and behavior of a good citizen are the same regardless of whether you are online or in the "real" world.

A commitment to act with respect, safety, and kindness toward yourself and others knows no boundaries. The knowledge of how to protect yourself from harmful words, whether you hear them or see them, is the same. The importance of staying mindful is relevant no matter where you are. And bullying is unsafe, disrespectful behavior, whether it happens in person, on paper, on film, or with electrons.

At Kidpower, we recommend that responsible adults say clearly to the children and teens in their care: "You have the right to be treated with safety and respect everywhere and with everyone—and you have the responsibility to act safely and respectfully toward yourself and others. This includes being a good digital citizen in all activities using technology such as computers and smartphones to interact through social media, gaming, texting, etc."

We recommend a written digital citizenship and technology use contract that kids sign with their parents and that can be updated each year. Kidpower.org provides a contract that you can download and adapt for your personal use.

4. Discuss what cyberbullying is and the harm it does with older children and teens

Ask kids who are actively using technology for communication what they already know about cyberbullying. They usually have a lot of information and strong ideas. Ask if this has ever happened to them or anyone they know.

Make sure that the young people in your life know that:

- Cyberbullying means using computers, mobile phones, or other technology to hurt, scare, or embarrass other people. Cyberbullying gets people in serious trouble at school and also with the law. In a growing number of places, certain forms of cyberbullying are illegal.

- Being mean is being mean, no matter how you do it. Don't ask if it's funny. Ask if it will make someone unhappy.

- Even if you think someone was mean to you, being mean back is not a safe way to handle the problem. Instead, get help from an adult you trust.

- Have the courage to speak up if you notice anyone cyberbullying. Say that this is wrong and that you are not going to keep it a secret.

- Use privacy settings, but never post anything in social medial or send anything out electronically that you don't want the world to see.

• If you get an upsetting message or see something that is attacking you: Do not reply. Do not delete. Save the message, get a screenshot, print it if you can and get help from an adult you trust. If one adult does not help you, keep asking until you get the help you need.

5. Be clear about what happens if young people misuse their technology privileges

For children and teens, the responsibility that goes with the right to use technology independently is to stay in charge of what they say and do, to make safe and wise decisions, to tell you about problems, and to get your agreement in advance about any changes. Treat the use of computers for anything except schoolwork as a privilege, not a right. Treat the use of mobile phones for anything except for emergencies and communication with responsible adults as a privilege rather than a right.

As one mother explained, "I was horrified when I learned that my daughter had texted embarrassing photos and attacking remarks about a couple of kids on her swim team. I heavily restricted her use of her devices until she wrote an essay about the harm done by cyberbullying and gave it in person along with an apology to her teammates and coach that she rehearsed with me ahead of time to make sure that it was respectful and clear. Although she was furious with me, I felt that my child needed to understand the seriousness of this kind of behavior and to make amends."

If young people in your life do something hurtful to another person either online or in person, have them apologize and make amends. Figure out what actions they took to create the problem, and coach them through a practice of making safer choices instead. Often, loss of the privilege to use the technology involved for a specific period of time is the most appropriate consequence. In addition, have kids do something active such as mail a handwritten letter of apology, do some research about the harm done by cyberbullying and write a paper, or do some volunteer work to make our world a better place.

6. Teach kids not to do anything online that they wouldn't want the world to see

One transgender teen was shocked when they found out that a boy they had trusted had encouraged them to text their feelings about their gender identity—and then forwarded these very personal messages to a bunch of other kids, along with sneering comments. The boy who spread the private messages his friend has trusted him with was shocked to discover that he got into big trouble for cyberbullying. He had thought no adult would ever know, especially since he had deleted the forwarded messages.

Young people need to understand that even though a communication seems very private and anonymous, and even if the developers claim their platform is private, whenever a person uses technology, what they do leaves an electronic footprint that can become public, including to potential employers or college admissions offices. In addition, even if it's deleted later, an electronic communication can spread very far and very fast, with much greater consequences than the user ever intended. Sending or receiving sexually explicit photos of anyone under 18 years old, even if intended to be privately shared, and even if the photos are "selfies," can be considered child pornography and trigger serious legal consequences.

With younger kids, you can use privacy settings but don't count on them. Remember that anything shared electronically with anyone can be shared publicly by anyone you send it to. Unless this is within a secure system of people who know each other, such as a school, avoid allowing children to post personal information or photos in an online friend's community, chat group, or anywhere else.

7. Teach young people how to take charge of their safety and well-being, online and everywhere else

Being safe online includes knowing how to act if you have a problem that harms the well-being of you or someone else. If you get or see a threatening or harmful message, don't answer back and don't delete. Take a screenshot and go tell an adult you trust. One boy, Max, asked his parents for help after a couple of former friends had put up a Facebook page saying "I hate Max" that was "liked" by hundreds of kids in his high school. As you can imagine, this experience was devastating. Max says, "What helped me was having the support of my parents who got Facebook to take the page down and who kept telling me that what happened was not my fault; going to a counselor; going to a Teenpower class to practice what to do when you have problems with people; and finding some new friends."

Practice Kidpower People Safety Skills such as how to: protect your feelings from hurtful words; set boundaries with yourself and others; communicate and connect with people in positive ways; stay in charge of what you say or do no matter how you feel inside; move away from trouble; and be persistent in getting help from busy adults. Practice ways to speak up, say "No" and "Stop," and use other peer-diversion tactics, and practice persisting in the face of negative reactions. Practice putting your hands down and stepping away from the technology when you feel tempted to post, agree with, or share something hurtful or disrespectful.

8. Provide support if a child is cyberbullied

The anonymous nature and widespread distribution of cyberbullying can be devastating. If your child is facing cyberbullying, provide emotional support by saying, "I am so sorry this is happening to you and so proud of you for having the courage to tell me. This is not your fault and we are going to do what we can to make it stop." Insist on action to correct the problem from school authorities, your Internet provider or mobile phone company, the social media company such as Facebook, and, if necessary, the police.

If your child seems traumatized by what happened, provide support through reassuring the child that this is not their fault and that things will get better; arranging professional counseling for the child and the family; providing protection from retaliation for telling and from further aggression; finding opportunities for the child to develop new relationships and to have fun with peers; and providing the child with 'People Safety' training of the kind offered by Kidpower.

9. Practice how to speak up to stop cyberbullying

After kids understand what cyberbullying might look like, practice how to speak up. Identify possible negative reactions from the other person. Then, practice respectful, powerful responses to persist in setting the boundary. Let youth make up their own story about the situation to use for the practice. Switch roles with them.

For example, a friend might say, "I can't stand Roger. Look, I got a photo of him going to the bathroom on the field trip. Let's see how many people we can send this to."

One way to speak up could be: "That's cyberbullying. It's wrong."

A common negative reaction to this boundary is, "But you have to admit that it would be funny."

An effective response might be, "Even though Roger is not my favorite person, I don't think it is funny to embarrass people. Besides, it is illegal."

10. Teach kids to get adult help anytime they see unsafe behavior online, while texting, or in person

Young people can have a huge impact and be safer themselves if they know that unsafe behavior online or anywhere else is an important time to get adult help. One of our Kidpower Teens, Laura, asked her mother for help because an online "friend" in a chat group was writing despairing comments about life not being worth living. With her mother's guidance, Laura told this girl that feeling this was not safe and encouraged her to call the Suicide Prevention Hotline. The next day the girl wrote to Laura that she had talked to a counselor there for a very long time. Although she didn't have clear answers yet, this girl was on the path to getting the kind of help she needed.

How to Pick a Good Self-Defense Program

Self-defense skills are essential to our personal safety. Choosing the right kind of program can greatly increase the confidence and competence of adults and kids alike in being able to protect themselves physically and emotionally from an attack.

Done well, self-defense workshops can be exciting, empowering, and life-changing. Done poorly, they can be boring, discouraging, or destructive. The quality of the program and approach of the instructor will make a huge difference in the results of any kind of training. Self-defense is no exception.

Here are some questions to consider when evaluating a self-defense program:

1. Is the content positive, accurate, comprehensive, and appropriate for the ages and life situations of the students?

The best programs will teach a range of 'People Safety' skills for being aware, taking charge of the space around you, getting help, setting boundaries with people you know, de-escalating conflict, and staying calm and making choices instead of just getting upset when you have a problem. Physical self-defense skills will be taught in a context of having first done everything possible to get out of a situation safely without fighting.

Look for programs that focus on the skills to learn rather than on reasons why we have to learn these skills. Realize that students can become traumatized by scary stories about bad things that happened to other people. People learn best if their teacher has a calm, matter-of-fact approach which makes it clear that they can keep themselves safe most of the time by learning how to do a few easy things.

Look for programs that are based on research from a wide variety of fields including mental health, education, crime prevention, law enforcement, and martial arts.

Look for endorsements from real people and credible organizations.

Look for programs that are willing to give credit for what they have learned from others rather than saying that they have invented "the best and only way to learning true self-defense."

Be wary of programs that give simplistic, absolute answers such as, "If you wear a pony tail, you are very likely to be assaulted" or "If you train with us, you will never have to be afraid again."

2. Is the teacher clear, respectful, in charge, enthusiastic, and able to adapt?

You and the children and teens in your life deserve to have teachers who are helpful rather than discouraging. Good teachers do not make negative remarks about their students or anyone else and do not allow others to do so, even as a joke.

Look for teachers who know how to be both firm and respectful when they set boundaries with students who are doing things that detract from the class.

The best teachers will change what they do to meet the needs of their students rather than having a standard, canned approach. Role-plays to demonstrate or practice skills should be described in terms of situations that students are likely to encounter. The way something is presented should be in terms that are meaningful to a student. Instead of telling a blind student to look at a potential attacker, for example, a teacher who knows how to adapt will say something like, "Turn your face toward Joe so that he knows you know he's there."

Good teachers will listen to your concerns with appreciation for your having the courage to raise them rather than with defensiveness. When possible, they will change what they do to make the class work better for you. At the very least, they will explain their reasons for what they do and why they cannot accommodate your wishes.

3. Is the approach more action-oriented or talking-oriented?

In general, people remember more about what they have seen than what they have been told. People are more likely to be able to do what they have practiced themselves than what they have been shown to do or told to do.

Look for programs that involve showing more than explaining and that provide lots of opportunity for learning by doing.

4. Is the learning success-based?

It can be destructive to students' emotional and physical safety if they feel as if they are failing when they are trying to learn self-protection skills. Success-based learning means that students are guided through what they need to learn in a highly positive way. Practices go step by step starting with where each student actually is. Success is defined as progress for each individual student rather than as perfection according to some standard of the teacher. Students are coached as they do the practices so that they can do them correctly as much as possible. They are given feedback about how to improve in a context that communicates, "mistakes are part of learning."

5. Is the approach more focused on traditional martial arts or on practical self-defense?

Martial arts programs, like other activities involving interactive movement such as sports and dance, can be wonderful for building confidence, character, and physical condition. However, for teaching personal safety skills, the approach of most martial arts is like long-term preventative health care. Practical self-defense is like emergency medicine, which teaches skills in a few hours in a way that is very focused on preventing and escaping from danger.

6. Is the program emotionally safe and trauma-informed?

When a person has experienced trauma, regardless of what kind, their power has been taken away. Providing people with disabilities, survivors of abuse and violence, and those with other difficult life challenges with an emotionally safe, relevant, and successful program that uses their mind, their bodies, and their voice is at the heart of Trauma-Informed principles.

7. How do *you* feel about the program?

The most important skill in choosing a good self-defense program is being able to act on your intuition without being stopped by feelings of confusion or fear. It can be hard to stay clear about what your needs are or what the needs of your children are when you are bombarded by often conflicting advice from experts. If something someone does seems wrong to you, even if you can't justify your feeling logically, leave rather than staying in a potentially bad situation. Keep looking until you find the type of program that answers to your satisfaction the kinds of questions described above.

Whether you are looking for a self-defense class or any other important training, pay attention to uncomfortable feelings you have about someone's approach, no matter how highly recommended the person is and no matter how much you like the teacher as a person. Often very well meaning, knowledgeable people try to teach through talking about what can go wrong rather than through helping their students practice how to use skills effectively. Remember that what programs actually do is more important than what their literature or representatives say they are going to do.

In Kidpower Teenpower Fullpower International, we do our best to uphold high standards for all of our services. Please let us know if ever we do not follow through on this commitment.

Acknowledgements

First of all, we want to express our heartfelt gratitude to Dan Heath for your eloquent and inspiring foreword—as well as for the wisdom and insights we have gained from all your exceptional books.

Thank you to our Kidpower colleagues Joe Connelly, Marylaine Léger, Erika Leonard, Kim Leisey, John Luna-Sparks, and Beth McGreevy for taking the time to read, discuss, and give us your valuable suggestions, feedback, perspectives, and stories—and to everyone in the Kidpower Teenpower Fullpower International community for your countless and essential contributions to our organization's values, curriculum, teaching methods, and services since 1989.

A special thank you to Maryjane Hayes for your powerful leadership as Kidpower North Carolina Center Director. Your vision and dedication are propelling the statewide program to new heights of excellence and growth and are also giving important support to Kidpower International's training programs and school projects. Because you took over as the Center Director so effectively, Amy has been able to direct her energy and time to writing our book and to sharing our work much more widely through creating exciting new training and speaking opportunities.

Special appreciation also goes to Kidpower California Program Director Erika Leonard and Kidpower International Special Projects Coordinator Marylaine Léger, who is also our Montreal Center Director, as well as our whole Central Office team, for your leadership, competence, and commitment. Thanks to your keeping our training programs and services thriving and successful, Irene has been able to focus on writing our book, developing new educational resources, and establishing important partnerships for Kidpower.

Amy sends deep gratitude to her Spark Productions team who makes sure that her work runs smoothly, especially during the creation of this book. Thank you Cynthia Fioretti, Christopher Sherman, and Michelle Pratico for your dedicated expertise.

Thank you to Redwoods Group Co-Founder and CEO Kevin Trapani and President Gareth Hedges; Positive Coaching Alliance Founder and CEO Jim Thompson; Darkness to Light; Cross Cultural Communications Trainer Lillian Roybal Rose; and many others included in our reference section for sharing such excellent tools and ideas from your own important work.

Thanks to Christi Hurt, Gina Maisto Smith, and Leslie Gomez of the UNC Title IX Task Force for your expertise, leadership, and encouragement of our work.

Amy sends her gratitude to many friends in the To-Shin Do ninjutsu martial arts community for your incredible support and teaching.

Gratitude to Lacey Mamak for thoughtful discussions about self-defense over two decades with Amy, and for insightful feedback and editing of early chapters.

Thank you to Kathi Dunn for your beautiful design of the interior and cover that has made this book much more attractive and accessible—and to editor Diane O'Connell for your keen eye and helpful changes.

And thank you most of all to our families for your patience, faith, and support during the journey it has taken us to bring this book to life.

Endnote References

Stories, concepts, and practices from the Kidpower Teenpower Full-power International programs and curriculum are featured and interwoven throughout *Doing Right by Our Kids,* and used with permission from Kidpower's founder and primary author Irene van der Zande. Since Irene van der Zande is a co-author of this book, we have not cited every instance of Kidpower material used or adapted from other sources.

Chapter 1: The Heart of Child Protection

[1] Academy on Violence and Abuse, "ACE Study DVD Pre-View" YouTube video, April 12, 2012, https://youtu.be/v3A_HexLxDY. See also, Academy on Violence and Abuse home page: http://www.avahealth.org/.

[2] David Finkelhor et al., "Children's Exposure to Violence: A Comprehensive National Survey: (640762009-001)" American Psychological Association, 2009, https://doi.org/10.1037/e640762009-001.

[3] Glenn Kessler, "One in Five Women in College Sexually Assaulted: An Update on This Statistic," *Washington Post,* December 17, 2014, sec. Fact Checker, https://www.washingtonpost.com/news/fact-checker/wp/2014/12/17/one-in-five-women-in-college-sexually-assaulted-an-update/.

[4] Quil Lawrence, "New Report Says Pentagon Not Doing Enough for Sexual Assault Victims," *NPR,* May 19, 2016, https://www.npr.org/sections/parallels/2016/05/19/478576716/new-report-says-pentagon-not-doing-enough-for-sexual-assault-victims.

[5] Catherine Townsend and Alyssa Rheingold, "Estimating a Child Sexual Abuse Prevalence Rate for Practitioners: A Review of Child Sexual Abuse Prevalence Studies," August 2013, 28. https://www.d2l.org/wp-content/uploads/2017/02/PREVALENCE-RATE-WHITE-PAPER-D2L.pdf

[6] Simone Robers et al., "Indicators of School Crime and Safety: 2013," 2013, 208.

7 David Finkelhor et al., "Prevalence of Childhood Exposure to Violence, Crime, and Abuse: Results from the National Survey of Children's Exposure to Violence," *JAMA Pediatrics* 169, no. 8 (August 2015): 746–54, https://doi.org/10.1001/jamapediatrics.2015.0676.

8 Centers for Disease Control, "Child Abuse and Neglect Cost the United States $124 Billion," February 1, 2012, https://www.cdc.gov/media/releases/2012/p0201_child_abuse.html.

9 Xiangming Fang et al., "The Economic Burden of Child Maltreatment in the United States and Implications for Prevention," *Child Abuse & Neglect* 36, no. 2 (February 1, 2012): 156–65, https://doi.org/10.1016/j.chiabu.2011.10.006.

10 "Bullying and Harassment of Students with Disabilities," PACER's National Bullying Prevention Center, http://www.pacer.org/bullying/resources/students-with-disabilities/.

11 The abbreviation "LGBTQIA+" refers to people who are lesbian, gay, bisexual, transgender, queer or questioning, intersexual, asexual, and other people who have expansive sexual orientations or gender identities.

12 "GLSEN Shares Latest Findings on LGBTQ Students' Experiences in Schools," GLSEN, https://www.glsen.org/article/2015-national-school-climate-survey.

13 FBI, "Latest Hate Crime Statistics Report Released," Story, Federal Bureau of Investigation, December 8, 2014, https://www.fbi.gov/news/stories/latest-hate-crime-statistics-report-released.

14 Katie Zezima and Susan Svrluga, "The Legacy of Newtown: Lockdowns, Active-Shooter Training and School Security," *Washington Post,* December 10, 2017, sec. National, https://www.washingtonpost.com/national/the-legacy-of-newtown-lockdowns-active-shooter-training-and-school-security/2017/12/10/cc538e74-dacd-11e7-a841-2066faf731ef_story.html.

Chapter 2: Kidpower's Core Safety Principles for Adults

The core Kidpower principles and skills in Chapters 2 and 3 are from several Kidpower publications/sources, including: *The Kidpower Book for Caring Adults: Personal Safety, Self-Protection, Confidence, and Advocacy for Young People; Kidpower Child Protection Advocate Workbook;* and the *Kidpower Comprehensive Program Manual.*

1 Amy Tiemann, "The Night Intuition Saved Four Lives on the Way Home from the Safety Seminar," *Doing Right by Our Kids* (blog), June 6, 2011, https://doingrightbyourkids.com/2011/06/06/the-night-intuition-saved-four-lives-on-the-way-home-from-the-safety-seminar/.

2 "10 Pieces of Wisdom from Desmond Tutu on His Birthday," *Desmond Tutu Foundation USA* (blog), October 7, 2015, http://www.tutufoundationusa.org/2015/10/07/10-pieces-of-wisdom-from-desmond-tutu-on-his-birthday/.

Chapter 3: Kidpower Tools for Protecting Children and Empowering Families

Expanded explanations of the material presented in Chapter 3 can be found in the *Bonus Toolkit: Kidpower Skills and Action Plans* starting on page 189.

Chapter 4: Taking Charge of Our Inner Circle: Safety with Family, Friends, Neighbors, and Babysitters

[1] Gavin de Becker, *Protecting the Gift: Keeping Children and Teenagers Safe (and Parents Sane)* (New York: Dell Pub., 2000), 206-210.

[2] Farnam Street, "Dan Ariely on How and Why We Cheat," *Farnam Street Psychology Blog* (blog), December 16, 2015, https://www.fs.blog/2015/12/dan-ariely-on-why-and-how-we-cheat/.

Chapter 5: Worthy of Trust: What Youth-serving Organizations Must Do to Keep Kids Safe

[1] Mark Davis, "Wrongful Death Lawsuit Settled for Teen Kayaker on Adventure Tour," Davis Levin Livingston, February 7, 2014, https://www.davislevin.com/in-the-news/wrongful-death-lawsuit-settled-teen-kayaker-adventure-tour/.

[2] Amy Tiemann, "Universities Realize That They Are Youth-Serving Organizations: A Starting Point for Creating Safety Policies," *Doing Right by Our Kids* (blog), July 13, 2013, https://doingrightbyourkids.com/2013/07/13/universities-realize-that-they-are-youth-serving-organizations/.

[3] John Guirey, "Camp Daggett Social Networking Policy," Camp Daggett website, http://www.campdaggett.org/summer-camp-reminders/social-netowrking-policy/.

[4] Kevin Trapani and Gareth Hedges interviewed by Amy Tiemann. See also: Redwoods Group, "Redwoods Group Safety Resources," http://www.redwoodsgroup.com/safety-resources/.

[5] Redwoods Group, "Aquatics Guidance & Tools," http://www.redwoodsgroup.com/safety-resources/aquatics-guidance-and-tools/.

[6] Redwoods Group, "Our Purpose Statement," http://www.redwoodsgroup.com/about-us/purpose/.

[7] Jolie Logan interviewed by Amy Tiemann. See also, Darkness to Light Website, https://www.d2l.org/.

Chapter 6: Kids Learn Best When They Feel Safe: Tools for Schools

[1] "Erin's Law Website," Erin's Law, http://www.erinslaw.org/.

[2] Sarah Stultz, "Area School Board Expels Student for Knife Found in Locker," *Austin Daily Herald*, April 25, 2014, https://www.austindailyherald.com/2014/04/611312/.

[3] Kelly Wallace, "6-Year-Old Suspended for Kissing Girl, Accused of Sexual Harassment," *CNN*, December 12, 2013, https://www.cnn.com/2013/12/11/living/6-year-old-suspended-kissing-girl/index.html.

[4] Susan Edelman, "City Pays Exiled Teachers to Snooze as 'Rubber Rooms' Return," *New York Post,* January 17, 2016, https://nypost.com/2016/01/17/city-pays-exiled-teachers-to-snooze-as-rubber-rooms-return/.

[5] "The BULLY Project: About the Film," http://www.thebullyproject.com/about_film.

Chapter 7: The JOY of the Game: Reclaiming Youth Sports

[1] Amy Tiemann, "Kids and Sports: Staying True to Our Core Values in a Sports-Crazed World," *Doing Right By Our Kids* (blog), April 17, 2017, https://doingrightbyourkids.com/2017/04/17/kids-sports-staying-true-core-values-sports-crazed-world/.

[2] Positive Coaching Alliance website, https://www.positivecoach.org/.

[3] "Protecting Youth Athletes from Sexual Abuse: Parents And Coaches," PCA Development Zone, https://devzone.positivecoach.org/resource/video/protecting-youth-athletes-sexual-abuse-parents-and-coaches.

[4] AP, "Coach Gained Parents' Trust with Skills before Abusing Kids," *USA Today,* November 26, 2016, https://www.usatoday.com/story/sports/soccer/2016/11/26/coach-gained-parents-trust-with-skills-before-abusing-kids/94479414/.

[5] USOC, "Team USA Safe Sport," Team USA, https://www.teamusa.org/about-the-usoc/safe-sport.

[6] Will Hobson and Steven Rich, "Every Six Weeks for More than 36 Years: When Will Sex Abuse in Olympic Sports End?" *Washington Post,* November 17, 2017, sec. Sports, https://www.washingtonpost.com/sports/every-six-weeks-for-more-than-36-years-when-will-sex-abuse-in-olympic-sports-end/2017/11/17/286ae804-c88d-11e7-8321-481fd63f174d_story.html.

[7] "Penn State Child Sex Abuse Scandal," *Wikipedia,* March 27, 2018, https://en.wikipedia.org/w/index.php?title=Penn_State_child_sex_abuse_scandal

[8] Tracy Connor and Sarah Fitzpatrick, "From 1997 to 2015, the Moments When Larry Nassar Could Have Been Stopped," *NBC News,* January 25, 2018, https://www.nbcnews.com/news/us-news/gymnastics-scandal-8-times-larry-nassar-could-have-been-stopped-n841091.

[9] Tim Evans, Mark Alesia, and Marisa Kwiatkowski, "Former USA Gymnastics Doctor Accused of Abuse," *Indianapolis Star,* September 12, 2016, https://www.indystar.com/story/news/2016/09/12/former-usa-gymnastics-doctor-accused-abuse/89995734/.

[10] Dan Barry, Serge F. Kovaleski, and Juliet Macur, "As FBI Took a Year to Pursue the Nassar Case, Dozens Say They Were Molested," *The New York Times,* February 3, 2018, sec. Sports, https://www.nytimes.com/2018/02/03/sports/nassar-fbi.html.

[11] Rachel Axon and Nancy Armour, "Entire USA Gymnastics Board Resigns in Wake of Larry Nassar Scandal," *USA Today,* January 31, 2018, https://www.usatoday.com/story/sports/olympics/2018/01/31/entire-usa-gymnastics-board-resigns-usoc-larry-nassar-scandal/1082855001/.

Chapter 8: Spiritual Safety: Places of Worship Should Be Safe for Kids

[1] The Investigative Staff of the Boston Globe, *Betrayal: The Crisis in the Catholic Church,* Updated edition (New York: Back Bay Books, 2015).

Chapter 9: Colleges: A Safe Place to Spread Their Wings

[1] Christopher Krebs et al., "The Campus Sexual Assault (CSA) Study," December 2007, https://www.ncjrs.gov/pdffiles1/nij/grants/221153.pdf.

[2] College Parents Matter website, http://www.collegeparentsmatter.org/.

[3] Emanuella Grinberg, "Student-Led Activists Movement Fights to End Rape on Campus," *CNN,* February 12, 2014, https://www.cnn.com/2014/02/09/living/campus-sexual-violence-students-schools/index.html.

[4] Anna Blackshaw, "UNC and Its Honor Court Have Failed Sexual Assault Survivors," *Indy Week,* March 27, 2013, https://www.indyweek.com/indyweek/unc-and-its-honor-court-have-failed-sexual-assault-survivors/Content?oid=3461355.

[5] U. S. Department of Education and Office of Civil Rights, "Dear Colleague Letter: Sexual Violence | National Sexual Violence Resource Center (NSVRC)," 2011, https://www.nsvrc.org/publications/dear-colleague-letter-sexual-violence.

[6] Carolina Alumni Review, "University Refines Policies on Sexual Violence—UNC General Alumni Association," August 28, 2014, https://alumni.unc.edu/news/university-refines-policies-on-sexual-violence/.

[7] FBI Uniform Crime Reporting, "Forcible Rape," FBI, 2010, https://ucr.fbi.gov/crime-in-the.s/2010/crime-in-the-u.s.-2010/violent-crime/rapemain.

[8] Susan Carbon, "An Updated Definition of Rape," January 6, 2012, https://www.justice.gov/archives/opa/blog/updated-definition-rape.

[9] Anonymous, "Dear Harvard: You Win," *The Harvard Crimson,* March 31, 2014, http://www.thecrimson.com/article/2014/3/31/Harvard-sexual-assault/?page=1.

[10] Susan Donaldson James, "Student Who Alleges Sexual Assault Slams Harvard University Policies," *ABC News,* April 2, 2014, http://abcnews.go.com/Health/harvard-student-claims-campus-sexual-assault-slams-university/story?id =23148803.

[11] Matthew Clairda and Madeline Conway, "Univ. Announces New Sexual Assault Policy Including Central Office, 'Preponderance of the Evidence' Standard," *The Harvard Crimson, July 3, 2014,* http://www.thecrimson.com/article/2014/7/3/new-sexual-assault-policies/.

[12] "Green Dot Bystander Intervention," *Wikipedia,* October 24, 2017, https://en.wikipedia.org/w/index.php?title=Green_Dot_Bystander_Intervention&oldid=806805832.

[13] Ryan Grim and Jason Cherkis, "Here's How You Can Help Stop A Sexual Assault Before It Happens," *Huffington Post,* July 9, 2015, sec. Politics, https://www.huffingtonpost.com/2015/07/08/bystander-intervention_n_7758118.html.

[14] "Map of Local Green Dots | Kent State University," https://www.kent.edu/greendot/map-local-green-dots.

[15] Grim and Cherkis, "Here's How You Can Help Stop A Sexual Assault Before It Happens."

[16] Keith Hautala, "Green Dot Effective at Reducing Sexual Violence." *UKNow,* November 20, 2015, https://uknow.uky.edu/research/green-dot-effective-reducing-sexual-violence.

[17] Byron Hurt, "About HAZING, Director's Statement," http://www.bhurt.com/films/view/hazing_how_badly_do_you_want_in.

[18] Susan Lipkins, "Inside Hazing. Definitions: What/Who/Where/When," Inside Hazing, https://www.insidehazing.com/definitions/.

[19] Leo Lambert, "Elon University Convocation" (Elon University, August 27, 2017).

Chapter 10: Overcoming Harmful Prejudice with Understanding, Determination and Courage

[1] Tyler Clementi Foundation, "Tyler Clementi Foundation Additional Resources and Partners," https://tylerclementi.org/more-resources/.

[2] *"New Jersey v. Dharun Ravi,"* *Wikipedia,* December 28, 2017, https://en.wikipedia.org/w/index.php?title=New_Jersey_v._Dharun_Ravi&oldid=817396166.

[3] German Lopez, "There Are Huge Racial Disparities in How US Police Use Force," *Vox,* December 17, 2015, https://www.vox.com/cards/police-brutality-shootings-us/us-police-racism.

[4] ACLU, "Derechos de Inmigrantes: Que Hacer Si Lo Paran" [Immigrant Rights: What to do if You are Stopped], YouTube video, January 31, 2017, https://youtu.be/MB1VEwmoEpE.

5 Irene van der Zande, "Understanding Institutionalized Oppression," Kidpower International, June 22, 2015, https://www.kidpower.org/library/article/understanding-institutionalized-oppression/.

Chapter 11: Giving Our Kids a Better World to Live In

1 NPR Staff, "Civil Rights Attorney on How She Built Trust with Police," *NPR*, December 5, 2014, https://www.npr.org/sections/codeswitch/2014/12/05/368545491/civil-rights-attorney-on-how-she-built-trust-with-police.

2 Robert Rogers, "Use of Deadly Force by Police Disappears on Richmond Streets," *East Bay Times,* September 6, 2014, https://www.eastbaytimes.com/2014/09/06/use-of-deadly-force-by-police-disappears-on-richmond-streets/.

3 Jermaine Spradley, "George Zimmerman Not Guilty: Jury Lets Trayvon Martin Killer Go," *Huffington Post,* July 14, 2013, sec. Black Voices, https://www.huffingtonpost.com/2013/07/13/george-zimmerman-not-guilty_n_3588743.html.

4 Black Lives Matter, "We Can End Police Violence in America," Campaign Zero, https://www.joincampaignzero.org/vision/.

5 Black Lives Matter, "Campaign Zero Solutions," Campaign Zero, https://www.joincampaignzero.org/solutions/.

6 Irene van der Zande, "Facing Prejudice with Compassion and Determination," Kidpower International, December 11, 2014, https://www.kidpower.org/library/article/facing-prejudice-with-compassion-and-determination/.

7 "Las Vegas Shooting: 58 People Killed, almost 500 Hurt Near Mandalay Bay," *NBC News*, October 2, 2017, https://www.nbcnews.com/storyline/las-vegas-shooting.

8 Eric Levnson and Joe Sterling, "These Are the Victims of the Florida School Shooting," *CNN,* February 21, 2018, https://www.cnn.com/2018/02/15/us/florida-shooting-victims-school/index.html.

9 German Lopez, "I've Covered Gun Violence for Years. The Solutions Aren't a Big Mystery," *Vox,* February 21, 2018, https://www.vox.com/policy-and-politics/2018/2/21/17028930/gun-violence-us-statistics-charts.

10 Hannah Fingerhut, "5 Facts about Guns in the United States," *Pew Research Center,* January 5, 2016, http://www.pewresearch.org/fact-tank/2016/01/05/5-facts-about-guns-in-the-united-states/.

11 Angela Wright, "Gun Violence Isn't Just a U.S. Problem—and Canada Isn't Immune," *Macleans, October 7, 2017,* http://www.macleans.ca/opinion/gun-violence-isnt-just-a-u-s-problem-and-canada-isnt-immune/.

12 Soraya Sarhaddi Nelson, "What's Worked, And What Hasn't, In Gun-Loving Switzerland," *NPR*, March 19, 2013, https://www.npr.org/2013/03/19/174758723/facing-switzerland-gun-culture.

[13] Emanuella Grinberg and Nadeem Muaddi, "March for Our Lives: How Parkland Students Pulled off a Massive National Protest in Only 5 Weeks," *CNN*, March 26, 2018, https://www.cnn.com/2018/03/26/us/march-for-our-lives/index.html.

[14] "5 Timeless Truths from The Serenity Prayer That Offer Wisdom in The Modern Age," *Huffington Post, March 18, 2014,* https://www.huffingtonpost.com/2014/03/18/serenity-prayer-wisdom_n_4965139.html.

Bonus Toolkit: How to Prevent and Stop Cyberbullying

[1] Julia Prodis Sulek, "Audrie Pott: Saratoga Teen's Suicide Spurs 'Audrie's Law' on Cyberbullying," *The Mercury News* (blog), March 6, 2014, https://www.mercurynews.com/2014/03/06/audrie-pott-saratoga-teens-suicide-spurs-audries-law-on-cyberbullying/.

[2] Mike Ribble, *Digital Citizenship in Schools, Third Edition: Nine Elements All Students Should Know,* Third edition (International Society for Technology in Education, 2015).

Bibliography

"5 Timeless Truths from The Serenity Prayer That Offer Wisdom in The Modern Age," *Huffington Post,* March 18, 2014. https://www.huffingtonpost.com/2014/03/18/serenity-prayer-wisdom_n_4965139.html.

"10 Pieces of Wisdom from Desmond Tutu on His Birthday." *Desmond Tutu Foundation USA* (blog), October 7, 2015. http://www.tutufoundationusa.org/2015/10/07/10-pieces-of-wisdom-from-desmond-tutu-on-his-birthday/.

Academy on Violence and Abuse. "ACE Study DVD Pre-View," YouTube video, April 12, 2012. https://youtu.be/v3A_HexLxDY.

Academy on Violence and Abuse website, http://www.avahealth.org/.

ACLU, "Derechos de Inmigrantes: Que Hacer Si Lo Paran" [Immigrant Rights: What to do if You are Stopped], YouTube video, January 31, 2017, https://youtu.be/MB1VEwmoEpE.

"ACLU Apps to Record Police Conduct." American Civil Liberties Union. https://www.aclu.org/issues/criminal-law-reform/reforming-police-practices/aclu-apps-record-police-conduct.

Anonymous. "Dear Harvard: You Win," *The Harvard Crimson,* March 31, 2014. http://www.thecrimson.com/article/2014/3/31/Harvard-sexual-assault/?page=1.

Associated Press (AP). "Coach Gained Parents' Trust with Skills before Abusing Kids." *USA Today,* November 26, 2016, https://www.usatoday.com/story/sports/soccer/2016/11/26/coach-gained-parents-trust-with-skills-before-abusing-kids/94479414/.

Axon, Rachel, and Nancy Armour. "Entire USA Gymnastics Board Resigns in Wake of Larry Nassar Scandal." *USA Today.* https://www.usatoday.com/story/sports/olympics/2018/01/31/entire-usa-gymnastics-board-resigns-usoc-larry-nassar-scandal/1082855001/.

Barry, Dan, Serge F. Kovaleski, and Juliet Macur. "As FBI Took a Year to Pursue the Nassar Case, Dozens Say They Were Molested." *The New York Times,* February 3, 2018, sec. Sports. https://www.nytimes.com/2018/02/03/sports/nassar-fbi.html.

Bass, Ellen, and Laura Davis. *The Courage to Heal: A Guide for Women Survivors of Child Sexual Abuse.* 4th ed., 20th anniversary ed. New York: Collins Living, 2008.

Black Lives Matter. "Campaign Zero Solutions." Campaign Zero. https://www. joincampaignzero.org/solutions/.

———. "We Can End Police Violence in America." Campaign Zero. https://www. joincampaignzero.org/vision/.

Blackshaw, Anna. "UNC and Its Honor Court Have Failed Sexual Assault Survivors." *Indy Week.* March 27, 2013. https://www.indyweek.com/indyweek/ unc-and-its-honor-court-have-failed-sexual-assault-survivors/Content?oid= 3461355.

"Bullying and Harassment of Students with Disabilities." PACER's National Bullying Prevention Center. http://www.pacer.org/bullying/resources/students-with-disabilities/.

Carbon, Susan. "An Updated Definition of Rape." US Department of Justice Archives, January 6, 2012. https://www.justice.gov/archives/opa/blog/updated-definition-rape.

Carolina Alumni Review. "University Refines Policies on Sexual Violence," UNC General Alumni Association. July 3, 2014, https://alumni.unc.edu/news/university-refines-policies-on-sexual-violence/.

Centers for Disease Control. "Child Abuse and Neglect Cost the United States $124 Billion," February 1, 2012. https://www.cdc.gov/media/releases/2012/p0201_child_abuse.html.

Childhelp National Child Abuse Hotline." 1-800-4-A-CHILD, https://www. childhelp.org/hotline/.

Clairda, Matthew, and Madeline Conway. "Univ. Announces New Sexual Assault Policy Including Central Office, 'Preponderance of the Evidence' Standard" *The Harvard Crimson.* March 27, 2013. http://www.thecrimson.com/article/2014/7/3/new-sexual-assault-policies/.

College Parents Matter website, http://www.collegeparentsmatter.org/.

Connor, Tracy, and Sarah Fitzpatrick. "From 1997 to 2015, the Moments When Larry Nassar Could Have Been Stopped." *NBC News.* January 25, 2018, https:// www.nbcnews.com/news/us-news/gymnastics-scandal-8-times-larry-nassar-could-have-been-stopped-n841091.

Darkness to Light website, https://www.d2l.org/.

Davis, Mark. "Wrongful Death Lawsuit Settled for Teen Kayaker on Adventure Tour." Davis Levin Livingston, February 7, 2014. https://www.davislevin.com/in-the-news/wrongful-death-lawsuit-settled-teen-kayaker-adventure-tour/.

de Becker, Gavin. *Protecting the Gift: Keeping Children and Teenagers Safe (and Parents Sane)*. New York: Dell Pub., 2000, 207-210.

———. *The Gift of Fear: Survival Signals That Protect Us from Violence*. New York: Delta, 1999.

Donaldson James, Susan. "Student Who Alleges Sexual Assault Slams Harvard University Policies." *ABC News*, April 2, 2014. http://abcnews.go.com/Health/harvard-student-claims-campus-sexual-assault-slams-university/story?id=23148803.

Edelman, Susan. "City Pays Exiled Teachers to Snooze as 'Rubber Rooms' Return," *New York Post*, January 17, 2016. https://nypost.com/2016/01/17/city-pays-exiled-teachers-to-snooze-as-rubber-rooms-return/.

Erin's Law Website, http://www.erinslaw.org/.

Evans, Tim, Mark Alesia, and Marisa Kwiatkowski. "Former USA Gymnastics Doctor Accused of Abuse." *Indianapolis Star*, September 12, 2016. https://www.indystar.com/story/news/2016/09/12/former-usa-gymnastics-doctor-accused-abuse/89995734/.

Fang, Xiangming, Derek S. Brown, Curtis S. Florence, and James A. Mercy. "The Economic Burden of Child Maltreatment in the United States and Implications for Prevention." *Child Abuse & Neglect* 36, no. 2 (February 1, 2012): 156–65. https://doi.org/10.1016/j.chiabu.2011.10.006.

Farnam Street. "Dan Ariely on How and Why We Cheat." *Farnam Street Psychology* (blog), December 16, 2015. https://www.fs.blog/2015/12/dan-ariely-on-why-and-how-we-cheat/.

FBI. "Latest Hate Crime Statistics Report Released." Federal Bureau of Investigation, December 8, 2014. https://www.fbi.gov/news/stories/latest-hate-crime-statistics-report-released.

FBI Uniform Crime Reporting. "Forcible Rape." Federal Bureau of Investigation, 2010. https://ucr.fbi.gov/crime-in-the-u.s/2010/crime-in-the-u.s.-2010/violent-crime/rapemain.

Fingerhut, Hannah. "5 Facts about Guns in the United States." *Pew Research Center* (blog), January 5, 2016. http://www.pewresearch.org/fact-tank/2016/01/05/5-facts-about-guns-in-the-united-states/.

Finkelhor, David, Heather A. Turner, Anne Shattuck, and Sherry L. Hamby. "Prevalence of Childhood Exposure to Violence, Crime, and Abuse: Results from the National Survey of Children's Exposure to Violence." *JAMA Pediatrics* 169, no. 8 (August 2015): 746–54. https://doi.org/10.1001/jamapediatrics.2015.0676.

Finkelhor, David, Heather Turner, Richard Ormrod, Sherry Hamby, and Kristen Kracke. "Children's Exposure to Violence: A Comprehensive National Survey: (640762009-001)." American Psychological Association, 2009. https://doi.org/10.1037/e640762009-001.

Friday, Sarah Stultz. "Area School Board Expels Student for Knife Found in Locker," *Austin Daily Herald,* April 25, 2014. https://www.austindailyherald.com/2014/04/611312/.

"GLSEN Shares Latest Findings on LGBTQ Students' Experiences in Schools." GLSEN, 2015. https://www.glsen.org/article/2015-national-school-climate-survey.

"Green Dot Bystander Intervention." *Wikipedia,* October 24, 2017. https://en.wikipedia.org/w/index.php?title=Green_Dot_Bystander_Intervention&oldid=806805832.

Grim, Ryan, and Jason Cherkis. "Here's How You Can Help Stop A Sexual Assault Before It Happens." *Huffington Post,* July 9, 2015, sec. Politics. https://www.huffingtonpost.com/2015/07/08/bystander-intervention_n_7758118.html.

Grinberg, Emanuella. "Student-Led Activists Movement Fights to End Rape on Campus." *CNN,* February 12, 2014. https://www.cnn.com/2014/02/09/living/campus-sexual-violence-students-schools/index.html.

Grinberg, Emanuella, and Nadeem Muaddi. "March for Our Lives: How Parkland Students Pulled off a Massive National Protest in Only 5 Weeks," *CNN.* March 26, 2018. https://www.cnn.com/2018/03/26/us/march-for-our-lives/index.html.

Guirey, John. "Camp Daggett Social Networking Policy." Camp Daggett website, http://www.campdaggett.org/summer-camp-reminders/social-netowrking-policy/.

Hautala, Keith. "'Green Dot' Effective at Reducing Sexual Violence." *UKNow,* November 20, 2015. https://uknow.uky.edu/research/green-dot-effective-reducing-sexual-violence.

Heath, Chip, and Dan Heath. *Switch: How to Change Things When Change Is Hard.* 1st ed. New York: Broadway Books, 2010.

Hobson, Will, and Steven Rich. "Every Six Weeks for More than 36 Years: When Will Sex Abuse in Olympic Sports End?" *Washington Post,* November 17, 2017, sec. Sports. https://www.washingtonpost.com/sports/every-six-weeks-for-more-than-36-years-when-will-sex-abuse-in-olympic-sports-end/2017/11/17/286ae804-c88d-11e7-8321-481fd63f174d_story.html.

Hurt, Byron. "About HAZING, Director's Statement." http://www.bhurt.com/films/view/hazing_how_badly_do_you_want_in.

Kessler, Glenn. "One in Five Women in College Sexually Assaulted: An Update on This Statistic." *Washington Post,* December 17, 2014, sec. Fact Checker. https://www.washingtonpost.com/news/fact-checker/wp/2014/12/17/one-in-five-women-in-college-sexually-assaulted-an-update/.

Kidpower website, "Kidpower Resource Library." https://www.kidpower.org/library/.

Krebs, Christopher, Christine Lindquist, Warner, Tara, Bonnie Fisher, and Sandra Martin. "The Campus Sexual Assault (CSA) Study," December 2007. htt;ps://www.ncjrs.gov/pdffiles1/nij/grants/221153.pdf.

Lambert, Leo. "Elon University Convocation." Elon University, August 27, 2017.

"Las Vegas Shooting: 58 People Killed, almost 500 Hurt Near Mandalay Bay." *NBC News.* October 2, 2017. https://www.nbcnews.com/storyline/las-vegas-shooting.

Lawrence, Quil. "New Report Says Pentagon Not Doing Enough for Sexual Assault Victims," *NPR,* May 19, 2016. https://www.npr.org/sections/parallels/2016/05/19/478576716/new-report-says-pentagon-not-doing-enough-for-sexual-assault-victims.

Levnson, Eric, and Joe Sterling. "These Are the Victims of the Florida School Shooting." *CNN.* February 21, 2018, https://www.cnn.com/2018/02/15/us/florida-shooting-victims-school/index.html.

Lipkins, Susan. "Inside Hazing. Definitions: What/Who/Where/When." Inside Hazing website. https://www.insidehazing.com/definitions/.

Lopez, German. "I've Covered Gun Violence for Years. The Solutions Aren't a Big Mystery." *Vox,* February 21, 2018. https://www.vox.com/policy-and-politics/2018/2/21/17028930/gun-violence-us-statistics-charts.

———. "There Are Huge Racial Disparities in How US Police Use Force." *Vox,* December 17, 2015. https://www.vox.com/cards/police-brutality-shootings-us/us-police-racism.

"Map of Local Green Dots," Kent State University." April 1, 2018. https://www.kent.edu/greendot/map-local-green-dots.

"New Jersey v. Dharun Ravi." *Wikipedia,* December 28, 2017. https://en.wikipedia.org/w/index.php?title=New_Jersey_v._Dharun_Ravi&oldid=817396166.

NPR Staff. "Civil Rights Attorney on How She Built Trust with Police." *NPR.* https://www.npr.org/sections/codeswitch/2014/12/05/368545491/civil-rights-attorney-on-how-she-built-trust-with-police.

"Penn State Child Sex Abuse Scandal." *Wikipedia,* March 27, 2018. https://en.wikipedia.org/w/index.php?title=Penn_State_child_sex_abuse_scandal&oldid=832698160.

Positive Coaching Alliance website, https://www.positivecoach.org/.

Prodis Sulek, Julia. "Audrie Pott: Saratoga Teen's Suicide Spurs 'Audrie's Law' on Cyberbullying." *The Mercury News* (blog), March 6, 2014. https://www. mercurynews.com/2014/03/06/audrie-pott-saratoga-teens-suicide-spurs- audries-law-on-cyberbullying/.

"Protecting Youth Athletes from Sexual Abuse: Parents and Coaches." PCA Development Zone. https://devzone.positivecoach.org/resource/video/protecting- youth-athletes-sexual-abuse-parents-and-coaches.

Redwoods Group. "Aquatics Guidance & Tools" The Redwoods Group. http:// www.redwoodsgroup.com/safety-resources/aquatics-guidance-and-tools/.

———. "Our Purpose Statement." http://www.redwoodsgroup.com/about-us/ purpose/.

———. "Redwoods Group Safety Resources." http://www.redwoodsgroup.com/ safety-resources/.

Ribble, Mike. *Digital Citizenship in Schools, Third Edition: Nine Elements All Students Should Know.* Third edition. International Society for Technology in Education, 2015.

Robers, Simone, Jana Kemp, Amy Rathbun, Rachel E Morgan, and Thomas D Snyder. "Indicators of School Crime and Safety: 2013," US Department of Education, 2013, 208 pages. PDF accessed via Bureau of Justice Statistics website, https://www.bjs.gov/content/pub/pdf/iscs13.pdf

Rogers, Robert. "Use of Deadly Force by Police Disappears on Richmond Streets." *East Bay Times,* September 6, 2014. https://www.eastbaytimes.com/2014/09/06/ use-of-deadly-force-by-police-disappears-on-richmond-streets/.

Sarhaddi Nelson, Soraya. "What's Worked, And What Hasn't, In Gun-Loving Switzerland." *NPR.* March 19, 2013. https://www.npr.org/2013/03/19/174758723/ facing-switzerland-gun-culture.

Spradley, Jermaine. "George Zimmerman Not Guilty: Jury Lets Trayvon Martin Killer Go." *Huffington Post,* July 14, 2013, sec. Black Voices. https:// www.huffingtonpost.com/2013/07/13/george-zimmerman-not-guilty_n_ 3588743.html.

"The BULLY Project: About the Film." The BULLY Project. http://www. thebullyproject.com/about_film.

The Investigative Staff of the Boston Globe. *Betrayal: The Crisis in the Catholic Church.* Updated edition. New York: Back Bay Books, 2015.

Tiemann, Amy, ed. *Courageous Parents, Confident Kids: Letting Go So You Both Can Grow.* Chapel Hill: Spark Press, 2010.

Tiemann, Amy. "Kids and Sports: Staying True to Our Core Values in a Sports-Crazed World." *Doing Right by Our Kids* (blog), April 17, 2017. https://doingrightbyourkids.com/2017/04/17/kids-sports-staying-true-core-values-sports-crazed-world/.

————. "The Night Intuition Saved Four Lives on the Way Home from the Safety Seminar." *Doing Right by Our Kids* (blog), June 6, 2011. https://doingrightbyourkids.com/2011/06/06/the-night-intuition-saved-four-lives-on-the-way-home-from-the-safety-seminar/.

————. "Universities Realize That They Are Youth-Serving Organizations: A Starting Point for Creating Safety Policies." *Doing Right by Our Kids* (blog), July 13, 2013. https://doingrightbyourkids.com/2013/07/13/universities-realize-that-they-are-youth-serving-organizations/.

Townsend, Catherine, and Alyssa Rheingold. "Estimating a Child Sexual Abuse Prevalence Rate for Practitioners: A Review of Child Sexual Abuse Prevalence Studies," August 2013, 28 pages. PDF accessed via Darkness to Light website, https://www.d2l.org/wp-content/uploads/2017/02/PREVALENCE-RATE-WHITE-PAPER-D2L.pdf.

Tyler Clementi Foundation. "Tyler Clementi Foundation Additional Resources and Partners." https://tylerclementi.org/more-resources/.

US Department of Education, and Office of Civil Rights. "Dear Colleague Letter: Sexual Violence | National Sexual Violence Resource Center (NSVRC)," 2011. https://www.nsvrc.org/publications/dear-colleague-letter-sexual-violence.

USOC. "Team USA Safe Sport." Team USA. https://www.teamusa.org: 443/About-the-USOC/Safe-Sport.

van der Zande, Irene. "10 Actions to Prevent and Stop Cyberbullying." Kidpower International. https://www.kidpower.org/library/article/prevent-cyberbullying/.

————. "Face Bullying with Confidence: 8 Kidpower Skills We Can Use Right Away." https://www.kidpower.org/library/article/prevent-bullying/.

————. "Facing Prejudice with Compassion and Determination." https://www.kidpower.org/library/article/facing-prejudice-with-compassion-and-determination/.

————. "How to Pick a Good Self-Defense Program." https://www.kidpower.org/library/article/self-defense/.

————. *Kidpower Child Protection Advocate Workbook*. CreateSpace Independent Publishing Platform, 2014.

————. *Kidpower Comprehensive Program Manual*. CreateSpace Independent Publishing Platform, 2013.

————. "Preparing Children for More Independence." https://www.kidpower.org/library/article/preparing-independence/.

————. *The Kidpower Book for Caring Adults: Personal Safety, Self-Protection, Confidence, and Advocacy for Young People.* Santa Cruz, CA: Kidpower Press, 2012.

————. "Understanding Institutionalized Oppression." https://www.kidpower.org/library/article/understanding-institutionalized-oppression/.

Wallace, Kelly. "6-Year-Old Suspended for Kissing Girl, Accused of Sexual Harassment." *CNN,* December 12, 2013. https://www.cnn.com/2013/12/11/living/6-year-old-suspended-kissing-girl/index.html.

Wright, Angela. "Gun Violence Isn't Just a U.S. Problem—and Canada Isn't Immune," *Macleans,* October 7, 2017. http://www.macleans.ca/opinion/gun-violence-isnt-just-a-u-s-problem-and-canada-isnt-immune/.

Zezima, Katie, and Susan Svrluga. "The Legacy of Newtown: Lockdowns, Active-Shooter Training and School Security." *Washington Post,* December 10, 2017, sec. National. https://www.washingtonpost.com/national/the-legacy-of-newtown-lockdowns-active-shooter-training-and-school-security/2017/12/10/cc538e74-dacd-11e7-a841-2066faf731ef_story.html.

Index

trust
    criteria for, 69
    within Inner Circle, 63–64
Tutu, Desmond, 35
Twain, Mark, 63
Two-Deep Leadership, 79
Tyler Clementi Foundation, 160

U
unintended negative consequences,
    102–103
University of North Carolina's Title IX
    Task Force, 141–143
Upstander Pledge, 160–161
US National Institute of Justice, 138
USA Gymnastics, 123–124
Use Your Awareness principle
    in child protection, 27, 28–31, 35
    effective actions from, 202
    Illusion of Safety and, 199–200
    intuition and, 30–31
    practice for, 193–194
    responsibility in, 83
    self-defense program choice, 256
    situational awareness, 59–62
    See also context; situational awareness

V
van der Zande, Irene, 15–17, 170–173,
    278
victim-blaming, 84, 142

violence
    advocacy against, 186
    civil disobedience vs., 183
    exposure to, 21–22
    school shootings, 184–185
vulnerability
    with faith community authority
        figures, 130
    in LGBTQIA+, 158–159

W
walking away, 155–156
Walking with Awareness and
    Confidence, 37. *See also* respectful
    confidence
#WhatsYourGreenDot, 146
Williamson, David F., 19
win-at-all-costs mentality, 114–116
"Wishing Technique", 81, 105
"Worrywart Technique", 81, 82

Y
youth sports
    abusive coaches in, 122–124
    adult egos in, 111–114
    choice of, 124–125
    coaches' actions in, 120–122
    organizational reform, 124
    PCA models for changes, 115–116
    win-at-all-costs mentality in, 114–115
youth-serving organizations (YSO). *See*
    organizations, youth-serving

Resources and Services from the Authors and Kidpower International

Kidpower Publications

Kidpower Online Library with over 300 articles, posters, handouts, videos and more

The Kidpower Book for Caring Adults: Personal Safety, Self-Protection, Confidence, and Advocacy for Young People

Solve Bullying with Kidpower: Proven Skills and Strategies to Keep Kids Safe from Cyberbullying, Harassment, Hazing, Shunning, and More

Earliest Teachable Moment: Personal Safety for Babies, Toddlers, and Preschoolers

One Strong Move: Step-by-step Self-Defense Lessons to Stop Attacks

Kidpower Child Protection Advocates Workbook

Kidpower Children's Safety Comics: Smart Safety Skills for Kids Ages 3 to 8

Kidpower Youth Safety Comics: Skills for Independence for Kids Ages 9 to 14

Fullpower Safety Comics for Teens and Adults: Stay Safe from Bullying, Abuse, and Violence

GIRLPOWER – Stay Confident!

Kidpower School Safety Curriculum Teaching Books series

For full list of books, please visit *Kidpower.org/books*

Dr. Amy Tiemann Books and Films

Mojo Mom: Nurturing Your Self While Raising a Family

Courageous Parents, Confident Kids: Letting Go So You Both Can Grow

High Water—a young adult wilderness adventure story

Executive Producer of socially-relevant documentaries including *The Rape of Recy Taylor* and *Olympic Pride, American Prejudice*

For more information, please visit *AmyTiemann.com*

Training, Workshops, and Consulting

Kidpower International provides instructor training programs, partnerships, safety conferences, and the Kidpower Child Protection Advocacy Institute—as well as consulting to families, schools, businesses, organizations, and agencies in how to adapt Kidpower's skills, strategies, and teaching methods for their specific needs. In communities worldwide, certified Kidpower instructors organize and teach positive and practical safety workshops each year for over 20,000 children, teens, and adults, including those with special needs. *www.kidpower.org*

Speakers and Media Experts

Both authors are talented and inspiring speakers for conferences and other special events and are available as experts for the media. Topics include child protection and personal safety solutions for issues such as bullying, harassment, abuse, sexual assault, kidnapping, domestic violence, prejudice, and other violence. *You can message Dr. Amy Tiemann through her website, AmyTiemann.com, or call 919-391-4899. To reach Irene van der Zande, email irene@kidpower.org or call 800-467-6997.*

About the Authors

Dr. Amy Tiemann leads at all levels. A Stanford-trained neuroscientist, Amy Tiemann is an educator at heart who connects with audiences as an author, speaker and trainer, and media producer.

Tiemann brought Kidpower training to her state, establishing the Kidpower North Carolina Center in 2008. As a nationally respected personal safety expert, she has consulted with K-12 schools and served on UNC-Chapel Hill's *Title IX Task Force* to improve the university's policies addressing sexual assault and domestic violence.

A sought-after speaker and commentator, Dr. Tiemann is a frequent guest expert on parenting websites, national radio tours, magazines from *Redbook* to *Glamour*, and TV including ABC News, the CBS *Early Show,* and NBC's *Today Show.*

Knowing the power of stories to create social change, she serves as an Executive Producer of socially relevant films through her company Spark Productions. Recent films include *The Rape of Recy Taylor* and *Olympic Pride, American Prejudice,* documentaries that tell important historical stories that have profound relevance to modern society's challenges.

In her free time, Amy enjoys martial arts. She is a black-belt practitioner of To-Shin Do ninjutsu who is proud to train alongside her husband and son as an "all-black-belt family."

Amy Tiemann's combination of perspectives gives her a unique ability to make an impact on individuals, families, and cultural standards to create positive social change.

Irene van der Zande empowers millions of people worldwide. She is the Founder and Executive Director of Kidpower Teenpower Fullpower International®, the global nonprofit leader in 'People Safety' education, providing positive and practical solutions to bullying, violence, and abuse. Since 1989, Irene has inspired an international movement of leaders, reaching over 5 million people of all ages, abilities, identities, and walks of life with effective, culturally-competent interpersonal and social safety skills.

Throughout Irene's three decades of leadership and collaboration, Kidpower has earned an outstanding reputation for developing, organizing, and presenting high quality child protection, positive communication, advocacy, self-defense, and personal safety programs and curriculum. She is an expert at adapting services to meet the needs of those facing increased risk of violence because of disabilities, poverty, and prejudice.

As Kidpower's lead author, Irene puts life-saving skills and lessons directly into the hands of parents and professionals. Her work has gained world-wide acclaim by experts in education, law enforcement, and health for being upbeat, experiential, age-appropriate, emotionally safe, trauma-informed, and relevant. Kidpower lessons have been presented in over 20 languages, across six continents.

Irene is an inspiring and entertaining speaker, trainer, and storyteller who is a master at preparing people to turn problems into successful practices; take charge of their safety and well-being; and develop joyful relationships that enrich their lives.

Please visit www.DoingRightByOurKids.com for more information about:

- Quantity discount book purchases for your book club, school, organization, or association

- Requesting customized training by the authors, offered either in person or by teleconferencing

- Inviting the authors to deliver a conference presentation, keynote, or other speaking engagement

- Media queries for the authors serving as expert sources